STILL IN THE SADDLE

Still in the Saddle

The Hollywood Western, 1969–1980

ANDREW PATRICK NELSON

University of Oklahoma Press : Norman

Verse from "Whatever Happened to Randolph Scott" is reprinted in the introduction. Words and music by Don Reid and Harold Reid. Copyright © 1973 Songs of Universal, Inc. Copyright renewed. All rights reserved. Used by permission. Reprinted by permission of Hal Leonard Corporation.

Verse from "Chisum" is reprinted in chapter 5. Words and music by Andrew Fenaday and Dominic Frontiere. Copyright © 1970 Warner-Barham Music LLC (BMI). All rights administered by Songs of Universal, Inc. (BMI). Exclusive worldwide print rights administered by Alfred Music. All rights reserved. Used by permission of Alfred Music.

Library of Congress Cataloging-in-Publication Data

Nelson, Andrew Patrick, 1982–
Still in the saddle : the Hollywood western, 1969–1980 / Andrew Patrick Nelson.
pages cm
Includes bibliographical references and index.
Includes filmography.
ISBN 978-0-8061-4821-2 (pbk. : alk. paper)
1. Western films—United States—History and criticism. I. Title.
PN1995.9.W4N47 2015
791.43'65878—dc23

2014043429

The paper in this book meets the guidelines for permanence and durability of the Committee on Production Guidelines for Book Longevity of the Council on Library Resources, Inc. ∞

For Leah,
who rides shotgun with me on the stagecoach of life

Contents

Illustrations

Figures

Tables

Acknowledgments

I am grateful to a number of people who aided and encouraged me in the completion of this book. Steve Neale has been an unfailing source of guidance over the years in which this project has taken shape. Peter Stanfield and Joe Kember offered insightful feedback on the project's first incarnation. Matthew Carter read chapter drafts and gave welcome reassurance that I was on the right track. Michael T. Marsden and Robin L. Murray provided thoughtful commentary on the manuscript, identifying crucial areas for improvement. At the University of Oklahoma Press, I am indebted to Thomas Krause for his enthusiasm and commitment; Stephanie Evans for attentively shepherding the book through the editorial process; and freelance copy editor Rosanne Howell for giving the manuscript some needed polish. For their collegiality, advice, and friendship over the years, thanks are due to Ed Buscombe, Sue Matheson, and Charlie Keil. Finally, for their love I thank my family—especially my wife and son, who sustain me in all that I do.

STILL IN THE SADDLE

Introduction

Born Game and Going Out That Way

We've got to start thinking beyond our guns. Those days are closin' fast.

—Pike Bishop, *The Wild Bunch* (1969)

Baby sister, I was born game and I intend to go out that way.

—Rooster Cogburn, *True Grit* (1969)

The Statler Brothers' 1974 song "Whatever Happened to Randolph Scott?" is a lamentation, of sorts, both for the scores of cowboy matinee idols like the eponymous Scott who had, by the 1970s, long since rode off into the sunset, and for the general state of moviemaking at the time. As the quartet's bass vocalist Harold Reid monotonously intones in the opening verse:

Everybody knows when you go to the show
You can't take the kids along
You've gotta read the paper and know the code
Of G, PG and R and X
And you gotta know what the movie's about
Before you even go
Tex Ritter's gone and Disney's dead
And the screen is filled with sex

In the chorus, all four Statlers go on to harmoniously inquire as to the whereabouts of their white-Stetson-and silver-spur-wearing heroes:

> Whatever happened to Randolph Scott,
> riding the trail alone?
> Whatever happened to Gene and Tex
> and Roy and Rex? The Durango Kid?
> Whatever happened to Randolph Scott,
> his horse plain as can be?
> Whatever happened to Randolph Scott
> has happened to the rest of me

The combining of tongue-in-cheek commentary on the present day with a nostalgic longing for the past is a hallmark of the Statler Brothers' music, and places them firmly in a country-and-western tradition of salty social commentary dating back to the original cowboy philosopher, Will Rogers. In this particular song, the contrasting vocal style of the verse and the chorus—monotone and harmony—is a clever stylistic touch that helps to emphasize the song's opposing of present and past. The opposition thus plays out at both the level of form (vocals) and content (lyrics).

Away from formal and historical observations, a question we might entertain is whether, if we look beyond the surface opposition of monotonous cynicism and harmonious wistfulness, there might be something *more* to this song than a humorously reactionary country music statement about how the past was good and the present, well, ain't. The song seems to imply that the absence of Randolph Scott and his pistol-packin' brethren is not only indicative of but also, in a way, *responsible for* the lamentable condition of the movies in the 1970s—implying, as it were, a causal relationship between the Western genre and the American film industry. Without Scott and his plain white horse standing dependably as a signifier of quality family entertainment, moviegoing becomes an adult exercise in planning and research. So goes the cowboy, so go the movies. And more, even, as the line "Whatever happened to Randolph Scott has happened to the rest of me" could be read as indicating an overarching connection between the Western and *society*—as though the absence of the traditional cowboy figure in contemporary cinema is reflective of larger societal deficiencies. Whatever "happened" to Scott has also "happened" to us, and so the state of the movies is ultimately a reflection of the society that produces and consumes them.

Of course, such an interpretation may be something of a stretch given that the song in question is still, ultimately, about old movie cowboys and the preponderance of "dirty" movies in the 1970s. And not to take anything away from the Statlers, but this is a musical group who, a few years earlier, warned listeners of the dangers of dating two women at the same time in the amusing "You Can't Have Your Kate (And Edith, Too)."

In the second verse of "Whatever Happened to Randolph Scott?" we find more of the same surly humor:

> Everybody's trying to make a comment
> about our doubts and fears
> True Grit's the only movie
> I've really understood in years
> You've gotta take your analyst along
> to see if it's fit to see
> Whatever happened to Randolph Scott
> has happened to the industry

While the knowing jab at the psychologically inflected nature of 1970s filmmaking could cause us to reconsider our earlier dismissal of a symptomatic reading of the song, of greater interest is the reference to director Henry Hathaway's 1969 Western *True Grit,* based on Charles Portis's novel about a precocious young girl who enlists an irascible, one-eyed U.S. Marshal to track down her father's murderer.

In a song that alternates between specific references to old Western movie actors and general commentary about the state of the movies, *True Grit* is the only picture singled out for attention by name. Without venturing out too far on an interpretative limb, we can draw two implications from this reference. First, *True Grit,* in its comprehensibility, is more like movies used to be—however that was. This is a suggestive idea, but the song itself does not provide much more than that: a suggestion. The second implication is weightier, given the subject of the song. In a moviemaking climate where all the frontier heroes of yesteryear have hung up their spurs, a lone cowboy remains: the star of *True Grit,* John Wayne.

As much as the Duke may be synonymous with the Western, he is unlikely to come to mind when discussing Western moviemaking during the period the Statlers are poking fun at. Instead, one term has come to dominate the discourse, both critical and popular, about the movie Western of the late 1960s and 1970s: *revisionist.*

Accounts of the Western's development from the late 1960s onward tend to go something like this: after the genre's signature filmmakers had either retired or moved on to other genres, a new generation of directors took the Western in a different, more violent direction, away from the simplistic frontier morality plays of an earlier age to scenarios that openly attacked the ethos of the mythic West while wrestling with contemporary politics disguised in turn-of-the-century dressings. Movies like *The Wild Bunch* (Sam Peckinpah, 1969), *Little Big Man* (Arthur Penn, 1970), *McCabe & Mrs. Miller* (Robert Altman, 1971), and *Heaven's Gate* (Michael Cimino, 1980), though dissimilar in many respects, have been read by critics and scholars as offering a critique of the genre's ideological underbelly. Whereas earlier Westerns celebrated America's westward expansion following the Civil War, these pictures inveighed against the violence, racism, and greed of the frontier experience—criticisms that took on added significance in light of current events both at home and abroad.

During this same period, however, the Duke continued to star in Westerns—ten of them, in fact, between 1969 and 1976, most of which earned more at the box office than contemporary "revisionist" Westerns. The very fact that Wayne continued to even *exist* into the 1970s may come as a surprise to some today yet, during an era characterized by "doubts and fears," there he was: older, but still in the saddle.

A particular term is also used to describe Wayne's later Westerns: *traditional.* This can't help but suggest opposing Western camps during the period. One imagines two queues at an imaginary cinema in 1969, one made up of pretentious, "socially conscious" young adults there to see *The Wild Bunch,* the other of old-timers shuffling along to see John Wayne in *True Grit,* upset that the tickets cost more than a nickel. A caricature, to be certain, but one not too far removed from some accounts of the later Western. The truth, of course, is far more complex. However politically redolent *The Wild Bunch* may have been, at the time *True Grit* was the more popular of the two pictures. Both, however, lagged far behind a third Western released the same year: *Butch Cassidy and the Sundance*

Kid (George Roy Hill), a film largely ignored in writing on the movie Western.

The differing treatment of these three films is a microcosm of critical discourse on the later Western. A veneration of new filmmakers, coupled with prevailing theories about how and why movie genres change over time, have led to the canonization of a small group of Westerns from 1969 to 1980 to the exclusion of dozens of others. Yet many of the most insightful analyses of the Western over the past decade have explored areas of the genre that have been neglected, including silent and early sound films.[1] A next step in the widening investigation of the Western is to turn our attention to films that fall outside or on the margins of the established canon but *within* its temporal boundaries.

This book aims to uncover the multiplicity and complexity of the Western genre between 1969 and 1980. This is the period most commonly associated with the revisionist Western, and is bookended by two significant films: *The Wild Bunch* and *Heaven's Gate.* Drawing upon a comprehensive filmography of American Westerns released between 1969 and 1980, considered in light of the visual tropes and narratives developed and reworked in the genre from the 1930s to the present, the analysis that follows reveals the diversity and abundance that belies our present understanding of the revisionist Western. Throughout, examinations of the later Western reveal not only connections between canonical and lesser-known works of the period, but also continuities between these and older Westerns—an ongoing, cyclical process of regeneration that transcends established divisions in the genre's history. The theme of regeneration also emerges in the films themselves and helps to reconceptualize divisions between "revisionist" and "traditional" Westerns: the latter emphasize the passing down of knowledge from one generation to the next, while the former see this as an impossibility.

The first part of the book, "Revision and Regeneration," is historiographical in nature, exploring where the prevailing history of the revisionist Western comes from, looking for cracks in its explanations, and positing an alternative. Rather than a simple review of existing literature, these chapters offer a narrative about the writing of film history and its consequences. Combined, they establish the necessary foundation for an informed and more inclusive analysis of Western films produced between 1969 and 1980. Chapter 1 opens with an investigation of the origins and uses of the term *revisionist* as applied to both the Western and film genres generally. The chapter carefully draws out the connections and contradictions in those histories of the Western that are considered to have established the "revisionist canon." This canon comprises a select group of later Westerns that meet certain criteria—such as being the product of an "auteur" filmmaker or using the genre's conventions for the purpose of social commentary—that correspond to larger narratives about Hollywood history and American culture. Upon examination, the canon proves to have its own internal divisions: certain films are subject to repeated analysis, while others are merely referenced as supplementary examples of the characteristics which the more favored films are held to exemplify. Chapter 2 begins with an analysis of *The Wild Bunch,* the most famous Western of the period, yet one that polarized critics and audiences and failed to recoup its production costs. The chapter situates some of the movie's purported "subversions" of Western convention within larger, general trends both within the genre and Hollywood moviemaking. That a movie said to be a reflection of the cultural anxieties of its time failed to find a wide audience prompts an investigation of which Westerns audiences *were* frequenting. An examination of box office and production data reveals that canonical revisionist Westerns represent not only a minority of Westerns produced, but also a minority of the most successful Westerns. What emerges is a very different vision of the period than that described in existing histories of the genre: one where the most active filmmakers are Burt Kennedy and Andrew V. McLaglen, and the biggest star is—or rather, *remains*—John Wayne. The variety of Westerns we find in the 1970s is in fact a reflection of the heterogeneity of Hollywood production at the time—a heterogeneity that bespeaks a heterogeneous audience that included both young and older patrons.

The second part of the book, "Critique and Convention," examines the revisionist Western: both the films themselves and the underlying criteria by which they have been elevated above other Westerns of the period, in particular the enduring notion that Westerns straightforwardly reflect American culture. Together, chapters 3 and 4 illustrate how accounts of the revisionist Western have selectively referenced only films that appear critical of earlier formal conventions or ideological positions, and, of these films, have focused repeatedly on those made by filmmakers associated with the "renaissance" of the Hollywood art film beginning in the late 1960s. Chapter 3 examines the representation of American Indians in Westerns of the 1970s, investigating the relationship between the genre and larger social and political phenomena, including America's military involvement in Vietnam and the tribal sovereignty movement. In "pro-Indian" movies of the period, such as *A Man Called Horse* (Elliot Silverstein, 1970) and *Ulzana's Raid* (Robert Aldrich, 1972), we find earnest attempts to portray indigenous cultures with greater complexity, but these attempts are nevertheless problematic, inasmuch as they work to challenge the genre's stereotypes they are still shaped by those stereotypes, as well as by changing norms of cinematic representation—in particular, increasing violence. Chapter 4 considers the representation of heroism in the genre, and includes analyses of the changing cinematic depictions of frontier legends Wyatt Earp and Jesse James, as well as an evaluation of the two Westerns made by director Robert Altman that offer critiques of Western heroism. Taking a broad view of the genre's history, the chapter demonstrates that the often-unflattering depiction of frontier heroes in canonical revisionist Westerns is less a reflection of societal disenchantment (as it is often argued) than part of an ongoing process of generic regeneration through which American heroes have been repeatedly "revised." By examining both celebrated and neglected revisionist films, and identifying in earlier Westerns the features most often associated with the revisionist Western, we see that the significance of these purported revisions stems from the context in which they are interpreted, rather than their place within the Western's history and their engagement with its conventions.

The book's third part, "Popularity and Preponderance," widens the focus of investigation beyond the revisionist canon through a consideration of alternative criteria by which a movie may draw attention to itself as being worthy of closer examination, including popularity, measured by box office performance or audience polling, and preponderance, looking at the number and kinds of Westerns produced during the period. These approaches lead us to an alternative conception of the period, where many of the most acclaimed revisionist Westerns did not find favor with audiences, while "traditional" Westerns were produced in greater number and, in general, had greater success. Chapter 5 focuses on the final Westerns of John Wayne. In nearly all of these features we find an emphasis on the legacy of the frontier hero and the need to pass this legacy from one generation to the next. Yet this concern with the frontier hero is not limited to "traditional" Westerns. It manifests in many Westerns of the period, including revisionist works. Films like *The Wild Bunch, McCabe & Mrs. Miller, The Culpepper Cattle Co.* (Dick Richards, 1972), *Lawman* (Michael Winner, 1971), and many others suggest the impossibility that the values of the Western hero can endure, with many films going so far as to stage scenes in which young characters are killed. From an extra-textual perspective, however, even traditional Westerns like those of Wayne or Clint Eastwood fail to regenerate the genre: while young characters may learn the appropriate lessons and inherit the hero's legacy, they are always played by second- or third-tier actors. Chapter 6 then takes us to the end of the period, opening with an analysis of *The Long Riders* (Walter Hill, 1980), a successful Western about Jesse James released in 1980 that was supposed to signal the return of the genre. This comeback failed to materialize, thanks to the notorious, monumental failure of director Michael Cimino's ambitious Western *Heaven's Gate*—or so the story goes. The chapter reconsiders that movie's role in the demise of both the Western and the Hollywood art film, and argues that the film's reputation as a Western improves after the genre "returns" in the mid-1990s following the success of Eastwood's *Unforgiven* (1992). Finally, the chapter scrutinizes the popular claim that the Western migrated to—or became—another genre, science fiction, in the 1980s.

Still in the Saddle proceeds from a basic but important observation about the Westerns produced between 1969 and 1980: they were far more diverse than histories of the genre acknowledge. This is significant because these same histories, although they reference a small number of films, argue that the Western *in general* reflected the hopes and fears of Americans, as the genre is argued to have done in earlier periods. The number of Westerns identified by critics as revisionist is small relative to the total number of Westerns produced during the period. If the numbers alone don't tell us something, they at the very least impel us to question how representative this small sample of films is. The answers have consequences not only for our understanding of the movie Western but also for arguments that use the revisionist Western as evidence for broad claims about American history and culture.

This book does not set out to dispute the fact that the Western died out as a popular form during this period, or to contradict general explanations of why this occurred (a confluence of factors, including shifting demographics, modified production patterns and processes, changing tastes and the failure to develop new stars). It does, however, offer a corrective to claims that the Western's decline was characterized or produced by an increasingly cynical self-consciousness, along with the notion that only a few revisionist Westerns were any good or resonated with audiences, and that even these types of Westerns quickly became unappealing. Instead, *Still in the Saddle* shows the later Western as it truly was: like John Wayne's character Rooster Cogburn in *True Grit,* born game and going out that way.

PART I

Revision and Regeneration

1

The Scattered Formula in Western Movie Criticism

Once, we happily accepted myths of Western heroes as honorable scouts who lived by codes. Then movies like "Little Big Man" said that the myths were lies and that Gen. Custer, for example, was really a genocidal maniac.
—Tom Shales, *The Washington Post*, January 28, 1980

Revisionist Westerns . . . dominated the decade of the 1970s, and through their emphasis on greed, genocide, and white guilt managed to kill off the Western film genre by decade's end.
—Paul Andrew Hutton, *Montana: The Magazine of Western History*, 1995

The traditional Western at its peak celebrated mainstream American values and ideology—the American Dream. In the 1960s darkness struck national innocence—the cultural, political and sexual revolutions, Vietnam, Watergate, assassinations, etc. Westerns continued to be made, but they were revisionist and began to speak less to the mainstream audience. The positivist, transcendental, triumphalist tone was lost.
—Jim Kitses, quoted in *GamePro*, June 22, 2010

In January of 2009, I attended a lecture by film scholar Ed Buscombe at the British Film Institute (BFI) in London as part of a retrospective of the films of Sam Peckinpah. The focus of the lecture was Peckinpah's Westerns, from *Ride the High Country* (1962) through to *Pat Garrett and*

Billy the Kid (1974). In a wide-ranging discussion, Buscombe reflected on the legacy of the auteur theory in scholarship on the Western and highlighted a number of key themes that recur over Peckinpah's Western oeuvre, including an emphasis on tragedy. After Buscombe concluded his talk, the floor was opened for questions. A man seated to my right rose to his feet, was handed the microphone, and asked Buscombe how Peckinpah's films related to the "revisionist Western."

It was a fair query, to be sure, and it was met with a few nods from others in the audience and a whispered "yes, good question" from a woman seated behind me. It is also worth noting, though, that at no point in his presentation had Buscombe used the term revisionist to describe Peckinpah's Westerns—or any other Westerns, for that matter.

In response to the gentleman's question, Buscombe first commented on the general imprecision of the term, but then said that if "revisionist" was taken to mean films that were purposefully critical of the genre, like Robert Altman's *McCabe & Mrs. Miller,* then he did not consider Peckinpah's Westerns to be revisionist.

This anecdote—short as it is—tells us a great deal about the Western. It tells us that a particular kind of Western, distinguished by the adjective "revisionist," exists—or is at least believed to exist by the kinds of people who attend lectures about movies. The adjectival modification also distinguishes these Westerns from *other* Westerns. Given that the idea of the revisionist Western was introduced in the context of a discussion about Sam Peckinpah, who made his Westerns in the 1960s and 1970s, and that the word "revisionist" signals a reexamination or correction of something that already exists, these other Westerns must be *older* Westerns, made before the likes of Peckinpah and Altman. This not only implies that the genre has changed over time, but that those changes can be organized along authorial or thematic lines. That is to say, what distinguishes the Westerns of this later period is that they look back on earlier Westerns by other filmmakers and revise them in some way. This is a common way of understanding both how and why film genres change over time: successive periods characterized by an increasing awareness of the genre's established conventions and themes.

Yet, in the face of this, the absence of the revisionist Western in Buscombe's talk and his subsequent skepticism about the term's usefulness are equally telling. As knowledgeable as the BFI audience may have been, Buscombe is a leading authority on the Western. This is not to say that one party is necessarily right and the other wrong; instead, it suggests a possible divide between popular and scholarly interpretation—or, at the very least, a difference of opinion. Moreover, simply because the Westerns of Peckinpah are not considered revisionist does not mean that there is no such thing as a revisionist Western. Buscombe's own example of *McCabe & Mrs. Miller* suggests that the revisionist Western may exist as a variant of the genre (provided that there are other Westerns like it). Yet if *McCabe & Mrs. Miller* is, or could be considered, a revisionist Western while other Westerns of its time are not, this indicates that there are also distinctions to be made within the genre at a particular point in time, rather than across time. This is a far less common conception of how movie genres operate.

Revisionism and Western Movie Criticism

That the revisionist Western was introduced not by Buscombe but an audience member is appropriate on several levels. The absence of the revisionist Western in Buscombe's lecture is consistent with his scholarship on the genre, where the concept is never employed. Yet he is in the minority. Today, the term is used in all varieties of writing on the Western, from scholarly essays to mainstream criticism. The revisionist Western is not a limited, specialist concept. It is, as the BFI example suggests, a *popular* one.

The term revisionist was first applied to the genre, occasionally, in trade journals and reviews in the 1970s, when critics begin to distinguish a series of new "'revisionist' Westerns . . . deliberately designed to destroy the previous myths of heroic cowboy literature and films."[1] *The Wild Bunch,* Peckinpah's violent lament for the end of the mythical west and its larger-than-life heroes, is frequently identified as the inaugurator of this trend. By the 1980s, the "revisionist Western" gains wider currency as a more general description for the genre in the preceding decade.

For their part, academics were not oblivious to the changes taking place in the Western in the 1970s, even if they did not initially characterize these changes as an outright revision. Indeed, what comes across most clearly in examinations of the genre from this time is the variety of Westerns being produced.

Writing in 1973, Jack Nachbar likens the formula of the contemporary Western to the "wide and confusing pattern" of a shotgun blast. He argues that the Western's standard plot structure, focused on the epic moment of confrontation between the forces of civilization and wilderness on the American frontier, had branched into four basic types: (1) a "traditional" type, starring saddle-hardened veterans like John Wayne and Burt Lancaster; (2) the "anti-Western," using the genre as a vehicle for social criticism; (3) the "new-Western," which eschews genre tradition in favor of realistic portrayals of frontier life; and, finally, (4) the "personal-Western," where auteur filmmakers like Peckinpah and Altman use the genre to express their unique viewpoints.[2] After delineating these divisions within the genre, Nachbar proposes that all four types are nevertheless contained by a new theme, exploring a different moment in history when "progress overcame the fundamental aspirations of the old pioneer and transformed him into someone irrelevant and out of place."[3]

Nachbar was not alone in observing a splintering of the genre. In a contemporary essay, John G. Cawelti agrees that it is no longer possible to speak of a single Western formula, but he sees the divisions within the genre somewhat differently. He proposes three types: (1) the violent, cynical Italian Western of Sergio Leone; (2) the "Western Godfather" of John Wayne, aiming to reaffirm the genre's traditional themes; and (3) a class of Western that seeks to create a new myth of the West more sympathetic to Indians and hostile to traditional heroes.[4] What unites these three types is "a disillusioned and pessimistic view of society and an obsession with the place of violence in it."[5]

In a 1982 essay about the "allusory" nature of 1970s American moviemaking, Noël Carroll describes *McCabe & Mrs. Miller* as "an example of the revisionist western which dates back to at least *The Wild Bunch.*" He offers the following definition of the type: "The revisionist western lives off the classical western, which it criticizes by decisive subversions of set genre plots, locales, and/or characters. The revisionist western assays these alterations for the sake of projecting a broad sentiment of social disenchantment by demystifying national myths and registering a sense of loss."[6] In a footnote, Carroll lists eight additional revisionist Westerns:

Little Big Man, The Ballad of Cable Hogue (Sam Peckinpah, 1970), *Bad Company* (Robert Benton, 1972), *The Culpepper Cattle Co., Dirty Little Billy* (Stan Dragoti, 1972), *The Great Northfield Minnesota Raid* (Philip Kaufman, 1972), *Pat Garrett and Billy the Kid* (Sam Peckinpah, 1973), and *The Missouri Breaks* (Arthur Penn, 1976). Like Nachbar and Cawelti, Carroll sees the revisionist Western as one of several types coexisting within the genre in the late 1960s and 1970s, alongside popular pictures like *The War Wagon* (Burt Kennedy, 1967) and Westerns like *The Shootist* (Don Siegel, 1976) that, he claims, reworked the genre without being revisionist.[7]

In 1987, Nachbar, writing with Michael T. Marsden, both revises and updates his classificatory model. His first two types, the traditional Western and the anti-Western, remain largely unchanged. On the impact of the anti-Western, the authors comment: "Because Westerns since the late '60s have presented a much less idealized picture of the frontier West, it appears that anti-Westerns were an important influence on the entire genre."[8] At the same time, Marsden and Nachbar argue that the Westerns of Clint Eastwood, the last major Hollywood star and filmmaker to be principally associated with the genre, also "reaffirm the ideals of the traditional Western." They write: "Eastwood's American films are known for their violence, which stems from the macho power of his tight-lipped heroes. Within such a context, however, Eastwood's Westerns develop a pattern of values that defends proper civilization as strongly as the oldest Western movies."[9] The new and personal Westerns are reconfigured into the "elegiac" and "experimental" Westerns. The former, with roots in 1950s Westerns like *The Gunfighter* (Henry King, 1950) and *Shane* (George Stevens, 1953), "mourn the loss of the frontier hero." The latter displays "a fascination with the Western itself," manipulating the genre to convey an authorial vision and extend the implications of earlier Westerns. According to the authors, Peckinpah's Westerns are elegiac, while Altman's are experimental.[10]

While Nachbar and Cawelti each describe what we could call "revisionism" occurring within the genre in the late 1960s and 1970s, these "revisions" follow no one set precept or objective. That there is disagreement among critics about how to characterize and classify both individual films and larger trends is a further indication of this. Yet the inter-genre divisions of the period delineated by Nachbar, Cawelti, and Carroll do contrast with an apparent unity the genre enjoyed in earlier times when it seems to have had a single formula or standard plot.

The idea that genres experience a classic phase or "golden age" is one of the most widely held and most scrutinized in the study of movie genres. It is also often bound to the notion that genres develop in particular ways, responding to internal or external forces (or some combination of the two). As it happens, the Western is very good at supporting such theories, so it is not surprising that, implicitly or explicitly, all three authors posit the existence of a classic Western from which the genre then splits apart into the diversity of types detailed above. Scholarship on the genre continues to refer to the "classic Western," typically as a rhetorical means of distinguishing between periods in the genre's history. John H. Lenihan writes that "*The Appaloosa* [Sidney J. Furie, 1966] and *The Hired Hand* [Peter Fonda, 1971] . . . differ from the classic western lyricism of the great outdoors (e.g., *Shane*) by removing any connotation of a promising civilization." Michael Coyne asserts, "*The Gunfighter* heralded the advent of true maturity within the classic Western." Patrick McGee argues that *The Man Who Shot Liberty Valance* (John Ford, 1962) "brings closure to the classic Western itself," whereas a later Western like *The Wild Bunch* dramatizes the "contradictions in the relationship between subjectivity and power in the postmodern world." Deborah Knight and George McKnight write, "The classic western tells the story about expansion westward. [*McCabe & Mrs. Miller*] tells what happened when the idealization of western expansion and the mystique developed around the figure of the western hero faltered in the late 1960s and early 1970s."[11]

Noted scholar of the Western Jim Kitses appears to dispute the idea of a Western golden age in his 1996 essay "Post-modernism and the Western," an ambitious attempt to account for the genre's development from the 1960s to the 1990s in light of postmodernist theory. Kitses asserts that the Western has never been a "monolith," and that there have always been deviations and dissents within it—a "revisionist shadow" of films including *The Ox-Bow Incident* (William Wellman, 1943), *The Gunfighter, Broken Arrow* (Delmer Daves, 1950), *High Noon* (Fred Zinnemann, 1952), and *Johnny Guitar* (Nicholas Ray, 1954). In an argument that recalls the work of Russian formalist literary critics, who held that art evolves through a continual process of minority trends supplanting majority ones—what they called the "canonization of the junior branch"—Kitses sees the 1960s as time when the sun sets and the Western's "revisionist shadow" becomes the mainstream: "In retrospect, it is possible to see these movies as precursors to a counter-tradition that the Western tradition itself generates, a revisionist shadow, a parallel track to the imperial mainstream with all its ideological baggage. Accumulating in fragments and on the margins, this practice shifts gears radically in the 60s, wherein America loses her innocence, the result of traumatic change—the Vietnam War, civil rights, imperial assassinations, Watergate."[12] The Western's ideological baggage includes racism and imperialism, which are directly opposed to emphases from the late 1960s onward on feel-good values like tolerance, inclusivity, and especially multiculturalism, which Kitses calls "America's official ideology marking the millennium . . . itself a revision of the melting pot thesis that underlay and underwrote the nation in the 20th century."[13] So, while revisionist tendencies have always been present in the Western in the form of critiques of frontier justice or the genre's treatment of Indians, it is ultimately cultural change that precipitates an about-face in the genre. America loses her innocence, and so does the Western.

Treating movies as reflections of the social conditions of their production has long been a standard approach in cinema studies. The work of the critic becomes to interpret, or "read," a film for what Kristin Thompson calls symptomatic meaning: "We also use interpretation to create meanings that go beyond the level of the individual work, and that help define its relation to the world. When we speak of a film's non-explicit ideology, or of the film as a reflection of social tendencies, or of the film as suggestive of the mental states of large groups of people, then we are interpreting its *symptomatic* meanings."[14] This particular methodology has been criticized on a number of grounds. While popular films undoubtedly reflect contemporary tastes to a certain degree, whether taste in movies can be taken as an accurate gauge of the mood of an entire nation is an open question. As Steve Neale points out, not only does such an approach ignore the role of institutional determinants, but the assumption that consumer decision-making, with its own multiplicity of determinants, can be considered a form of "cultural expression" is a questionable one.[15] David Bordwell observes that reflectionist accounts often overlook how "movies are made by particular people, all with varying agendas," who will rework any given idea or concept in myriad ways during a movie's development from concept to script to screen—a process that can take years. How representative the personnel of the movie industry are of wider society is also a relevant question. Writes Bordwell, "[T]hese workers, we are constantly reminded, are far from typical, living their superficial lives in Beverly Hills. How can the fears and yearnings of the masses be adequately 'reflected' once these atypical individuals have finished with the product?"[16] Yet, in spite of objections about the general viability of such approaches in the study of cinema, symptomatic readings have dominated criticism of the Western from the late 1960s to the present.

In scholarly writing on the Western, the idea of the American frontier as the site of contestation between the competing values of civilization and savagery continues to resonate. This critical conception of what defines the movie Western is employed in the influential early work of a number of scholars, including Kitses (1969), Cawelti (1971), Peter Wollen (1969), and Will Wright (1975), but also owes an often-unacknowledged debt to the "Frontier Thesis" of historian Frederick Jackson Turner, first articulated in an address to the World's Congress of Historians and Historical Students at the Columbian Exhibition in Chicago in 1893. In the published version of his talk, Turner states:

> Behind institutions, behind constitutional forms and modifications, lie the vital forces that call these organs into life and shape them to meet changing conditions. The peculiarity of American institutions is, the fact that they have been compelled to adapt themselves to the changes of an expanding people—to the changes involved in crossing a continent, in winning a wilderness, and in developing at each area of this progress out of the primitive economic and political conditions of the frontier into the complexity of city life.[17]

Turner's conception of the frontier as a border between conflicting values—the meeting point between savagery and civilization—posits a binary opposition at the heart of the American experience. This conflict is emphasized in subsequent scholarship that proceeds from the position that the popular stories of modern societies, based on underlying narrative "structures," function like myths did for earlier societies, both expressing and providing imaginary resolutions to deep-rooted, fundamental cultural conflicts. In the case of the Western, it is the mythical frontier lawman who straddles the structural divide between savagery and civilization, embodying the best of both worlds and thereby reconciling them in the American imaginary.

Perhaps the key reason why the westward expansion that followed the American Civil War has enjoyed a privileged place in American history—and the Western a privileged place among American genres—is that the pioneer experience is seen as quintessentially American in nature. It is *the* American experience. As such, the Western is more than simply one myth of American popular culture—it is *the* American myth. Even as the "New Western History" movement of the 1980s moved analyses of the historical American frontier away from the Turner Thesis towards a consideration of economic conditions and issues of race, class, and gender—concerns at the fore of Kitses' postmodernist critique of the later Western—popular representations of the mythical American West continue to be interpreted symptomatically. For example, in *Gunfighter Nation* (1992), the final volume in Richard Slotkin's comprehensive study of the myth of the frontier, Hollywood Westerns figure prominently as evidence of the prevalence and enduring influence of a racialist theory of white ascendancy and supremacy in twentieth century American culture.

Given the continued adoption of cultural approaches to the study of the Western, it is not surprising that in their initial analyses both Cawelti and Nachbar argue that we can account for the fracture of the Western formula in the late 1960s on cultural grounds. Nachbar sees the fragmentation of the Western as a reflection of an ideological fragmentation of American society that began in the 1960s, while Cawelti contends that, even if changes to the American film industry are taken into account, there are "still enough differences in the form and content of current western films to suggest that the western themes and patterns of action that so deeply engaged American filmmakers and audiences for some twenty years after World War II have lost much of their interest. It seems to me that the diversity of contemporary westerns reflects a quest for new themes and meanings to revitalize the traditional western formula."[18] As explained in later scholarship, the Western's decline (or death) represents the failure of this search for new cultural resonance, where, as Richard Maltby writes, "the Western has ceased to function as a vehicle for American culture to tell itself the stories it needs to hear."[19]

Although Kitses' "counter-tradition" productively posits the coexistence of competing trends within a single genre, and implies that the relationship between Westerns and American culture was therefore not as straightforward as other theories may suggest, he is silent on the matter of how, or why, the Western generated its "revisionist shadow." How did such forward-looking, consensus-defying movies come to be?

Existing scholarship on cinema genres suggests two possible approaches that could account for this development. The first holds that genres develop not in response to cultural changes but according to *internal* forces. The second holds that change in a genre's trajectory is the result of intervention by innovative film artists.

The idea that genres change following a particular pattern is a common one in film criticism, but it finds its strongest articulation, regarding both the Western and genres in general, in Thomas Schatz's influential 1981 book *Hollywood Genres.* Writes Schatz: "Because continued variation tends to sensitize us to a genre's social message, our interests, and those of the filmmakers, gradually expand from the message itself to its articulation, from the tale to the visual and narrative artistry of its telling."[20] Schatz uses the Westerns of director John Ford to demonstrate how the genre evolves from a state of formal transparency to one of opaque, self-conscious formalism—an internal pattern of evolution that he argues is a common feature of all movie genres. Drawing on a diverse range of influences, a genre first goes through a period of experimentation during which its conventions are isolated and established. Experimentation eventually produces a golden age of stability and formal transparency. This is followed by a period of increasing self-consciousness, where conventions and themes are embellished and refined. Finally, self-consciousness gives way to self-reflexivity and parody.

Schatz's evolutionary model provides a useful way of conceptualizing the history of the movie Western. Cinema's early and silent periods produced a number of successful or notable films that contained cowboy imagery or frontier themes, but were not "Westerns" in the later sense.[21] Eventually, elements from these movies coalesced in a remarkable series of A-pictures released in 1939 and 1940, including *Stagecoach* (John Ford, 1939), *Jesse James* (Henry King, 1939), *Union Pacific* (Cecil B. DeMille, 1939), *The Westerner* (William Wyler, 1940), and *The Return of Frank James* (Fritz Lang, 1940), which established formal and thematic conventions that would endure for more than twenty years. In the 1950s, the genre began to refine these conventions, although not yet to the point of self-critique. In films like *Shane* and *The Searchers* (John Ford, 1956) the Western hero is distilled to his essence—a man with a gun, devoid of sentimental attachments—and a greater attention to costume and staging lends proceedings a ceremonial importance. Over the course of the 1960s and into the 1970s, the genre turns its attention inward, first in self-reflection, as in *The Man Who Shot Liberty Valance* or *The Wild Bunch,* and finally in self-mockery, as in *Cat Ballou* (Elliot Silverstein, 1965) and *McCabe & Mrs. Miller.* The model is thus able to account for a lengthy Western golden age as well as the genre's swift decline. Thus, everything from *Dodge City* (Michael Curtiz, 1939) to *Rio Bravo* (Howard Hawks, 1959) is classic Western territory, whereas only five years separate *The Wild Bunch* from *Blazing Saddles* (Mel Brooks, 1974). This says nothing about a counter-tradition, though. Where is it to be found?

While evolutionary accounts of genre are often expressed, simplistically, as a succession of discrete blocks of films, a more nuanced account, like that espoused by the Russian formalists, could acknowledge that generic evolution is an incremental, overlapping process. Thus a picture like *Shane,* while it emerged during the genre's golden age, could be seen to presage later Westerns in its requiem for the solitary cowboy hero or its suggestive formal minimalism. Looked at this way, the Western's "revisionist shadow" comprises early examples of movies that evince the characteristics that will come to typify a later period in the genre's evolution. Significantly, these precursory pictures emerge not as the product of cultural stimulus, but according to immutable laws of genre evolution.

Our second potential explanation for the appearance of a Western counter-tradition—that generic change is the product of artistic intercession—is not altogether incompatible with a model of genre evolution. Schatz states that it is in the interest of filmmakers to refine a genre as its "social message" becomes increasingly well known, and his examination of the Western focuses on the films of a single director, John Ford. Kitses' seminal study of the Western, *Horizons West,* also examines authorship in the Western. The original 1969 monograph included chapters on Anthony Mann, Budd Boetticher, and Sam Peckinpah, and a revised edition released in 2004 added chapters on John Ford, Sergio Leone, and Clint Eastwood. Expectedly, the revisionist Westerns Kitses names in

"Post-modernism and the Western" as most interesting are each defined along authorial lines: "[t]he hugely influential achievements of Peckinpah and Leone, key figures, Arthur Penn's work and especially *Little Big Man,* Robert Altman's *McCabe & Mrs. Miller,* Clint Eastwood and *The Outlaw Josey Wales* in particular . . . and finally, Michael Cimino's *Heaven's Gate.*"[22]

Historically, the study of the movie Western has by and large been a study of specific directors. As much the Western genre has been taken as embodying certain recurring themes that relate to enduring tensions in American society, which movies are understood to incarnate these themes has frequently been defined as the product of a select group of filmmakers.[23] A focus on authorship not only accounts for exemplary Westerns that change the course of the genre's history, but also more eclectic pictures—including some that Kitses names as part of the genre's earlier counter-tradition. Westerns like *Johnny Guitar, Rancho Notorious* (Fritz Lang, 1952), and *Forty Guns* (Samuel Fuller, 1957) are inextricably linked to their eccentric directors.

Consider how the perceived change the Western undergoes in the late 1960s corresponds to a change in who is making Westerns. John Ford, Anthony Mann, Howard Hawks, and other esteemed veterans of the 1940s and 1950s give way to the likes of Sam Peckinpah, Robert Altman, and Arthur Penn. Moreover, just as those studio veterans are associated with a larger era—"Classical Hollywood"—so, too, are these later directors part of a subsequent period of American cinema history, dubbed the "Hollywood Renaissance."

Led by a group of young, liberal-minded filmmakers, the late 1960s to the mid-1970s are remembered, as Geoff King writes, as "an era in which Hollywood produced a relatively high number of innovative films that seemed to go beyond the confines of conventional studio fare in terms of their content and style and their existence as products of a purely commercial and corporate system."[24] This renaissance in American moviemaking corresponds nearly exactly to the revisionist Western—not only chronologically, but also in its roster of auteur filmmakers. Fittingly, it is director Michael Cimino's calamitous *Heaven's Gate,* the epitome of the authorial excesses of the period, which is held responsible for killing off both the Hollywood art film *and* the Western. Just as Peter Biskind melodramatically eulogizes the years 1967 to 1980 as "the last time it was really exciting to make movies in Hollywood, the last time people could be consistently proud of the movies they made," so does David A. Cook comment, "More and more, it begins to seem that the period 1969–1980 was the Western's last great moment."[25]

The Wild Bunch and *Heaven's Gate,* then, provide a convenient periodization for this "last great moment" that resonates on multiple levels.

The Problematic Confluence of Genre Methodologies

At this point, we have in hand three broad methods by which the Western has been appraised and which account for the emergence of the revisionist Western in the late 1960s:

1. A structuralist approach that treats genre as myth, articulating and resolving tensions in American culture.
2. A teleological approach that considers genres as developing according to an internal logic of increasing formalism.
3. An auteurist approach that treats genres as a vehicle for the expressions of great filmmakers.

A plurality of critical approaches is undeniably a good thing. While a given examination of the Western should certainly be persuasive on its own terms, it need not preclude the possibility of alternative accounts of the genre. Yet what is remarkable about the Western, and the revisionist Western in particular, is how it is able to provide evidence in support of each method *at the same time.* Increased formal consciousness corresponds with social change, social change corresponds with new filmmakers, new filmmakers correspond with increased formal consciousness—and so on. What results is the genre theory equivalent of a perfect storm. However a given critic contends that movie genres "work," the revisionist Western confirms it. We would do well, though, to bear in mind the old adage that correlation does not necessarily equal causation.

Rather than complementing the prevailing structuralist account of why genres change, teleological and auteurist theories in fact controvert it. Kitses, for example, argues that the Western's revisionist turn is precipitated by factors external to the genre, namely cultural change and young filmmakers. While Kitses does appeal to the notion of a transcendental conflict at the core of American culture, his argument about the revisionist Western is still historical, holding that features of and changes to a genre are the product of contextual factors. By contrast, Schatz argues that the same development is the product of an *internal* process of evolution that proceeds apace regardless of circumstance. As Raphaëlle Moine has observed, a model of genre evolution does not totally ignore historical factors, but "subordinates them to a general schema that assumes an inescapable development from classical equilibrium towards decline."[26] To see the correlation of the structuralist and authorial explanations for the revisionist Western, both of which are largely historical, with that of the teleological model, which is largely ahistorical, as causation is to suggest that all of human activity is developing in accordance with the same general evolutionary schema—a grand, if dubious, proposition.

Structuralist and authorial explanations for genre development have historically enjoyed a greater compatibility. While cinematic genre study is often conceived of as a kind of antidote to authorship studies for its ability to bring attention to films that do not have the benefit of an auteur director, the two approaches often work hand-in-hand. After all, celebrated filmmakers are often associated with particular genres, and scholarship on the Western has, again, traditionally placed a strong emphasis on the roles of individual filmmakers. In *Horizons West,* Kitses envisions a reciprocal relationship between auteur directors and the Western genre: "Rather than an empty vessel breathed into by the film-maker, the genre is a vital structure through which flow a myriad of themes and concepts. As such the form can provide a director with a range of possible connections and the space in which to experiment, to shape and refine the kind of effects and meanings he is working towards."[27] The Westerns of Peckinpah, Mann *et al* express the essence of the genre, and those filmmakers have each found their own essence within the Western.

Given our natural inclination to equate change with youth (in the arts and elsewhere), it is not surprising that younger filmmakers are thought to express contemporary concerns better than their older peers. This thinking is evident in accounts of both the revisionist Western and the Hollywood Renaissance, which emphasize the contributions of younger moviemakers like Altman, Penn, and Cimino. In placing young auteur filmmakers at their center, however, these accounts imply that artists neither change their views nor adapt their styles over time, which is patently not true. We need look no further than the long careers of either Ford or Altman for evidence of this. While Kitses' later valorization of the Westerns of Peckinpah, Leone, Penn, Altman, Eastwood, and Cimino as the most interesting of the 1960s and 1970s suggests that he subscribes to the Renaissance account's adulation of new filmmakers, in *Horizons West* he originally emphasized the need to "be prepared to entertain the idea that *auteurs* grow, and that the genre can help to crystallize preoccupations and contribute actively to development."[28]

In recent years, the Renaissance account of 1960s and 1970s Hollywood has come under closer scrutiny, and with good reason. It is true that movies like *Bonnie and Clyde* (Arthur Penn, 1967), *Easy Rider* (Dennis Hopper, 1969), and *Five Easy Pieces* (Bob Rafelson, 1970) were stylish and innovative, and made good money—but not as much money as more "traditional" fare like *The Love Bug* (Robert Stevenson, 1969), *Airport* (George Seaton, 1970), or *Fiddler on the Roof* (Norman Jewison, 1971). The overstated centrality of the movies of Renaissance auteurs in histories of the period calls into question whether those filmmakers or their films did, in fact, express the zeitgeist. Thompson notes that, despite the critical attention they receive, auteurist works like *McCabe & Mrs. Miller* constituted a small minority of the films released by Hollywood firms during the 1970s; a look at the highest-grossing films of the period reveals a "business as usual" pattern dominated by genre films like *Patton* (Franklin J. Shaffner, 1970), *Love Story* (Arthur Hiller, 1971), and *The Poseidon Adventure* (Ronald Neame, 1973).[29] In a similar vein, Steve Neale has pointed to the "continued appeal of family-, female-, or adult-oriented films with classical ideology and narrative values" in the 1960s and 70s, including comedies, war pictures, and lavish musicals.[30]

In "Post-modernism and the Western," Kitses observes that Buscombe, in *The BFI Companion to the Western,* does not use the term *revisionist* to describe any period of the Western's development. Kitses remarks that "attempts to avoid taxonomies in general are certainly understandable," but nevertheless argues that "there now seems a strong argument for recognition of the revisionist Western as a discrete, dominant type."[31] While this suggests that there may be other "types" of coeval Westerns, Kitses does not mention any—even though he has done so for the previous phase of the genre's history. As much as he wants to acknowledge that taxonomies are problematic, he, like others, finds the revisionist idea so appealing because it confirms the notion that the Western responds to cultural change. He wants to have it both ways, and postmodernism by its very nature allows him to do this. He writes: "[I]f post-modernism is hostile to separate, linear models, to categorization, it also dearly loves contradiction. Whatever the limitations of revisionism as a classification system, the need to point to an ongoing stream of works that play off the traditional, push against the past, and erect a counter-myth, is self-evident."[32] Kitses goes so far as to stake out a defensive position against unnamed critics who see revisionism as unwelcome. He detects a "strain of denial" manifest in discussions of genre as it has darkened, a "doomed last stand against the encroachment of the revisionist films, often seen as doing violence to *the* Western—the classical model."[33]

While there is no shortage of essays and articles appreciative of older Westerns, it is not entirely clear where this strain of denial is to be found. Certainly, some 1970s Westerns like *Soldier Blue* (Ralph Nelson, 1970) and *Doc* (Frank Perry, 1971) are panned for their leaden attempts at criticizing the genre's conventions and myths. But whether this derision is in fact a knee-jerk defense of the genre by lovers of old Westerns, rather than fair valuations of uneven movies made by pretentious filmmakers, is debatable. While Nachbar's 1973 appraisal of the genre is tinged with melancholy, he acknowledges that Westerns like *McCabe & Mrs. Miller* and *The Wild Bunch* were already being acclaimed as classics.[34] Around the same time, Cawelti sees the most promise in those Westerns that address, or redress, aspects of the genre that he finds objectionable in earlier Westerns, like the treatment of Indians. Indeed, many of the movies frequently invoked in discussions of the revisionist Western are still considered to be among the greatest Westerns ever made—indeed, some are considered to be among the greatest *movies* ever made.

In the American Film Institute's 2007 ranking of the top ten Westerns of all time (table 1), five are from the 1960s and later, including *The Wild Bunch* and *McCabe & Mrs. Miller.*[35] Out of the 50 Westerns that were eligible to be voted for, 20 were released in the 1960s and 70s—compared to 19 released in the 1940s and 50s.[36] This is despite the fact that over *five times* as many Westerns were released in the 1940s and 50s as in the 1960s and 70s.[37] On another AFI list, *The Wild Bunch* placed 80th on a 1998 ranking of the 100 best American movies of all time. When the

Table 1. The American Film Institute's Top 10 Westerns (2007)

1. *The Searchers* (1956)	6. *The Wild Bunch* (1969)
2. *High Noon* (1952)	7. *Butch Cassidy and the Sundance Kid* (1969)
3. *Shane* (1953)	8. *McCabe & Mrs. Miller* (1971)
4. *Unforgiven* (1992)	9. *Stagecoach* (1939)
5. *Red River* (1948)	10. *Cat Ballou* (1965)

Source: "AFI's 10 Top 10: Top 10 Westerns," http://www.afi.com/10top10/category.aspx?cat=3.

AFI revised this list in 2007, *The Wild Bunch* retained its ranking. Less fortunate was John Ford's *Stagecoach* (1939), which was dropped from the list entirely! Clearly, the revisionist Western occupies a privileged place in contemporary valuations of the genre.

There is now a confluence between scholarly accounts of the later Western and the popular conception of the revisionist Western that emerged by the 1980s. It is this conception of the Western that persists to this day. Clint Eastwood's 1992 Western *Unforgiven*, for example, was widely described as revisionist, as have been the majority of Westerns released since.[38]

As time has passed, the Westerns of the late 1960s and 1970s have become characterized in a manner comparable to the classic Western: as a unified generic entity, comprising a select group of films and filmmakers. Rather than constantly changing, the Western is seen as progressing incrementally in distinct, stable periods. As we have seen, this is a central tendency in genre criticism that transcends individual critical methodologies.

In contrast to much writing about the classic Western, however, accounts of the revisionist Western place the relationship between the genre and contemporary social and political forces in the foreground. Yet the nature of the relationship between the Western and its wider context depends on the historical perspective of the critic. Nachbar, writing in the 1970s, sees ideological fragmentation producing a diversity of new types of Westerns. Later writers see the same cultural tumult, but they see it as producing a single, dominant type of film.

There are precedents for this kind of change in the history of criticism of the Western. *Shane* may be, in the words of Will Wright, "the classic of the classic Westerns," but French critic André Bazin, writing twenty years earlier, saw it and other Westerns of the 1950s as a lamentable move away from the classical perfection the genre had achieved in the late 1930s and 1940s.[39] Over time, these distinctions have been subsumed by a conception of an overarching Western golden age.

Is it the case that, with the benefit of twenty years of hindsight, later critics are able to more accurately judge and describe the state of things—finding order within what initially seemed chaos? Or is this act of description, in fact, delimitation—the deliberate crafting of an orderly narrative by a process of selection and exclusion? The initial appraisals of the later Western by Nachbar, Cawelti, and Carroll indicate as much, as does the recurring suggestion that there are other types of Westerns in the late 1960s and 1970s.

A closer inspection of the dominant cultural methodology used to account for the Western's revisionist break also turns up cracks. Kitses claims that America lost her innocence in the 1960s, yet the standard narrative he and others draw upon—where Vietnam, Watergate, and civil rights begin to move the nation from melting pot to multiculturalism—is a simplified sketch of the decade. The Vietnam War was initially supported by a majority of the American people. Richard Nixon was unquestionably a divisive figure who met a scandalous end, but he won a comfortable victory in the 1968 presidential election and a decisive one in 1972. The civil rights movement brought about positive change for many Americans, but not all groups benefited equally.

If we accept that the types of movies produced will reflect, in some way, a nation's social and political climate, then it is reasonable to expect a diversity of material given the complexity of this historical picture. It could also be that the variety of Westerns produced at the time is more appropriately explained on industrial, rather than cultural grounds: that, in trying to perpetuate the genre, filmmakers and producers were attempting to appeal to a heterogeneous audience that included both younger and older patrons. The pursuit of profit in this context explains why, for example, a studio like Warner Bros. would produce and distribute *The Wild Bunch* in 1969; a John Wayne Western, *Chisum* (Andrew V. McLaglen), in 1970; and *McCabe & Mrs. Miller* in 1971. Or why Cinema Center Films would produce revisionist pictures *Little Big Man* and *A Man Called Horse* (Elliot Silverstein, 1970) at the same time as traditional Westerns *Big Jake* (George Sherman, 1971) and *Rio Lobo* (Howard Hawks, 1970).

That this diversity is seen to mark a departure from an earlier period of stability still presents a problem, however. If the inter-genre fragmentation identified as characteristic of the later Western reflects ideological fragmentation, it would then follow that the unity and stability the genre experienced during its classic period was a reflection of ideological unity and stability. Although the late 1940s and 1950s are frequently presented as a tranquil period of post-war cultural consensus, this is just as much an oversimplification as the late-1960s narrative criticized above. While there was no war in Vietnam, no hippies, and no President Nixon in the 1950s, there was war in Korea, beatniks, and Congressman, Senator, and Vice President Nixon. Harry Truman never experienced anything like Watergate, but he did leave office in 1952 with what remain to this day some of the lowest approval ratings ever recorded.

The idea raised by Kitses that there are precedents within the Western's history for the types of Westerns that emerge in the 1970s also challenges the divisions that have been established by genre critics and historians. Although Kitses states that there was a "shadow" of movies in the Western's history that heralded the revisionist Western, he offers no explanation of this conceit beyond naming sample movies, and, as we've seen, attempts to explain it using common critical methodologies prove unsatisfactory. By insisting that these precursors exist as alternatives to an "imperial mainstream," Kitses actually affirms the existence of a Western golden age from which the revisionist Western can properly depart. Terms like "shadow" and "counter" denote otherness, thus reinforcing the norm of the classic Western. Yet, as with *Shane* possibly anticipating subsequent elegiac Westerns, the films that Kitses identifies as presaging the advent of the revisionist Western are far from marginal works. While none are directed by John Ford or Anthony Mann, they all are A-pictures made by well-known filmmakers, and most were popular hits. If a nostalgic movie like *Shane,* often regarded as the apotheosis of the classic western, anticipates the Westerns of Peckinpah—as Marsden and Nachbar claim—it suggests that there are continuities across the genre's history independent of particular filmmakers or historical context.

The Revisionist Western in Context

Asserting the importance of the revisionist Western, Kitses writes: "The totality of remarkable works corrective of America stretching back to the 60s has not eroded or diminished or killed off the Western, it now *is* the Western."[40] And yet, accumulating in fragments and on the margins—to borrow Kitses's phrase—is a body of evidence that suggests that revisionism is only part of the story.

As much as it may be commonplace for small selections of exemplary movies to come to represent entire genres or periods in movie history, in the case of the later Western these selections have proved to be remarkably durable, and the revisionist account of the period has avoided the kind of critical reexamination that the Hollywood Renaissance has been subject to. We have seen, however, that the popular histories and established methodologies upon which the revisionist Western rests prove to be selective and inconsistent. Despite repeated indications, explicit in early accounts and implicit in later writing, that there were other types of Westerns in the late 1960s and 1970s, as well as claims for thematic connections that both transcend and challenge existing categories, little has been done to directly challenge the prevailing conception of the Western of the late 1960s and 1970s as dominated by auteur-made films that self-consciously critique the conventions and ideologies of earlier works.

The methodological underpinnings of most scholarship on the Western have roots in critical approaches to the study of cinema that came to prominence in the 1960s and 1970s, and whose influence extended far beyond the examination of individual genres. For example, we have seen how the dominant conception of the later Western as "revisionist" has been shaped in accordance with established narratives about late 1960s and 1970s Hollywood history that emphasize the contributions of individual filmmakers and the purported reflection in films of social unrest and cultural uncertainty. The decades since the ascendancy of auteurist and structuralist methodologies have brought new trends and "turns" in the field of cinema studies, and these have had an impact on the study of the Western. Just as histories of the American West began to view the past through the lens of gender and race, so too did studies of the movie Western begin to focus on these neglected aspects of the genre, particularly during its "classic" period. A related concern for areas that standard cinema histories had overlooked or excluded led, as noted above, to insightful analyses of early and silent Westerns, as well as of cycles of B-Westerns, singing cowboy films, and Westerns produced outside of the United States.[41]

Given that the overarching concern of much of this work is a more thorough and nuanced account of the Western genre, it may come as a surprise that no study has dedicated itself to reconsidering the revisionist Western in the broader context of contemporary Western movie production. If, however, we consider the more specific trends within recent scholarship, it is not difficult to see why the revisionist Western has not emerged as a target for closer examination. The Western's development from 1939 to the 1970s is intertwined with well-worn accounts of the history of Hollywood moviemaking. As such, one could be forgiven for thinking that there are not the same opportunities for the discovery or recovery of important movies in the history of a "mainstream" genre like the Western as there are in the study of industrial contexts outside of the major studio system, or in cinema's early and silent periods.

The trend in recent scholarship toward the inspection of the ideological aspects of commercial cinema is actually in sympathy with the perceived remedial intentions of many later Western movies, especially with regard to the representation of racial difference. Looked at this way, New Western History–style analyses of the revisionist Western are redundant, whereas older Westerns offer a far richer source to mine for sociological subtext about racial or gender inequality. And yet the Western movies favored by these newer studies are films like *Shane* and *High Noon*—the same films favored by earlier accounts that had ostensibly different aims, thereby giving the impression that the movie Western is not a deep mine but a shallow well.[42] Thus, we again find that studies of the Western continue to return to the canon of celebrated films for evidence to support wider claims about the character of the genre.[43] The frequency with which this occurs cannot help but reinforce the notion that there are no discoveries or recoveries of movies to be made within the genre's established history, and that new insights about the classic or revisionist periods can only come from continually reinterpreting the same small number of Westerns in isolation from wider developments in the genre.

How the films from this small selection of Westerns are reinterpreted also needs to be addressed.

Recent scholarship on the movie Western largely accords with the broader disciplinary lineage that has been traced by Bordwell, in which structuralist methodologies began to be supplanted in the mid-1970s by "Grand Theories" that frame their discussions of cinema "within schemes which seek to describe or explain very broad features of society, history, language and psyche."[44] Bordwell identifies two overarching Grand Theories: subject-position theory, largely based on psychoanalytic approaches, and culturalism, which "holds that pervasive cultural mechanisms govern the social and psychic functions of cinema."[45] The most influential variant of culturalist theory, Cultural Studies, treats culture as a site of contestation among different groups. Bordwell explains: "A culture is conceived as a network of institutions, representations and practices which produce differences of a race, ethnic heritage, class, gender/sexual preference and the like. These differences are centrally involved in the production of meaning."[46] The influence of culturalist theory in recent scholarship on the Western is particularly evident in the trend towards ideological readings of the genre. Even the Western's wane in popularity is seen as culturally meaningful because it confirms that the myth of the frontier no longer resonates with the modern experience, and thus tells us something about changes within American society.

We have, of course, seen how earlier studies of the Western that drew upon structuralist procedures were concerned with the genre's relationship to American culture. Bordwell acknowledges this, citing Henry Nash Smith's 1950 study *Virgin Land: The American West As Symbol and Myth* as a prototype for subsequent cultural approaches to the movie Western.[47] While analyses of the genre—as of cinema, more generally—have largely abandoned the overt structuralism of Cawelti, Kitses, and Wright, they continue to rely on various modes of symptomatic interpretation.

The Western's privileged status as the foundational myth of American society certainly helps to account for the insistence that studies of the genre must provide insight into American culture. The requirement that the findings of new film research must have a cultural component is not, however, unique to examinations of the Western. As Bordwell has observed, "For many educated people, the most important questions about cinema revolve around its relation to culture."[48] These questions persist despite the many limitations of cultural analysis already noted, from the assumption that the decisions of moviegoers straightforwardly express the cultural zeitgeist to glossing over the specificities and complexities of the filmmaking process.

The rejoinders of Neale, Thompson, and others to the prevailing Renaissance account of American moviemaking of the 1960s and 1970s draw upon a view of the period that is both more inclusive and expansive. Taking into consideration the diversity of movies produced not only sheds light on neglected and undervalued films, but also forces the analyst to judge favored movies against others that are excluded from dominant narratives but that were equally popular or financially successful. Such approaches accord with the "middle level" research program advocated by Bordwell in his and Noël Carroll's collection *Post-Theory* (1996). As an alternative to Grand Theories, which rest upon suppositions about the fundamental nature of society and history, middle level research devotes itself to the analysis of specific phenomena in a focused, problem-driven (rather than doctrine-driven) fashion that favors proximate influences over transcendental ones.[49]

With respect to the Western, a middle level approach could certainly produce an alternative to the broad cultural interpretation that characterizes most studies of the genre. Yet one could easily classify many of the studies of the Western criticized above as middle level research. Bordwell counts empirical studies of individual genres as among the "most established realms of middle-level research," along with "revisionist" or "new" film histories that began to appear in the 1980s.[50] We have seen, however, that addressing one's inquiry to a particular problem, area, or period within an individual genre and conducting empirical research does not in and of itself preclude cultural interpretation. Studies of specific genre topics can arrive at far-reaching conclusions.

Arguments against symptomatic cultural interpretation—like Neale's on genre or Bordwell's on cinema, broadly—are apposite but general. They address the tendency itself, rather than specific instances of its application. As such, cultural analyses of particular movies, filmmakers, genres, periods, and trends continue to be produced in great numbers. New cultural examinations of the Western take their place within a tradition of scholarship that is largely unchallenged. As much as rigid structuralism is now seldom practiced, what remains is the broad supposition that films will reflect the culture that produces and consumes them. Yet the exact nature of the relationship between cinema and culture is often imprecise and, in a sense, undertheorized—as if, in place of a Grand Theory, there is now an absence of theory.

For evidence of this development we can point to the dominant idea that the changes we can observe in the Western in the late 1960s and 1970s reflect changes in American society. As the epigraph to this chapter makes clear, this conception of the revisionist Western has not only remained unchanged for more than thirty years, but also transcends any division between scholarly and popular criticism. This suggests that the cultural meanings ascribed to the revisionist Western have not been arrived at through any sophisticated method of cultural exegesis, and instead simply accord with the general supposition that popular movies can, or must, tell us something about the culture that produces and consumes them.

A middle-level approach to the later Western certainly holds promise. While reappraisals of particular films have appeared over the years, no study has dedicated itself to considering the revisionist Western in the broader context of contemporary Western movie production. It is not enough, however, to simply articulate at outset the limitations of existing accounts of the period and then carry on with one's own analysis. Those earlier examinations, and the premises upon which they rest, must be directly challenged.

Loading the Canon

Around twenty Westerns are regularly referred to as revisionist. These movies do not, however, all receive equal billing on the marquee. At the top are *The Wild Bunch*, *McCabe & Mrs. Miller*, and *Little Big Man*. In different ways, these films are seen to exemplify the characteristics of the revisionist Western, including a more graphic representation of violence, more realistic mise-en-scène and period detail, more sympathetic portrayals of Indians, and a more skeptical, if not outright pessimistic, attitude towards the genre's established conventions. They are also each the product of a celebrated auteur director. The subsequent Westerns of these filmmakers fall below the top three—Peckinpah's *The Ballad of Cable Hogue* and *Pat Garrett and Billy the Kid*, Altman's *Buffalo Bill and the Indians, or Sitting Bull's History Lesson* (1976), and Penn's *The Missouri*

Breaks—along with *Heaven's Gate,* whose director was also, at least up to the movie's release, an acclaimed auteur. Finally, there is an assortment of movies that also display revisionist characteristics, in some cases very prominently, that have not achieved the status of those above. These include *Bad Company, The Culpepper Cattle Co., Dirty Little Billy, Doc, The Great Northfield Minnesota Raid, A Man Called Horse, Monte Walsh* (William A. Fraker, 1970), *Soldier Blue, Tell Them Willie Boy Is Here* (Abraham Polonsky, 1969), and *Ulzana's Raid.* Clint Eastwood's American Westerns are often referred to as revisionist, yet there is disagreement about this.

Given that the number of movies increases steadily as we move down this list, the revisionist canon resembles a three-tiered pyramid. Yet, despite the large number of Westerns at its base, the pyramid is top-heavy, as the number of films in each tier is inversely proportional to the critical attention they have received. The marquee analogy proves apt: like the opening credits of an old movie, the typeface gets progressively smaller as we go from a few top-billed stars to the supporting cast to, finally, bit players. This conspicuous inequality amplifies questions about how representative this group of films is of the Western during the 1970s.

"Third tier" revisionist Westerns are frequently referred to in discussions of this period in the genre's history, but they are seldom examined in any detail. Instead, they are cited as other examples of the type of Western which the "big three" are said to exemplify. Noël Caroll's article "The Future of Allusion" is a good example. In the course of his analysis of *McCabe & Mrs. Miller,* he calls the picture an example of the revisionist Western, offers a definition of the revisionist Western, lists other examples of the type as evidence, and then returns to his principle analysis.

Many of these "third tier" revisionist Westerns received favorable reviews upon release, and a few have been subject to critical reexamination in the years since (and not always on the grounds that they are revisionist Westerns). Yet, unlike the constituents of the upper two tiers of the revisionist canon, monographs on individual titles and studies of their makers have not appeared, nor are they likely to. Instead, these movies subsist largely on occasional mentions in film criticism—or in some cases they have achieved lasting notoriety because they are especially violent.

Presenting a list of titles as evidence to support the prevalence of a certain type of movie is a common enough tactic in film criticism, but in the case of the revisionist Western the evidence is not very persuasive.

Remember that we are talking about over half of the revisionist canon here—the majority of an already small group of pictures. More than anything else, these Westerns seem guilty of "revisionism by association." If one wants to argue that the revisionist Western is not only a distinct type of Western but also one that dominated the genre in the late 1960s and 1970s, it cannot be on the strength of eight or so films, however exemplary they may be.

Why should the third tier revisionist Westerns be consistently cited, but never examined? It is not because they are unavailable. Of the titles listed above, only one, *Dirty Little Billy,* has been unavailable commercially until recently.[51] Given the dominant methods by which the revisionist Western has been appraised, a number of possible explanations present themselves. One is that these movies are revisionist in nature, but not in the same way or to the same degree as those higher up the chain. This leads to two related possibilities: that the films do not meet some other criteria, or that they are simply not as good or interesting as those above them. As we have seen, the discourses surrounding the revisionist Western emphasize the role of extra-filmic factors like innovative young filmmakers, or a movie's perceived sympathy with contemporary cultural issues. Furthermore, most scholarly writing on cinema, the Western included, is actually quite adept at avoiding outright appraisals of a given film's interest or worth, even if such judgments are often implicit in the choice of which films to write about (and which not to).

A cursory look at these movies confirms their status as revisionist Westerns. *Doc, Dirty Little Billy,* and *The Great Northfield Minnesota Raid* are thorough dressing-downs of frontier legends Wyatt Earp, Billy the Kid, and Jesse James that reveal each man to be far, far less than his legend suggests. Similarly, *The Culpepper Cattle Co.* and *Monte Walsh* offer unglamorous, melancholy portraits of the lives of cowpunchers and range hands. *Tell Them Willie Boy Is Here, Soldier Blue, A Man Called Horse,* and *Ulzana's Raid* in different ways attempt to portray indigenous cultures with greater sensitivity and complexity.

In light of the revisionist characteristics detailed above, it is not immediately clear how any of this "revisionism" is different from that found in *The Wild Bunch, McCabe & Mrs. Miller,* or *Little Big Man.* The general demythologization of the mythic frontier experience is as prevalent a theme in the bottom ten as it is in the top three. If these Westerns do evidence revisionist qualities, we may then assume that their relegation to the base of the pyramid is due, at least in part, to the *nature* of their revision of the genre's established narratives and conventions. Perhaps they are not as sincere in their debunking of Western legends and heroes? Or are not as unflinching in their depiction of frontier violence? Or do not engage with contemporary political and social issues, like the Vietnam War, as earnestly?

Not necessarily.

In what may come as a surprise, upon closer examination some of these pictures initially appear to be *better* examples of the qualities typically ascribed to the revisionist Western. Arriving at this assessment depends on first establishing the characteristics of those films higher up the pyramid, beginning at the very top, with *The Wild Bunch.*

2

A Conflict of Visions, or What If They Staged a Revision and Nobody Came?

> I must say that when I received the script I didn't read into it all of these controversial things. . . . So many significant things are now being read into it that perhaps there is a moral suggestion here.
>
> —Ernest Borgnine, on *The Wild Bunch*, 1969

Looking beyond the revisionist canon detailed in the preceding chapter, we find dozens of other Westerns released during between 1969 and 1980. With one or two exceptions, like Howard Hawks's final film *Rio Lobo*, these films do not have the benefit of auteur filmmakers, and they do not have the same veneer of social commentary and self-reflexive critique. They do, however, meet two other criteria: there are more of them, and, in many cases, more people went to see them. In film criticism, artistic and cultural worth nearly always trumps preponderance and popularity. Yet, if the Western is indeed a "reflection" of the state of American culture, should this zeitgeist not also be reflected in the movies which audiences more actively patronized? To determine this, we need to actually look at these other neglected Westerns.

There are, however, other ways to gauge a given Western's popularity—number of mentions in cinema histories, for example, or centrality to larger arguments about the genre. Let us begin, then, with the most-analyzed Western released during the period under investigation—a film that also sits atop the revisionist canon.

The Wild Bunch

When it comes to writing about the later Western, or even the Western in general, there is no riding around *The Wild Bunch.* With the exception of the celebrated films of John Ford, no Western has received more critical attention. Since its release in 1969, the movie has accrued a reputation as one of the greatest Westerns ever made, and has been an ongoing subject of debate on a range of other topics, from movie violence to the representation of women on screen. In both scholarly and popular criticism, *The Wild Bunch* stands as the Western's benchmark of the period, at once a savage break from tradition and the inaugurator of a brief, final flourish of innovation in the early 1970s, after which the genre quickly faded into an obscurity from which it has yet to rebound.

Just how savage a break from Western tradition was *The Wild Bunch?* In his analysis of the film in *Gunfighter Nation,* Richard Slotkin devotes a great deal of attention to the movie's title sequence, where the Bunch ride into the town of Starbuck disguised as U.S. Cavalry officers with the intention of robbing the railroad office. As each credit title appears on screen, the image freezes and "abstracts" to black-and-white.

Each change in image corresponds to a change in the soundtrack. Slotkin writes: "The music emphasizes the break with the 'normal' world of color by shifting abruptly to a 'chilly,' suspended phrase played by strings. Faces in these freeze-frames appear more skull-like and sinister than the colored originals, suggesting a view into some deathly substructure of the normal world."[1] For Slotkin, the presentation of the titles in this fashion is one of several ways that the movie immediately sets out to defy audience expectations by violating established genre conventions. On the outskirts of the town a group of "innocent" children are revealed to be gleefully lording over a battle between two white scorpions and a horde of red ants, a "disconcerting vision of an amoral and disordered universe" that foreshadows the Bunch's ultimate demise in Mexico. In town, a meeting of the Temperance Union is presided over by a preacher raving against the evils of strong drink, but we "recognize him as a pious flannel-mouth who knows nothing of real evil." And, of course, the cavalry officers are revealed to be a gang of thieves and killers willing to use innocent women to shield themselves from enemy fire, thereby breaking one of the genre's most sacred taboos.[2] What these repeated violations

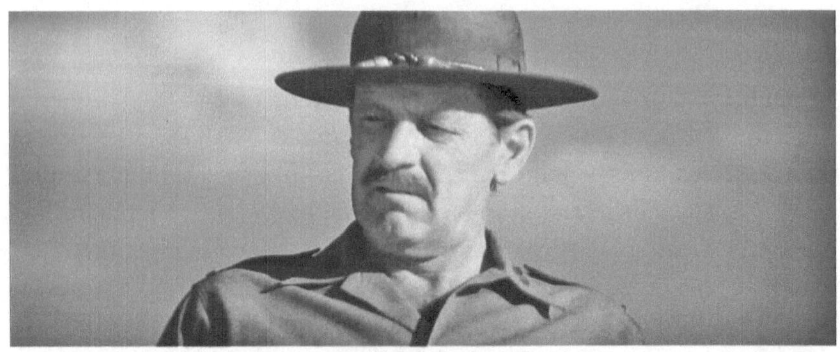

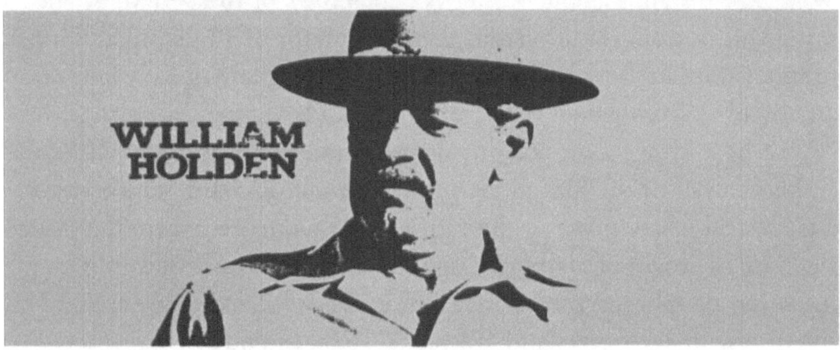

The opening titles of *The Wild Bunch* (1969)

amount to, according to Slotkin, is a subversion of social order and a commentary on the failure of traditional American ideology. Michael Coyne reaches similar conclusions in his analysis of the film, arguing that the power of *The Wild Bunch* results from its uncompromising assault on Hollywood conventions. He writes, "Peckinpah is intent on shattering the entire framework of clichés and candy-coated myths in which movies customarily traffic as a prettified alternative to life."[3]

While it is possible to take issue with aspects of Slotkin's argument—when in a Western has the Temperance Union been anything other than sanctimonious or hypocritical?—there is little question that the opening of *The Wild Bunch* purposely sets out to give viewers an aggressive jolt by defying their expectations. Yet one component of the opening sequence that viewers familiar with the Western are unlikely to have found surprising is the use of the black-and-white images described by Slotkin.

In the 1960s and 1970s it was common for illustrations to be incorporated into the title sequences of Western movies. These images generally take one of two forms: painted color canvasses that evoke the work of artists like Frederic Remington and C. M. Russell, or black-and-white images that recall old photographs and newspapers. We find examples in a range of Westerns, including *El Dorado* (Howard Hawks, 1967), *The Scalphunters* (Sydney Pollock, 1968), *Paint Your Wagon* (Joshua Logan, 1969), *Monte Walsh,* and *The Culpepper Cattle Co.* Other contemporary Westerns like *Butch Cassidy and the Sundance Kid* and *Big Jake* also use old-fashioned imagery for thematic effect in their opening title sequences, and Robert Altman's aim in *McCabe & Mrs. Miller* was to give the majority of the film the antiquated look of a worn photograph.

What Slotkin does not mention about the title sequence of *The Wild Bunch* is that the very first shot in the film is not from the "world of color." It is in black-and-white. Following Slotkin's line of argument, this would mean that the Bunch is riding out of some deathly netherworld and into our own. If, however, the black-and-white images are taken to be from an old newspaper, or an old illustration—a fair assumption, given the prevalence of the technique at the time—then the Bunch are instead riding out of the *past*—out of a world that exists, imperfectly, in recorded history. Like many Westerns, then, *The Wild Bunch* establishes a relationship with the past by drawing on conventions that signal it will offer a "historical" representation of life on the American frontier.

Over the course of the 1960s, ideas about increased cinematic realism frequently entailed more graphic depictions of violence. Without understating the degree to which *The Wild Bunch* was exceptionally violent for the time, it still needs to be understood in this broader context. As Stephen Prince has argued, although Peckinpah "pushed screen violence to unprecedented levels," the director was benefiting from "a trend [toward increased violence] that was already established and well underway and was driven by powerful industry incentives."[4]

Well before the release of *The Wild Bunch,* Motion Picture Association of America (MPAA) president Jack Valenti was defending the film industry's new artistic freedom on the grounds that the industry was simply coming in line with current social trends. Prince writes: "Valenti's line of defense against condemnations of film brutality entailed emphasizing how filmmakers were inevitably responding to, and reflecting, a revolution in social mores that was underway in the culture, a defense that implicitly acknowledged the economic incentives for filmmakers to mirror these changes on screen."[5] This defense involved contextualizing increased screen violence in relation to the Vietnam War, "a brilliant rhetorical move that was effective because of the undeniable connections between the revolution in movie violence and the late-sixties crucible of sociopolitical violence."[6]

At a press conference held following the premier of *The Wild Bunch* for American film critics, members of the production defended the movie on similar grounds. Star William Holden was incredulous when members of the press accused the film of promoting violence. "I just can't get over the reaction here," he said. "Are people surprised that violence really exists in the world? Just turn on your TV set any night. The viewer sees the Vietnam War, cities burning, campus riots; he sees plenty of violence."[7] "The era of escapism is over; the era of reality is here," said producer Phil Feldman. "Truth is not beautiful; dying is not beautiful. The entertainment industry has a right and a duty to depict reality as it is."[8] What we have, then, are filmmakers justifying increased violence on the same grounds that critics will later account for it in retrospect: as concern for increased realism, reflection of changing cultural norms, response to social and political events.

As Prince points out, the motivations of filmmakers were implicitly pecuniary. Whatever the financial incentives were for Hollywood to produce more violent films, however, there were also clearly risks. Surveying the initial critical response to *The Wild Bunch,* Garner Simmons observes: "Almost universally, reviewers called the film the bloodiest ever made; they were split, however, over whether this was good or bad."[9] Some critics called the movie a masterpiece, while others questioned why it had been made at all. Moreover, the picture was not a financial success. With a negative cost of $6.24 million, *The Wild Bunch* earned $5.3 million in rentals, placing it well outside the top 20 earners for 1969.[10] If the film did reflect in its cynicism and violence the zeitgeist of the United States in the late 1960s—as countless critics have argued—it is certainly fair to question why comparatively few people went to see it. We would do well to recall the observations of Thompson and Neale that, despite an emphasis in film history on the Hollywood Renaissance, the most successful films of the 1960s and 1970s were genre movies with broad appeal. The emphasis on *The Wild Bunch* in histories of the Western is similarly misleading.

Assertions about purported influence of *The Wild Bunch* on subsequent Westerns are also often wide of the mark. Richard A. Maynard exaggerates when he claims that "many of the violence techniques of *The Wild Bunch* (including scenes of wholesale killing in slow motion) have become the stock-in-trade of later Westerns."[11] In truth, very few 1970s Westerns so much as approach the aestheticized bloodshed of the climax of *The Wild Bunch*—which should come as little surprise given the polarized response to the movie owing to its graphic violence. While we can note a more frequent employment of a formal device like slow motion cinematography in subsequent Westerns, it is often used in markedly different ways than in *The Wild Bunch.* In *The Hired Hand*, slow motion is combined with kaleidoscope-like optical effects to give the movie's opening sequence a lyrical character. *Bite the Bullet* (Richard Brooks, 1975) uses slow motion selectively during scenes of horseback riding in the open desert, near-freezing rider and horse into Remington-like poses. *Hannie Caulder* (Burt Kennedy, 1971) abruptly switches to slow motion during a confrontation between bounty hunter Price (Robert Culp) and one of the villainous Clemens brothers. Another brother, hiding to Price's left, throws his knife at the gunman. Price wheels around, draws his sidearm, and fires at the concealed man. As in *The Wild Bunch,* slow motion is used to heighten the action, but here the elongation of time is used to create suspense—who will connect first?—rather than prolong visceral impact.

Many of the narrative and thematic elements found in *The Wild Bunch* that feature in subsequent Westerns were also already long-established conventions of the genre. Variants on the plot of experienced gunmen venturing south of the border, used to great thematic effect in *The Wild Bunch,* do feature in many 1970s Westerns. We also find heroes venturing down Mexico way in *Two Mules for Sister Sara* (Don Siegel, 1970), *Big Jake, Wild Rovers* (Blake Edwards, 1971), *The Deserter* (Burt Kennedy, 1971), *The Revengers* (Daniel Mann, 1972), *The Deadly Trackers* (Barry Shear, 1973), and *Goin' South* (Jack Nicholson, 1978). In the comedic Western *Dirty Dingus Magee* (Burt Kennedy, 1970), Dingus explains his rationale for heading to Mexico as follows: "When you steal money that's where you go. It's the code of the west!" Before taking the prevalence of this scenario as a sign of self-consciousness, or of the genre running out of ideas, however, we should consider how this plot had also been used countless times before in earlier Westerns.

Two of the most successful Westerns of the 1960s, *The Magnificent Seven* (John Sturges, 1960) and *The Professionals* (Richard Brooks, 1966), each feature protagonists who recognize their days and ways are numbered but see opportunity in mercenary exploits in Mexico. We need not wait until the 1960s to find other examples. In *Buchanan Rides Alone* (Budd Boetticher, 1958), the eponymous hero has made his fortune selling his gun in Mexico, while *Vera Cruz* (Robert Aldrich, 1954) features rival soldiers of fortune offering their services to the highest bidder during the Mexican Revolution. In as early an example as *Stagecoach,* Mexico represents a new "final frontier" for the Western hero who no longer has a place in the modernizing west.

These examples also indicate that using the closing of the frontier as a dramatic device does not mean the genre is itself nearing the end of the line. Given the short historical timeframe within which most Westerns operate—roughly 1865 to 1900—the "end of the West" is never more than thirty-five years away, a fact acknowledged in many Westerns. *Devil's Canyon* (Alfred L. Werker, 1953), for example, opens with the following title: "Arizona Territory in 1897 was the last of the old frontier. The story we are about to tell is well known to historians. Names have been changed but the lust and brutality, the love and sacrifice of the people involved remain for the record unchanged. The woman outlaw and her lovers belong now to folklore—in 1897 they lived." In *Last Train from Gun Hill* (John Sturges, 1959), the first scene with lawman Matt Morgan (Kirk Douglas) has him telling a story of his exploits in the rough and tumble past to a group of youngsters, who have not only heard the story before but lament the passing of more exciting times—those times being only "eight or ten years ago," as Morgan's deputy later explains.

The place of *The Wild Bunch* in genre history says nothing of its purported social commentary, of course. Could the movie's invocation of conventional Western narratives and iconography not be a critical commentary on those elements? Some see it that way. Despite his wealth of knowledge about the Western as a narrative form, the lens through which Slotkin analyzes *The Wild Bunch* and other movies of the period is less the genre's conventions than the Vietnam War. This is a common way of addressing the film. An article from 2000 in the *New York Times* asserts that *The Wild Bunch* "allegorically inscribed the failure of America's anti-Communist mission in Vietnam, and in so doing proposed a counter-myth to the western's myth of righteous progressivism from which the genre has never recovered."[12] To his credit, Slotkin keeps the movie's relationship to the Vietnam War in better perspective than many critics who interpret the film as a straightforward commentary on the War. For him, Peckinpah's critique of Western convention may only have been possible in light of Vietnam (and the Tet Offensive, in particular), but because those conventions are so well established and ideologically inscribed, the critique is not just of America's military involvement in southeast Asia, specifically, but of the larger myth of benign interventionism.

Although there is little doubt that Peckinpah intended some degree of social commentary, we may question whether the aim of *The Wild Bunch* is really such a rigorous rebuking of the ethos of the Western. Recall that Buscombe, in his talk at the British Film Institute, claimed that Peckinpah's Westerns were *not* revisionist because they did not deliberately criticize the genre. When asked in 1969 why he did not elect to make a movie expressly about the Vietnam War, Peckinpah replied, "The western is a universal frame within which it is possible to comment on today."[13] As evocative as that remark may be when taken in the context of the late 1960s, in terms of the Western this is far from a new development. As we'll see in chapters 3 and 4, in earlier decades filmmakers frequently used the genre to comment on the social and political concerns of the present. Furthermore, the Western is certainly not unique among American movie genres in transposing the concerns of today onto yesterday.

That Peckinpah would operate in a fashion comparable to earlier Western moviemakers is not surprising, given his association with and affection for the genre. One factor that distinguishes Peckinpah from the other directors whose movies make up the revisionist canon is that he is identified, first and foremost, as a maker of Westerns. This cannot be said for any other revisionist Western filmmaker.[14] Although Peckinpah also worked in other genres, his best films are unquestionably Westerns.

In the new edition of *Horizons West,* Kitses observes that Peckinpah's proponents are at pains to distance him from the "conventional" Western. "[A]dvocates of the director who repeatedly refer to the Western *films,* rather than simply the Westerns, reinforce the snobbish hair-splitting suggested here. . . . [T]he persistent qualification of 'films' is meant to hint at profound difference, evidence of a polemical and transparent strategy to lift the film-maker clear of any relationship with the common oater, horse opera and shoot-'em-up."[15] A similar impulse is found in attempts to group Peckinpah in with the Hollywood Renaissance, positioning him as more than simply a genre filmmaker, standing alongside other directors at the vanguard of a revolution in Hollywood cinema. In each case, change is emphasized over continuity.

Peckinpah is something of an awkward fit in the roster of Renaissance auteurs, though. While his personal reputation for off-screen debauchery puts him in good company with other celebrated 1970s filmmakers, the perceived right-wing tendencies of his films, along with accusations of bigotry and misogyny, certainly do not. Attempts to distance his Westerns from the "common" Western are equally problematic. In line with our earlier observations about *The Wild Bunch*'s continuities with established Western themes and conventions, Kitses argues that Peckinpah's Western oeuvre is not only saturated with references and allusions to older films, but engages those films with a measure of sophistication far greater than simply critique or revision, concluding that the director's "indebtedness to the collective tradition of the Western is everywhere apparent."[16]

The Way It Is

Like the revisionist Westerns of the late 1960s and 1970s, Fred Zinnemann's celebrated 1952 Western *High Noon,* about a lawman who leaves his wife on their wedding day to protect his town from an old villain, is remembered chiefly for its reflection of contemporary cultural concerns. Screenwriter Carl Foreman, who refused to "name names" before the House Un-American Activities Committee and would later be blacklisted by the film industry, intended the picture to be an allegory about the hunt for communists in Hollywood led by Senator Joseph McCarthy: protagonist Will Kane finds himself alone and outnumbered, abandoned by those he thought were his friends. In a 1971 interview, John Wayne denounced the picture as "the most un-American thing I've ever seen in my whole life."[17]

The movie's politics are actually not as straightforward as this information would suggest. In spite of the movie's liberal pedigree, in 1994 the *National Review* magazine ranked *High Noon* number fifty-seven on a list of "best conservative movies."[18] When the movie was released, some interpreted Kane's refusal to walk away from confrontation as an affirmation of America's mission in Korea. The Duke had also once been more appreciative of the picture. Accepting the 1952 best actor Oscar on behalf of the film's star Gary Cooper, Wayne said, "I'm going back and find my business manager and agent, producer, and three-name writers and find out why I didn't get *High Noon* instead of Cooper."[19] What any fixation on the picture's Cold War politics tends to obscure, however, are the ways in which *High Noon* is, above all else, a Western, and in particular how its "last man" scenario becomes one of the most common Western plots of the 1960s and 1970s.

High Noon offers an early reassessment of the myth of the prototypical frontier lawman—essentially, it speculates on what happens if Wyatt Earp, after defeating his enemies, avenging his brother's murder, and making the prairie safe for the advance of civilization with its churches and schools, does not ride out of town at the end of *My Darling Clementine* but instead chooses to stay. Influential elements from *High Noon* were responded to or adopted by a number of subsequent Westerns, most notably Howard Hawks's *Rio Bravo* (1959)—famously made as a somewhat-belated answer to *High Noon* and, less-belatedly, *3:10 to Yuma* (Delmer Daves, 1957). What Hawks disliked most about these films was what he perceived as an unheroic, almost cowardly portrayal of their respective protagonists. About the actions of Will Kane in *High Noon,* Hawks said:

> I didn't think a good sheriff was going to go running around town like a chicken with his head off asking for help, and finally his Quaker wife had to save him. That isn't my idea of a good Western sheriff. I said that a good sheriff would turn around and say, 'How good are you? Are you good enough to take the best man they've got?' The fellow would probably say no, and he'd say, 'Well, then I'd just have to take care you.' And that scene *was* in *Rio Bravo.*"[20]

In *Rio Bravo,* Sheriff John T. Chance (John Wayne) rejects the help of all but an eclectic group of gunmen—numbering a recovering alcoholic, an old coot, and Ricky Nelson—to defend his town's jail against a band of outlaws determined to break in and free their boss's no-good murderin' brother. The picture was a success, and helped to reinvigorate the genre at a time when its popularity was waning. While 1958 had seen the release of a number of notable Westerns, including the sprawling *The Big Country* (William Wyler) and *The Left Handed Gun* (Arthur Penn's directorial debut, which Hawks thought was "silly"), there were no popular successes on par with 1957's *Gunfight at the O.K. Corral* (John Sturges, 1957).

Rio Bravo is held to mark an important shift in the types of stories Westerns films tell. As detailed most notably by Will Wright in his structural study of the genre, *Sixguns and Society* (1975), beginning with *Rio Bravo* Western movie narratives increasingly centered on groups of "professionals" who defend society only as a job they accepted for pay, for love of fighting, or out of friendship. Becoming less common were solitary heroes purely committed to the ideals of law and justice.[21] In these "professional" Westerns, Wright argues, "[t]he social values of justice, order and peaceful domesticity have been replaced by a clear commitment to strength, skill, enjoyment of the battle, and masculine companionship."[22] Looked at this way, *Rio Bravo* is a forerunner to later Westerns like *The Magnificent Seven, The Professionals,* and *The Wild Bunch.* What neither Wright nor other critics takes into account, however, is how the idea of the professional band is itself "revised" in varying ways.

In *Rio Lobo* (1970), Hawks's second retelling of *Rio Bravo* following 1967's *El Dorado,* the odds are decidedly not in the four heroes' favor as they head into the final confrontation against a large gang of desperados. But unlike their counterparts in *The Wild Bunch,* the heroes do not ultimately find themselves alone and outnumbered. Instead, when they arrive at the rendezvous they find a half dozen of the town's men, armed and waiting to help—help that is gladly accepted by John Wayne and company, not because the men assert their ability to "take the best man they've got" but because they're all former soldiers. *A Man Called Sledge* (Vic Morrow, 1970) includes the formation of a group of experienced gunmen to pull off the theft of a gold shipment. As Sledge (James Garner) tells a member of his gang who voices concern about the 40 armed riders who guard the shipments: "Forget it. They aren't professionals. *We are.*" But after the successful robbery, the members of the group turn on their leader, leaving Sledge to defend himself against the entire gang. While this could be taken as a critique of the notion of outlaw brotherhood—bad men will turn on one another—the scenario, where a single "good"/reformed member of an outlaw gang is pitted against his former accomplices, also recalls Westerns of the 1940s like *Yellow Sky* (William A. Wellman, 1948) and *Blood on the Moon* (Robert Wise, 1948).

In the prequel *Butch and Sundance: The Early Days* (Richard Lester, 1979), the outlaw pair assembles a team to rob a train. Their plan is to board the train at a whistle-stop while it takes on water. Unfortunately, only Butch and Sundance are able to negotiate their way out of the water tower and onto one of the train cars—leaving the pair back where they started, forced to hold up the train as a duo. Whether two constitutes a gang is debatable, but the pair certainly evince "masculine companionship." What this distillation of the gang to its core elements points to is the undemocratic nature of most bands of expert gunmen. At the heart of these gangs we often find a central pair who serve as foils for each other: Pike and Dutch in *The Wild Bunch,* Cogburn and young Mattie Ross in *True Grit,* Butch and Sundance in *Butch Cassidy and the Sundance Kid,* Rico and Bill in *The Professionals,* Chris and Vin in *The Magnificent Seven,* and Chance and Dude in *Rio Bravo.* More so than the "professional plot," this emphasis on the camaraderie between two leads marks a notable shift from tendencies evident in earlier Westerns.

In many Westerns of the late 1940s and 1950s, the villain is often portrayed as the hero's evil opposite. An early example is found in *Pursued* (Raoul Walsh, 1947), but later Westerns like *Shane, Drum Beat* (Delmer Daves, 1954), *The Searchers,* and director Anthony Mann's collaborations with James Stewart in the 1950s also feature heroes who must confront their own inner demons as they are manifest in the villain. Yet, from the mid-1950s onward, the hero's savage double is increasingly found not in his adversary but in his ally. Examples include *Vera Cruz, Tennessee's Partner* (Allan Dwan, 1955), *The Tin Star* (Anthony Mann, 1957), *3:10 to Yuma,* and, perhaps most notably, *Gunfight at the O.K. Corral.*

In contrast to John Ford's earlier take on the Wyatt Earp legend, *Gunfight at the O.K. Corral* is less the tale of Earp avenging his brother's murder than the story of the friendship that develops between Earp (Burt Lancaster) and his friend Doc Holliday (Kirk Douglas). The first half of the picture, ostensibly about Wyatt pursuing various badmen across a couple of towns, focuses on the developing trust and friendship between the straightlaced lawman and the eccentric (and ailing) gambler. Unlike *My Darling Clementine,* only in the second half of the picture does the pair, along with most of the villains we have encountered over the

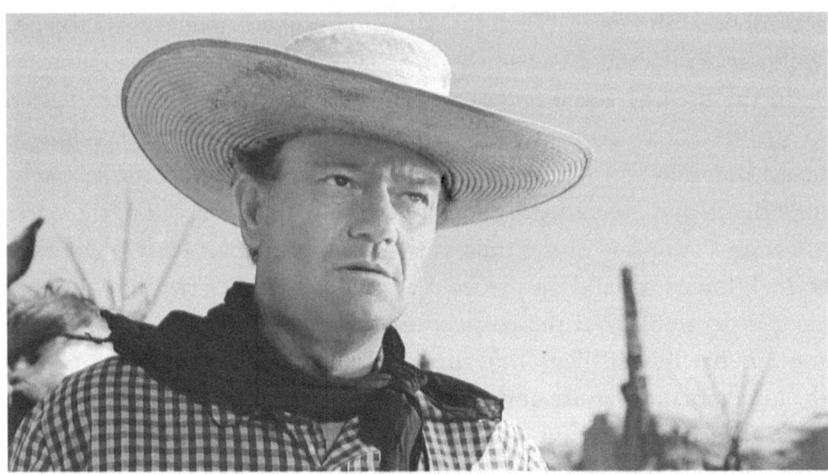

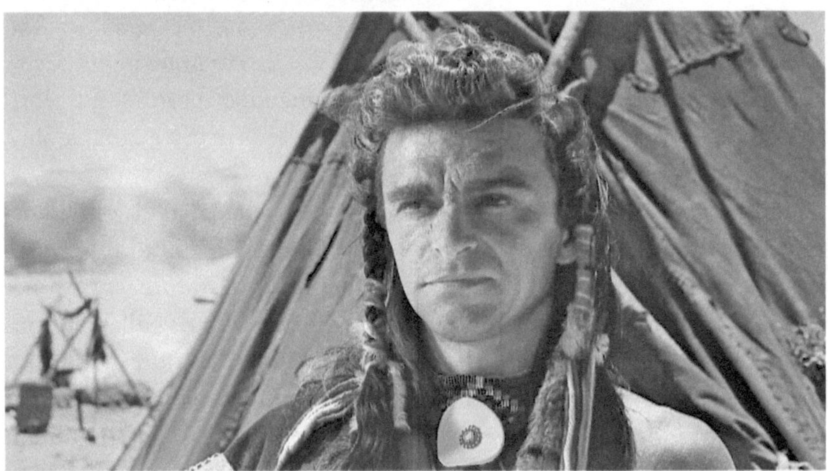

The hero meets his savage double in *The Searchers* (1956)

course of the movie, arrive in Tombstone. From very early in the picture, it is clear that Holliday's observations to Earp that the two are much alike, though tinged with sarcasm, ring true. The relationship is made clear near the end of the movie, where successive scenes feature a graphic match of each man's reflection framed in the same mirror. Similar symbolic imagery is used to introduce Earp in 1971's *Doc.* After Holliday arrives in Tombstone, he retires to his room. When he falls asleep, footsteps are heard coming from outside. The camera slowly pans from the sleeping Holliday, across the room, to the door, which gradually opens, first revealing the reflection of Earp in a mirror next to the door. This is the first we see of the lawman. As Richard Coombs notes in his review of the movie, *Doc* presents Earp and Holliday "less as individuals than opposing halves of a social crisis."[23] Friendship, love, or mutual love of combat is not always enough to preserve tenuous relationships between gunmen. That this scenario resembles much earlier Westerns points to a loosely cyclical, rather than stringently evolutionary, pattern of development.

Rio Bravo's relationship with *High Noon* is telling in another respect. Note that, in expressing his objection to *High Noon,* Hawks does not say he was responding to aspects of the movie that he found *politically* disagreeable—such as the movie's McCarthyist allegory—but rather to aspects of the movie's narrative and characterization: principally, the "cowardly" marshal. It is elements such as the ticking clock, or the scenario of a lone lawman pitted against a gang of villains and an apathetic town, that are the generic legacy of *High Noon,* not its politics. The scenario is recast not only in *Rio Bravo,* but also in *3:10 to Yuma, Silver Lode* (Allan Dwan, 1954), *Bad Day at Black Rock* (John Sturges, 1955), *Terror in a Texas Town* (Joseph H. Lewis, 1958), and *Last Train from Gun Hill,* among other films. We also find variations on this plot employed in a range of Westerns released between 1969 and 1980, including *Death of a Gunfighter* (Allan Smithee, 1969), *Young Billy Young* (Burt Kennedy, 1969), *The Good Guys and the Bad Guys* (Burt Kennedy, 1969), *Lawman, The Culpepper Cattle Co., The Life and Times of Judge Roy Bean* (John Huston, 1972), *High Plains Drifter* (Clint Eastwood, 1973), *Posse* (Kirk Douglas, 1975), and *Tom Horn* (William Wiard, 1980). In a case of generic circularity, many of these later pictures feature what we could call "ersatz Earps," characters clearly modeled on the famous lawman but given different names, with some explicitly referencing earlier Earp Westerns.

Young Billy Young stars Robert Mitchum as Ben Kane, a former sheriff on the hunt for his son's murderer, and Robert Walker (Jr.) as Billy Young, a hired killer abandoned by his partner Jess (David Carradine) after the pair assassinate a Mexican general. Angie Dickenson rounds out the top of the cast as dancehall girl Lily Benoit, a role reminiscent of her memorable turn as Feathers ten years earlier in *Rio Bravo.* Based on the novel *Who Rides with Wyatt?* by Will Henry, the movie gives us, in the guises of Kane and Billy, a hypothetical friendship between Wyatt Earp and Billy Clanton, the youngest of the infamous ranching family who squared off against Earp and his allies in Tombstone. Yet the link to the historical personages, or even the fictional renditions found in other movies, is very loose. Kane has no Doc Holliday or brothers to stand by him during the final shootout, nor does Billy have any familial relations to speak of. This is largely the point, though, as Kane and Billy develop a father–son relationship.

Like many of his predecessors, Kane encounters resistance from most of the citizenry, who are reluctant to cross the town's boss, Behan (Jack Kelly), and are skeptical of Kane's motivations. Young Evvie Cushman (Deana Martin) voices her concerns to the marshal:

> EVVIE: Look Mr. Kane, I don't like your kind any more than you like mine.
>
> KANE: What kind am I, Miss Cushman?
>
> EVVIE: A hired killer.
>
> KANE: Let me tell you something, Miss Cushman. Something for you and all the other gentle hearts of Lordsburg to think about. I've been indicted for murder in every town I've ever worn a badge, not by the ones I hunted, but by the people I was paid to protect. Like you, Miss Cushman. You're all alike. You hire a man and then you grab his gun arm and tell him to hold off, let the bad ones shoot first, so's you can make damn good and sure they're bad, even if it means getting a hole blown in that tin star they pin on you.
>
> EVVIE: But you don't work that way.
>
> KANE: I'm alive.

A similar exchange happens in *Lawman,* an effective Western about a straitlaced marshal on the hunt for a group of cowmen who drunkenly shot up his town three months earlier, accidentally killing a man in the process. Jarred Maddox (Burt Lancaster) tracks the men to Sabbath, where he learns from washed-up marshal Cotton Ryan (Robert Ryan) that the cowmen he seeks are in the employ of Vincent Bronson (Lee J. Cobb), the town's benevolent despot. A group of the town's leading men, upset at Maddox and what they perceive to be his murderous intentions, talk themselves up into action, take to arms, and confront the marshal in the saloon. Maddox coolly eyes the group, his expression betraying little other than the hint that he's been in this situation before. He slowly rises from his chair, drops his napkin on the table, and steps towards them.

> Which one has the words? You're the storekeeper. Luther Harris, isn't it? Let me say them for you. You want me out of your town. What happened some other time, some other place ain't your trouble. I've seen men like you in every town in the west. You want the law, but you want it to walk quiet, you don't want it to put a hole in your pocket. You take courage from each other and you come armed. Well, there are enough of you. All you need is one man with enough stomach to die first. I'm not leaving till what I came for is done. So if you plan to do anything about it, do it now or go home.

Gun-for-hire Clay Blaisdell (Henry Fonda) makes a similar speech in *Warlock* (Edward Dmytryk, 1959), about how the town will eventually turn on him. Even *Rio Bravo,* as much as it is a response to other aspects of *High Noon,* is part of the lineage of this plot. One element from *High Noon* that the movie does not object to, but rather embraces, is the weakness and reticence of the society the hero is paid to protect. The riposte in *Rio Bravo* is not to have the town rally to its sheriff's defense in his time of need—which does happen at the end of *Warlock,* incidentally—but for the sheriff to not even bother asking for help. Society is, in fact, conspicuously absent from *Rio Bravo.* If *High Noon* exposes the hypocrisy that lurks beneath *My Darling Clementine*—the frontier town is not simply weak but cowardly, unwilling to defend itself, and may turn on its lawman under the right circumstance—*Rio Bravo* does nothing to counter the revelation. In failing to act against the villains, society is still complicit in their actions.

Because the frontier town's disenchantment with the hero is one of the oldest plots of the genre, it is not, in and of itself, a reflection of any kind of societal disenchantment with the mythical frontier lawman and the values he embodies. As much as other conventions and archetypes of the genre are "revised" over the years, the scenario of the unwanted lawman proves both remarkably durable and surprisingly adaptable.

The Life and Times of Judge Roy Bean begins with an overhead shot of a map of Texas—a map presumably from around the turn of the last century—that promptly zooms in on the Pecos River. The Pecos, as the ensuing title crawl informs us, "marked the boundaries of civilization in western Texas. West of the Pecos there was no law, no order, and only bad men and rattlesnakes lived there." Unto this, the infamous Judge Roy Bean (Paul Newman), self-appointed "law west of the Pecos."

If rank in the pantheon of American frontier heroes is to be judged by appearances in theatrical Westerns, Bean, despite being a colorful character, falls somewhere near the bottom. Aside from the film in question, the notorious hanging judge of Vinegaroon features in two other movies of note: *The Westerner,* where the judge, played by Walter Brennan, matches wits with Gary Cooper, and *A Time for Dying* (Budd Boetticher, 1969), played by Victor Jory. In both films, Bean is played mostly for laughs (although the character's unrequited love for the actress Lillie Langtry lends a tragic note to Brennan's performance).

Perhaps the best-remembered aspect of *The Life and Times of Judge Roy Bean* is a bit of text from the opening credits: " . . . Maybe this isn't the way it was . . . it's the way it should have been." At the sight of these words, viewers even vaguely familiar with the Western are likely to think of newsman Maxwell Scott's famous refusal in *The Man Who Shot Liberty Valance* to print "the truth" about hero-turned-politician Ransom Stoddard: "This is the west, sir. When the legend becomes fact, print the legend." The sentiment is similar, only now the semantics are clearer.

It may be tempting to make a giant rhetorical leap to claiming that it is appropriate to apply this sentiment to the genre as a whole: that Westerns—despite the countless claims to veracity and fidelity made over the years—have in fact always been in the business of presenting an (honestly) idealized representation of the past, nay-saying historians and their inaccuracies be damned. Such an approach has been adopted, implicitly, by examinations that take a "mythical" approach to the study of genre. Yet the resulting rhetorical gloss applied to the genre as a whole tends to obscure the constructed and multiply determined nature of the historical representations found in the Western.

In the case of *The Life and Times of Judge Roy Bean,* consider that this statement introduces a movie made during a period of the Western's development popularly referred to as "revisionist." At the time when the

Western was—supposedly—self-consciously criticizing its own conventions (and their ideological implications), here we have a movie that is openly embracing an idealized (and, on balance, comic) presentation of history. Not only does the movie play fast and loose with history, it grafts the story of its protagonist onto a conventional plot seen countless times before in earlier Westerns.

As he was not a gunman of any renown—in contrast to most top-flight Western heroes—it is perhaps understandable that Bean did not find himself the subject of more Westerns. As far as heroics go, the judicial branch is not particularly exciting. *The Life and Times of Judge Roy Bean* attempts to strike a balance between earlier comedic portrayals of the character and a more conventional frontier narrative. Here Bean is presented as an agent of change: the man who brings law to the wilderness, but whose brand of justice quickly places him at odds with emerging civilization around him, to the point where he is unceremoniously dismissed like countless heroes before him. As evidenced by the number of Westerns that draw on it, the story of the unwanted gunfighter is clearly a productive and versatile narrative.

In a way, then, this *is* the way it was.

Bias and Box Office

Why, in the revisionist Western, is the use of the genre as a vehicle for social criticism seen as the same thing as criticizing the genre? This is a product of prevailing interpretive methodologies. If we subscribe to the durable notion that the Western is a core American myth, with subject matter that is spiritually entwined with American culture, then any commentary in a Western on American society is inevitably a commentary on the genre itself. If there have always been some Westerns that use the genre's conventions for the purpose of extra-textual commentary, the question then becomes why those earlier pictures did not bring about the demise of the genre.

We can begin by inspecting the common equation of genre revisionism with a genre's degradation. (The specific nature of this connection will depend on which critical methodology one favors—is revisionism a response to a genre's decline, or a symptom of it, or both?—but the relationship is causal nonetheless.) While descriptions of new Westerns as "revisionist" appear as early as the 1970s, appraisals linking this revisionism to the genre's decline are made in retrospect, secure in the knowledge that the Western had ceased to be a popular movie genre by the start of the 1980s. Cawelti and Nachbar initially saw the Western of the 1970s as *changing*, not dying. The "search for meaning" Cawelti describes is really a regenerative process the Western had undergone, successfully, many times before. Looking back, though, the task becomes explaining how the "best" Westerns of the decade, some of which were hailed as masterpieces, failed to sustain the genre.

Kitses relates attempts to distance Peckinpah from the "ordinary" Western to a broader tendency in criticism to distinguish between the classic and revisionist Western, which he says "has often led commentators to suggest that the latter are not true Westerns or are anti-Westerns or that the Western is dead—as if the classical is the whole of the genre."[24] The revisionism of later Westerns is seen to signal a profound break with tradition, where any temporary reinvigoration, because it relies on a self-reflexive attack, actually hastens the genre's decline. Looked at this way, revisionist Westerns were not intended to maintain the genre, but to destroy it. And, if we go by the dearth of Westerns released in their wake, they succeeded.

As we have seen, Kitses takes issue with attempts to divorce revisionist movies from the Western proper, arguing that a counter-tradition of oppositional Westerns—a "revisionist shadow"—existed alongside the genre's mainstream in earlier decades. As a result of the cultural upheavals of the 1960s, this counter-tradition asserted itself as the genre's new mainstream going forward. One potential benefit of this account of the genre's history is that it could explain how earlier Westerns that engaged in social commentary did not precipitate the destruction of the genre. Unlike the later revisionist Western, these pictures did not represent the genre's dominant form, so their criticisms would not have threatened it in the same way.

Kitses does not, however, outright link genre revision with decline. While adhering to a cultural mode of interpretation, he argues that the Western did not die at the end of the 1970s, and that the revisionist Western survives well into the 1990s. The optimism of this take is certainly refreshing, but it is the product of even greater hindsight, coming after a Western revival in the mid-1990s spurred by the success of *Dances with Wolves* (Kevin Costner, 1990) and *Unforgiven.* Between 1993 and 1996, fourteen Westerns were released theatrically in the United States, a level of output not experienced since the 1970s. This cycle of Westerns is often described as a second period or wave of revisionism, a claim that deserves much greater scrutiny than can be afforded here. With that said, some initial observations are still in order—not about the 1990s Westerns themselves, but about the manner in which they have been assessed.

The Western of the 1990s is described as analogous to the Western of the 1970s in both its origins and objectives. A 1996 essay on *Unforgiven* by Leighton Grist is worth quoting at length:

> The previous major period of revisionism in the Western, impelled by the ideological upheavals of the 1960s and 1970s, effectively ended the genre's central role in Hollywood production. An analogous, if less seismic context may, following the reactionary eighties, be responsible for the nineties revival. Witness the incidence of increasingly overt racial and sexual tensions, the rise (for good or ill) of political correctness, and the election in 1992 on a comparatively 'progressive' platform of the first Democratic president for twelve years. Within this context, reworking the Western, whatever its commercial possibilities, has a certain logic. Of all the major genres, the Western is most concerned with American history, with representing the establishment of social and national order and, crucially, with defining dramatically the terms of such an order. Challenging the conventions of the Western thus offers the opportunity to query the dominant order at its source.[25]

The Western, because of its special relationship with American history and culture, is a vehicle for grappling with the ideological and political tensions of the day. As with the "first" period of revisionism in the late 1960s and 1970s, changes we can observe in the Western—in this case, a revival of the genre—are thus the result of cultural change. As it happens, the number of Westerns released in the 1990s is also comparable to the number of 1970s revisionist Westerns referenced in writing on the genre, reinforcing the notion that the two periods are related.

Having said that, how representative the revisionist Western is of the genre during the 1970s is open to debate. While the genre's decline from the 1960s onward as a proportion of Hollywood's annual output has been well documented, Westerns continued to be produced with regularity well into the 1970s. The implication here—that the emphasis on revisionism in Western criticism may be obscuring the number of movies produced during this period—is borne out by data on the number of Westerns released between 1969 and 1980.

The most widely cited figures for numbers of Westerns produced come from a table in the appendix of *The BFI Companion to the Western,* which covers the years 1921 to 1977.[26] According to this table, 156 Westerns were produced between 1969 and 1977. The cited source of this data is Phil Hardy's invaluable *Western Movies* (1983), which was republished in 1985 as *The Encyclopedia of Western Movies.*[27] Hardy, who deliberately casts a very wide net, includes foreign, contemporary, sex, and hybrid Westerns in his year-by-year account of the genre, making his total number of Westerns released from 1969 to 1980 much higher: 212.[28] Because the *BFI Companion* table gives only numbers and not film titles, it is not clear how its figures have been derived from Hardy. The *BFI Companion* numbers certainly include Italian-made Westerns—the numbers could not be as high without them—but because the numbers for a given year are sometimes higher and sometimes lower than Hardy's, without knowing titles it is impossible to deduce what other criteria were used to either add or subtract movies.

If we exclude from Hardy all foreign, television, sex, and hybrid Westerns, and exclude movies with contemporary settings, we arrive at a total of 110 films (table 2). Going by the number of Westerns that are referred to, even infrequently or controversially, as revisionist, as a "type" the revisionist Western comprises no more than 25 percent of the total number of Westerns released between 1969 and 1980. This would appear to invalidate claims that the revisionist Western "dominated" the period. Dominance, however, can be defined in ways other than numerical superiority. This is especially true when discussing Hollywood cinema, where supremacy is often measured in dollars.

Of the 110 American Westerns released from 1969 to 1980, thirty-two earned at least $4 million in rentals in the United States and Canada (table 3).[29] Of these, only six are from the revisionist canon detailed in

Table 2. Western Production, 1969–1980

Year	Hardy	BFI	Hardy (U.S.)
1969	35	20	20
1970	33	22	19
1971	44	24	20
1972	27	25	14
1973	16	16	9
1974	9	13	3
1975	12	20	5
1976	12	26	8
1977	7	7	3
1978	4	0	1
1979	7	0	4
1980	6	0	4
Total	212	173	110

chapter 1. *Little Big Man, The Wild Bunch*, and *McCabe & Mrs. Miller* all rank, but the latter two fall on the bottom half of the list. Clint Eastwood stars in five Westerns, two of which he also directed. Arthur Penn and Don Siegel also directed two films each, but, with three movies—*The Undefeated, Cahill: United States Marshall*, and *Chisum*—Andrew V. McLaglen is the most represented filmmaker on the list. The son of actor Victor McLaglen, Andrew V. McLaglen started out as a second unit director in the 1950s, frequently working under William A. Wellman, before transitioning in the 1960s first to directing television series and then feature films. A workmanlike reputation for competence and efficiency kept McLaglen busy for the remainder of his career. Between 1965 and 1980 he directed twenty theatrical features, many of them Westerns, while continuing to work in television. The common denominator in McLaglen's three Westerns on the above list is also the period's most prominent personality: actor John Wayne, who stars in nine of the Westerns on the list. Out of the ten Westerns that Wayne made between 1969 and 1976, only one, *The Train Robbers* (Burt Kennedy, 1973), earned less than $4.0 million in rentals.[30]

Admittedly, a list of highest earning Westerns may not be the best representation of which pictures were financially successful, given that

Table 3. Highest Earning Westerns, 1969–1980

Title	Year	Rentals (millions of dollars)
Blazing Saddles	1974	47.8
Butch Cassidy and the Sundance Kid	1969	45.9
Jeremiah Johnson	1972	22.6
Little Big Man	1970	15.0
Paint Your Wagon	1969	14.5
True Grit	1969	14.3
The Outlaw Josey Wales	1976	13.5
The Villain	1979	9.9
The Life and Times of Judge Roy Bean	1972	8.1
Rooster Cogburn	1975	8.0
Big Jake	1971	7.5
The Cowboys	1972	7.5
High Plains Drifter	1972	7.3
The Missouri Breaks	1976	7.0
Joe Kidd	1972	6.7
The Long Riders	1980	6.1
Chisum	1970	6.0
A Man Called Horse	1970	6.0
The Shootist	1976	5.9
The Wild Bunch	1969	5.3
The Frisco Kid	1979	5.3
Bite the Bullet	1975	5.2
The Cheyenne Social Club	1970	5.2
Support Your Local Sheriff!	1969	5.1
Two Mules for Sister Sara	1970	5.1
The Duchess and the Dirtwater Fox	1976	4.9
Goin' South	1978	4.7
Tom Horn	1980	4.4
Rio Lobo	1970	4.3
McCabe & Mrs. Miller	1971	4.1
Cahill: United States Marshal	1973	4.1
The Undefeated	1969	4.0

Table 4. Westerns Placing among the Top Twenty Yearly Earners, 1969–1980

Title	Year	Yearly rank	Rentals (millions of dollars)
Blazing Saddles	1974	2	47.8
Butch Cassidy and the Sundance Kid	1969	1	45.9
Jeremiah Johnson	1972	5	22.6
Little Big Man	1970	7	15.0
Paint Your Wagon	1969	7	14.5
True Grit	1969	8	14.3
The Outlaw Josey Wales	1976	18	13.5
The Life and Times of Judge Roy Bean	1972	13	8.1
Big Jake	1971	15	7.5
The Cowboys	1972	13	7.5
High Plains Drifter	1972	20	7.3
Chisum	1970	17	6.0
A Man Called Horse	1970	18	6.0

Westerns compete less against each other than against movies from other genres. Table 4 ranks Westerns from 1969 to 1980 that placed among the top twenty highest earning movies for their respective release years. Even though the total number of Westerns falls from 32 to 13, it does not substantially alter the complexion of the period. John Wayne makes the most appearances, followed by Clint Eastwood. Three canonical revisionist Westerns rank, but only one, *Little Big Man,* is from the revisionist "big three."

During a period that is supposed to be their heyday, revisionist Westerns constitute a minority of both total Western production and highest-earning Westerns. Increasingly, the "dominance" of the revisionist Western appears confined to analyses of the genre, and we should, therefore, be skeptical of such accounts.

Two allied objections to this point are foreseeable. First, critics and historians are not beholden to the whims of fashion, so are under no obligation to write only about the most popular or successful films; their task is to weigh evidence, look for patterns, and make judgments, which may lead to conclusions that appear to contravene surface appearances or defy conventional wisdom. Second, it could be that characteristics of revisionism are endemic to most Westerns of the time, but those traits are exemplified—as determined by the process just described—in a small number of movies. Because they are the strongest evidence, those Westerns are then used as the basis for arguments about the genre.

The second objection essentially proposes that there is a fourth level to the revisionist pyramid—a basement, you might say, of films that go without mention. As evidence of the prevalence of a particular kind of film, this is even weaker stuff than the large number of "guilty by association" revisionist Westerns that merit only scant attention. In this way, the criteria used by critics prove to be self-serving: including certain films as evidence while at the same time excluding them from analysis. Wide claims about both the genre and its relationship with American culture are based on a narrow sample of films—a sample that makes some puzzling exclusions.

Butch Cassidy and the Sundance Kid, a Western that also explores the end of the west and the fate of the frontier hero, was the highest-grossing film of 1969 by a significant margin, earning over $20 million more in rentals than the closest rival, *The Love Bug.* It is also a Western in which the heroes, Butch (Paul Newman) and Sundance (Robert Redford), famously elect to run away—all the way to Bolivia—rather than turn and face their pursuers, a "super posse" of experienced lawmen. Screenwriter William Goldman has yet to tire of recounting how this narrative twist was met with consternation by one producer, who said he would buy Goldman's script only if the ending were changed to have the duo stand and fight. Goldman responded that the real Butch and Sundance did flee to South America, to which the producer replied, "I don't give a damn what they did, all I know is John Wayne don't run away."[31]

The unnamed producer's unwillingness to countenance a Western hero running from a fight suggests that *Butch Cassidy and the Sundance Kid* is distinct from earlier Westerns (and also any contemporary Western that happens to star John Wayne). Goldman's concern for neglected aspects of America history—in this case, personalities who don't conform to conventional notions of heroism—is also suggestive. The screenwriter claims to have come across the Butch and Sundance story in the late 1950s, and found the material appealing because it was unknown. This is something of an exaggeration. Butch and Sundance and their gang "the Wild Bunch" were certainly less well known than some other heroes in the frontier pantheon, but they nevertheless appear on screen as early as the 1930s, and feature in a number of Westerns in the 1940s, 1950s, and 1960s, including *Return of the Bad Men* (Ray Enright, 1948), *The Texas Rangers* (Phil Karlson, 1951), *The Maverick Queen* (Joe Kane, 1956), *Cat Ballou*, and *Return of the Gunfighter* (James Neilson, 1967). The characters were familiar enough for the filmmakers to feel the need to change the name of the duo's outlaw band from the Wild Bunch to the Hole in the Wall Gang, after the gang's secret mountain hide out, to avoid confusion with Peckinpah's *The Wild Bunch.* Nevertheless, Goldman's stated aim of telling a story that the genre had neglected (and telling it as it really happened) is in keeping with ideas about the revisionist Western, and the movie certainly lives up to its reputation of defying Western convention.

Given that *Butch Cassidy and the Sundance Kid* explores similar subject matter to *The Wild Bunch* but was a more popular film, it may reasonably strike us as a better candidate for the inaugurator of the revisionist Western, or for critical reflections on the Western's status and relationship to contemporary culture. How, then, do we explain the comparative neglect of *Butch Cassidy and the Sundance Kid* in histories of the Western?

Not unlike the less esteemed Westerns of the revisionist canon, *Butch Cassidy and the Sundance Kid* was made by a filmmaker not associated with the Hollywood Renaissance. George Roy Hill would, however, go on to be one of the most successful directors of the 1970s. Continuing to work with Redford and Newman (either together or individually), he followed *Butch Cassidy and the Sundance Kid* with a string of successful, critically acclaimed movies in the 1970s, including *The Sting* (1973), for which he won the Oscar for Best Director, and *Slap Shot* (1977). Hill's exclusion from studies of the Western places him in good company. A comparable example is Sydney Pollock, who directed *Jeremiah Johnson,* the period's third-highest-earning Western, as well as *The Way We Were* (1973), *Three Days of the Condor* (1975), and *The Electric Horseman* (1979).

There is a growing sense that success or popularity risks disqualifying a Western from serious critical consideration. While it is the critic's or historian's prerogative to select his or her own evidence, the relative neglect of these factors is odd given that the advent of the revisionist Western—whether conceived as a distinct break in the genre's evolution or the ascendancy of a hitherto minor tradition—is said to be the result of cultural change. This is not to suggest that an examination limited to the most popular movies will produce a more reliable or illuminating take on the culture that produced and consumed them. The choices individual consumers make are, again, influenced by a multitude of factors. That these choices somehow reflect a larger social consciousness—because successful movies are those that have been selected through a kind of collective response—is a specious argument that relies on a restricted vision of moviegoing as an activity.[32] Yet, if one did want to make the argument that an unconscious expression of cultural anxieties and ideological tensions could be found in popular cinema, would it not make sense to at least consider either the movies that more people went to see or the types of movies that were produced in greater numbers?

The fact that critical accounts of the Western have tended to downplay popular and successful films implicitly acknowledges that consumer preferences—reflected in production figures or box office data—are not considered to be the same thing as cultural expression, but this also suggests a suspicion of popular tastes and the attendant mechanisms by which films are brought to the marketplace.

The canonization by scholarship of a small group of later Westerns—to the exclusion of dozens of others—is the product less of their typicality for the period or financial success or even critical acclaim than of a form of symptomatic criticism that relies on a combination of veneration of Hollywood Renaissance auteur directors and *a priori* assumptions about how movie genres reflect cultural change—in this case, the aftermath of the Civil Rights movement and the growing opposition to America's military involvement in Vietnam. The shortcomings of this approach multiply when this small group of movies is used as the basis of arguments about the culture or mental state of large groups of people at a particular point in history, which, as we have seen, is a common move in genre criticism. In the case of the revisionist Western, the burden of proof falls on an increasingly small group of Westerns, as the means by which the canon is established lead to a progressive focus on the strongest examples. This means that even some Westerns initially identified as revisionist have been largely forgotten. A good example is *Bad Company*, an entertaining film from 1972 about two young draft-dodgers-turned-outlaws set during the Civil War. The subject matter is topical, and the film's remedial intentions were perceived to be akin to those of other Westerns of the time. In his review of the picture, critic Robert Ebert appreciatively lumps it and

The Great Northfield Minnesota Raid in with *The Wild Bunch* and *McCabe & Mrs. Miller* as Westerns that "pretend to be about the West as it really was"—in contrast to "romantic fantasies with no connection to a real West that never existed."[33]

The Westerns that make up the revisionist canon actually confirm that these movies do have much in common with other contemporary Westerns, but the commonality is not revisionism—at least not in the sense favored by critics. That these commonalities transcend the history of the genre further challenges the idea that this later period was a distinct break or turn in the Western's development.

The Last Hard Men

Looking at the two lists of highest-earning Westerns, the most obvious feature that transcends the history of the genre is the continued and repeated presence of John Wayne. Between 1969 and 1976, Wayne made twelve movies, ten of which were Westerns—a detail infrequently commented upon in existing literature on the genre. When the actor's later Westerns are discussed, one term is repeatedly used to describe them: *traditional.* As we saw in chapter 1, both Cawelti and Nachbar identify a "traditional" variant of Western in the 1970s alongside more modern types. More recent appraisals of the genre by Steve Neale and David A. Cook also distinguish a traditional Western amid a more general trend towards revisionism. In all of these accounts, Wayne's later Westerns are not only representative of the traditional Western, they are largely responsible for it.

> The traditional Westerns that were still produced in the mid-to-late 1960s and early 1970s catered for a traditional but dwindling adult audience. They were almost solely reliant on the ageing John Wayne, and Wayne was to make his last Western, *The Shootist,* in 1976.[34]

> American-produced traditional Westerns continued to be popular during the decade, many of them owing to the presence of John Wayne . . . whose star power remained considerable throughout the

> 1970s, despite strong competition from such newcomers as Clint Eastwood . . . and Robert Redford.[35]

Wayne was far from the only Hollywood elder still sporting spurs and a six-gun. Many of the genre's other established stars from the 1950s and 1960s continued to make Westerns in the 1970s: Burt Lancaster, Henry Fonda, Robert Mitchum, Kirk Douglas, James Stewart, Gregory Peck, Glenn Ford, Dean Martin, and Lee Marvin all remained active in the genre.[36]

Wayne's association with the Western, particularly in his later years, was admittedly much stronger than any of these other actors, but what also distinguished him was his continued appeal. Right up to his death, Wayne remained one of Hollywood's most popular and bankable actors, consistently placing in surveys of the ten most popular film stars.[37] If the presence of an admired actor increases the likelihood that a movie will be successful, it is not surprising that Wayne's Westerns would rank alongside those of other popular stars like Robert Redford, Paul Newman, and Clint Eastwood. With that said, there is both a demographic and political dimension to Wayne's popularity that distinguishes him from most other top stars of the day.

"Traditional" is a suggestive term, bringing to mind other words like old-fashioned, conservative, simple, even boring—all of which could be used to describe a particular film's style, theme, or subject matter. But therein lay a problem: when used to describe a film (or group of films), "traditional" risks coming across, however unintentionally, as pejorative. The films against which "traditional" films are contrasted are usually described in superlatives, as is the case with the innovative and stylish Westerns of the 1970s privileged by critics. It is well known that Wayne's personal politics were out of step with the supposed liberal sensibilities of Hollywood in the 1960s and 1970s. Cook states that the four Westerns made by Wayne's Batjac production company in the 1970s "were extremely conservative in their approach to the genre (unsurprisingly, given Wayne's ultra-rightist politics)."[38] It was Wayne's clout, then, that enabled him to make—or keep making—traditional Westerns. The success of any of these pictures is then explained to be the result of an aging star's enduring appeal to an audience that, like the Duke himself, was growing old. Times may have changed, but the Duke kept making Westerns like it was 1956, giving the old folks what they wanted to see. As a result, these movies can be discounted with relative ease as remnants of an earlier age—and of a filmmaking time that has already been accounted for.

This is a clever move, because it allows the critic to both characterize and dismiss a group of films without having to closely analyze them. When thorough evaluations of genre classics like *Red River* (Howard Hawks, 1948), *The Searchers*, and *The Man Who Shot Liberty Valance* already exist, there is little need to look at outmoded retreads like *Chisum, Big Jake*, or *The Shootist* (Don Siegel, 1976). Of course, we have already seen how other attempts to pare down the later Western to its essence are problematic, leading to the neglect and even loss of many Westerns.

Gary Wills contends in his biography *John Wayne's America* (1998) that the role of Rooster Cogburn in *True Grit* provided Wayne with the last of three personas he assumed over the course of his filmmaking career, on-screen and off. First came the naïve young hero, initially forged by director Raoul Walsh in *The Big Trail* (1930) and later epitomized in Ford's *Stagecoach*. Then came the older, somber authority figure of *Red River* onward. This persona began to wear thin, however. Says Wills: "During the 1960s [Wayne] was in danger of becoming a figure of fun until his last identity emerged—the lone survivor of a past heroic time. The conscious anachronism."[39] According to Wills, it was this identity that Wayne was able to make use of throughout the 1970s.

One drawback to this formulation is immediately apparent. Positing *True Grit* as establishing the persona that Wayne adopted in his remaining films unavoidably downplays how unconventional the character of Marshal Cogburn is. Without discounting the differences between Wayne's other roles in the period, it is certainly fair to assert that "one-eyed fat man" Cogburn is without question the most idiosyncratic character he played in the latter part of his career, if not his entire career. Given how Wayne is often criticized for playing essentially the same character over and over again, it may come as a surprise that, following the success of *True Grit*, he did not seek out roles that afforded him the same opportunity for burlesque.

Wills's idea of Wayne as "conscious anachronism" ultimately lacks precision. In spite of the significant thematic correspondences we find across Wayne's 1970s films, Wills examines only three—*Big Jake, Rooster Cogburn*, and *The Shootist*—as pictures that "gave him new symbolic vitality."[40] While a suggestive notion, Wills never elaborates on how these specific roles accomplished this. No indication is given as to why these three Wayne Westerns qualify while the other five made during the decade do not. Moreover, what first appears to be an anachronism may actually indicate *awareness*—not only of the Western genre's traditions, but also its more contemporary developments.

The Train Robbers (1973) was filmed in the spring of 1972 under the direction of Burt Kennedy, who also wrote the movie's screenplay. This was Kennedy's second time directing Wayne, after *The War Wagon* in 1967. Their association went further back, though. In 1955, Wayne's Batjac production company purchased Kennedy's script for a Western feature called *Seven Men from Now.* The movie was directed the following year by Budd Boetticher and starred Randolph Scott. Boetticher and Scott would go on to make six more Westerns in quick succession, three of which were scripted by Kennedy. In 1961, Kennedy moved into the director's chair. Over the next forty years, he would continue to work steadily, first in the cinema and then, from the late 1970s onward, increasingly in television.

The Train Robbers stars Wayne as Lane, a Civil War veteran who enlists the help of two old war buddies and three younger men to accompany a young widow, Mrs. Lowe (Ann-Margaret), to recover and return a gold shipment stolen by her late husband. Her aim is to clear the husband's name before a gang of his old partners beats them to the treasure. The movie opens with a striking series of shots that survey the desolate town of Liberty, Texas. The town is composed of only five buildings—a livery, a saloon, a hotel, a railway station, and a water tower with windmill—situated in the middle of a barren, sun-scorched landscape. There is no non-diegetic music. Instead, the only sound we hear over the carefully composed shots is the blowing of the wind and whatever objects it animates. Signs creak back and forth. Saloon doors bat open and shut. Rocking chairs sway slowly forward and back. Seated at the railway station is Jesse (Ben Johnson), awaiting the arrival of the train. He is the only person visible in the entire town.

With its exclusive use of diegetic sound and the setting of a frontier whistle-stop, the sequence clearly brings to mind the opening sequence of another recent Western: Sergio Leone's *Once Upon a Time in the West,* released four years earlier.

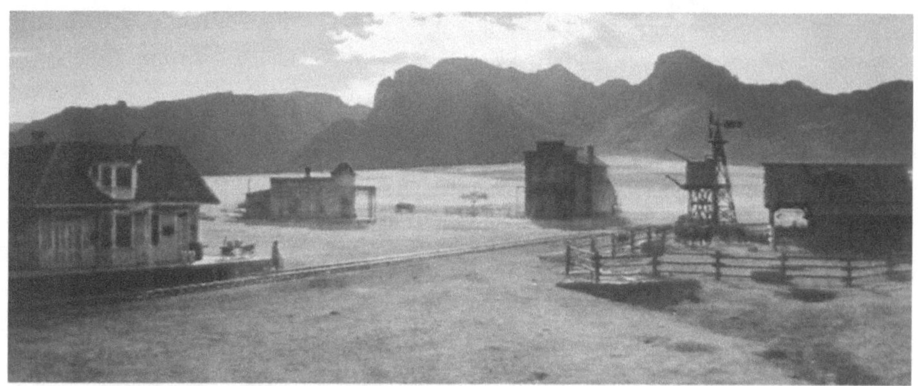

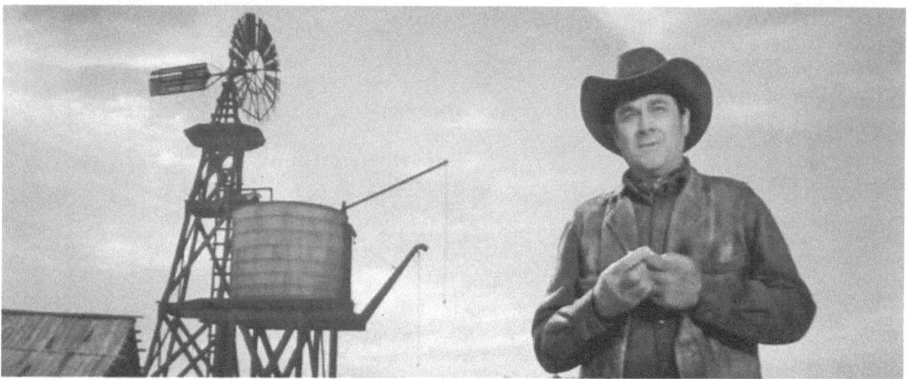

Opening shots from *The Train Robbers* (1973)

Yet before anyone decries Kennedy's effort as a rip-off, some genre archaeology is in order.

As famous as the opening to *Once Upon a Time in the West* may be, it is itself an obvious and well-known play on *High Noon,* in which a gang of outlaws awaits the arrival of their leader Frank Miller at the town's train station.

Leone's Westerns are each famously packed with references like these. Christopher Frayling detects no fewer than fifty-seven "explicit citations of American Westerns" in *Once Upon a Time in the West* alone.[41] In spite of this, Kennedy's choice of so recent a Western as "source" in *The Train Robbers,* coupled with a patent formal mimicry, mean that the motivation behind the reference could be taken for opportunism—that is, exploiting contemporary, ostensibly better Westerns. Such charges are, in

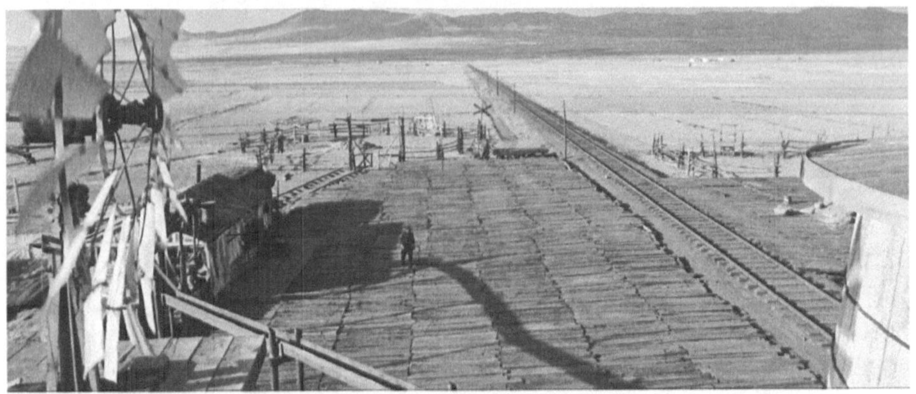

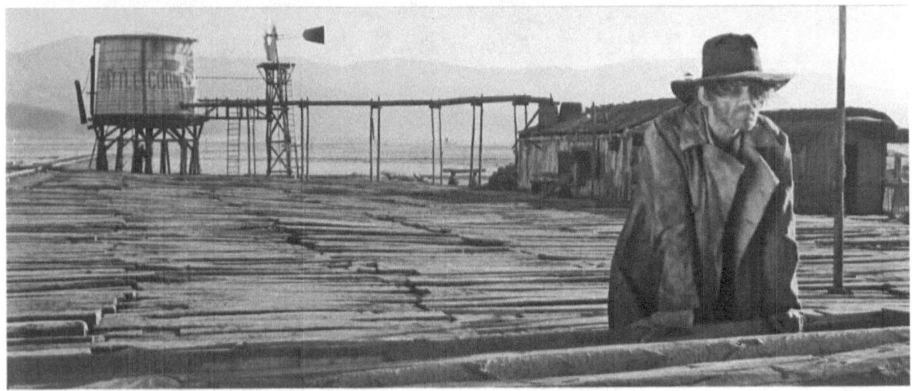

Opening shots from *Once Upon a Time in the West* (1969)

fact, common in the relatively rare instances when any of John Wayne's later pictures are written about. Noting superficial similarities between the character types found in *Rio Bravo* and four of Wayne's subsequent films, Michael Coyne writes: "This knee-jerk dependence on tried and tested movie formulae was commercially safe, politically conservative and artistically unadventurous."[42] In his book *Wild West Movies,* critic Kim Newman says of Wayne's later Westerns: "[In the late 1960s and 70s] the Duke is just going through the motions in an era when the West was the province of Leone and Peckinpah, not lazy comics like Andrew V. McLaglen and Burt Kennedy."[43]

That McLaglen and Kennedy, genre veterans though they may be, are not Leone or Peckinpah is true, but largely misses the point. Practically speaking, when Newman states that the genre was the "province"

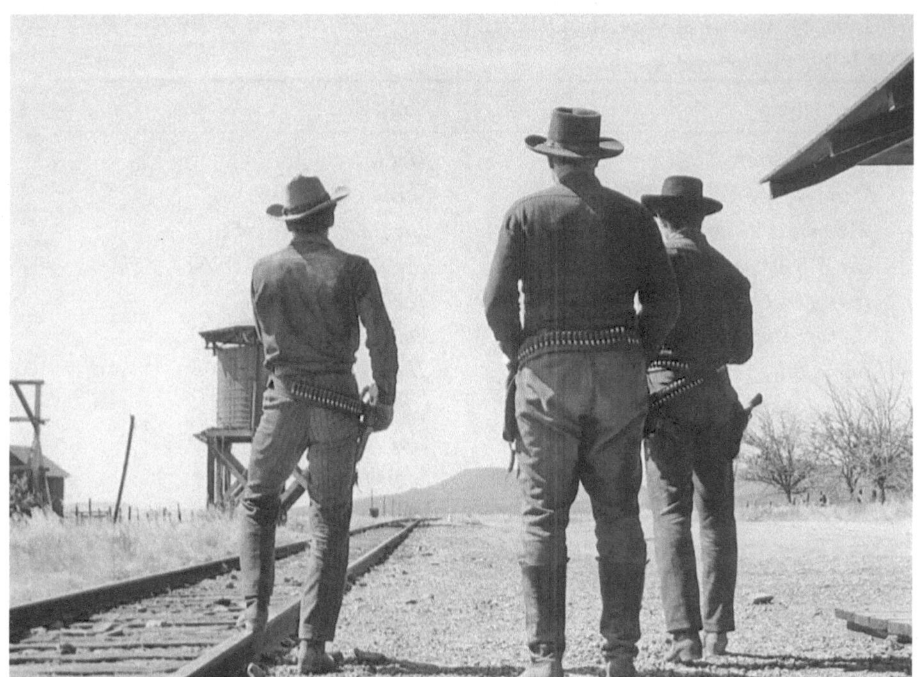

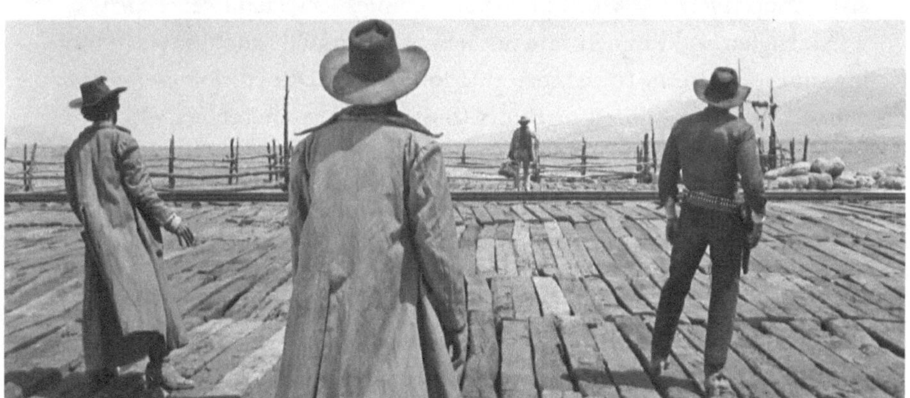

Waiting on a train: *High Noon* (1952) and *Once Upon a Time in the West* (1969)

of Leone and Peckinpah, he means that their movies have been valorized and canonized by scholars and critics on the grounds of decreed artistic or cultural merit, as opposed to other criteria like financial success or number of movies made. The top-earning Westerns of the era were not those of Leone or Peckinpah; they were, in general, those starring Wayne.

Table 5. Theatrical Westerns Directed by Burt Kennedy and Andrew V. McLaglen

Kennedy	McLaglen
The Canadians (1961)	*McLintock!* (1963)
Return of the Seven (1966)	*Shenandoah* (1965)
Welcome to Hard Times (1967)	*The Rare Breed* (1966)
The War Wagon (1967)	*The Ballad of Josie* (1967)
The Good Guys and the Bad Guys (1969)	*The Way West* (1967)
Support Your Local Sheriff! (1969)	*Bandolero!* (1968)
Young Billy Young (1969)	*The Undefeated* (1969)
Dirty Dingus Magee (1970)	*Chisum* (1970)
Hannie Caulder (1971)	*One More Train to Rob* (1971)
Support Your Local Gunfighter (1971)	*Something Big* (1971)
The Deserter (1971)	*Cahill: United States Marshal* (1973)
The Train Robbers (1973)	*The Last Hard Men* (1976)

In the 1960s and 1970s, Leone and Peckinpah directed five and six Westerns, respectively; Newman's two "lazy comics" directed twelve *each.*

McLaglen and Kennedy are not names one usually encounters in writing on the Western. In the introduction to the 2004 edition of *Horizons West,* Kitses lists a dozen directors (outside of the chosen six who make up his auteur-centered study) who have made significant contributions to the genre. Included are Robert Altman and Arthur Penn, who directed two and three Westerns, respectively. There is no mention of either McLaglen or Kennedy. Despite his lengthy association with the Western, even Wayne is unlikely to garner more than a brief mention in discussions of the genre's later years. Yet Andrew V. McLaglen, Burt Kennedy, and John Wayne were names Western moviegoers encountered with far greater frequency than those whose films have come to typify the period in question.

In the same year that *Once Upon a Time in the West* was citing *High Noon* (among other films), one of Kennedy's Westerns was also looking back at *High Noon,* albeit in a rather different fashion. *The Good Guys and the Bad Guys*—the third of three Kennedy-directed Westerns released in 1969, following *Support Your Local Sheriff!* and *Young Billy Young*—also features the familiar scenario of a group of outlaws awaiting the arrival of a train. Here the villains are planning to steal a gold shipment destined for the town's new bank—that is, until the entire town parades to the train station, complete with marching band, ready to greet the same shipment with an entirely different sort of fanfare.

Here Kennedy's take on the train station scenario may be less stylish than Leone's, but it is arguably more knowing. Whereas Leone's Westerns display a tendency to reference earlier Westerns in an exhibitionist fashion, Kennedy's invocation of the genre's conventions is more thematic, concertedly linking iconography to narrative concerns. The plot of *The Good Guys and the Bad Guys* centers on a town that decides it no longer requires the services of its renowned lawman, and unceremoniously dismisses him. This is, of course, the basic scenario of *High Noon. The Good Guys and the Bad Guys* provides not only a variation on a well-known Western set piece, but also situates it, unlike *Once Upon a Time in the West,* within a developing narrative tradition that derives from the same source. In the scene from *The Train Robbers,* consider how the frontier town of Liberty, as presented to the viewer, has in effect been stripped down to its most basic elements: again, a livery, a saloon, a hotel, a railway station, and a water tower. In one shot, as the camera tracks rightward following Jesse as he walks from the railway station to the water tower, we see the charred ruins of another building behind the saloon, suggesting the removal of another, superfluous structure. What this opening sequence establishes is a stylistic and thematic minimalism that permeates the remainder of the movie.

As these two examples illustrate, it should not be enough to simply note that a film has introduced an element that we are able to account for by recognizing it from earlier pictures, and then dismiss that film if the reference does not appear to be in service of critical or liberal or revisionist purposes. Regardless of the film's existing designation as revisionist or traditional, we must ask ourselves, *to what end?* What is the *function* of this device we have detected? In doing so, we have the potential to reveal not the zeitgeist or cultural anxieties but the richness and complexity of the Western.

PART II

Critique and Convention

3

Hugger of Trees, Scalper of Whites

Opposing Stereotypes in the "Pro-Indian" Western

> Our official position is that we are in Vietnam to honor a commitment. But let us not forget that we have signed 400 treaties with the Indians, violating them all, one after the other.
>
> —Ralph Nelson, 1970

Historically, one of the most problematic aspects of the movie Western is its treatment of Indians. The genre's depictions of America's indigenous peoples are best described not as conventions but stereotypes, and it is the Western that is largely responsible for propagating these stereotypes to the wider culture. Although some Westerns in the 1950s began to offer more sympathetic portrayals of Indians, it is revisionist Westerns, and in particular three films released in 1970, that are held to mark a pronounced break from the genre's traditional, stereotyped representations of Indians, moving the genre toward a more nuanced and historically truthful presentation of Indian life and customs. Despite such noble intentions, these new "pro-Indian" films have much in common with earlier Westerns, and not always in a positive way.

Westerns of the 1950s ostensibly sympathetic to the plight of the American Indian have been read as using that plight as an allegory about the present-day treatment of African Americans. In an influential 1981 essay titled "*The Searchers:* An American Dilemma," Brian Henderson writes that the celebrated John Ford film, generally regarded as the greatest Western ever made, "has to do with 1956, not with the 1868–1873 period in which it is set."[1] He argues that the film's depiction of race relations—an unambiguously racist hero searches for his niece, who has been kidnapped by Comanche Indians and made the wife of their chief—was motivated by contemporary anxieties about miscegenation and black civil rights, particularly in the wake of the Supreme Court's May 1954 ruling against segregation in public schools in the case of *Brown v. Board of Education*.[2] In similar fashion, later Westerns also use the conflict between Indians and the United States government as a parable about present-day hostilities, albeit hostilities taking place on a different frontier. John O'Connor observes that political subject matter found its way into Westerns of the late 1960s and early 1970s "in the form of Indian allegories of the American experience in Southeast Asia." He continues: "The Indian movies made then, such as *Little Big Man* and *Soldier Blue* (both 1970), films that indicted the American Army for practicing genocide on the Native American, were partly the expressions of the producers' and directors' feelings about Vietnam. Even more important, however, they were commercial products aimed at the moviegoing public of young adults who, by profitable coincidence, also represented the age group most deeply involved in the antiwar movement."[3] This raises questions about the degree to which these films are actually *about* American Indians. At the same time, attention to liberal allegory obscures a shift in the genre during the 1960s towards rectifying past shortcomings, a trend that continues into the 1970s but has shortcomings of its own.

Soldier Blue

Perhaps the most notorious Western released in the 1970s is *Solider Blue,* directed by Ralph Nelson. Released in the summer of 1970, the movie is a fictionalized account of the events surrounding the infamous Sand Creek Massacre of 1864, where Colorado militia wiped out a village of Cheyenne and Arapaho. The movie opens with the decimation of a troupe of United States cavalry by a band of Cheyenne. The only survivors are Honus Gant (Peter Strauss), a young private, and Cresta Marybelle Lee (Candice Bergen), a white woman formerly held captive for two years by the Cheyenne. Low on supplies, the pair set out for the cavalry's base camp at Fort Reunion. As they travel, the foulmouthed Cresta reveals that she was the wife of Spotted Wolf (Jorge Rivero), head of the raiding party that attacked Gant's company. Gant is initially repelled by Cresta's sympathy for the Cheyenne and disdain for the U.S. government, and she by his naïveté, but affection between them grows as they endure several trials. Menaced by a Kiowa band, the pair is allowed to proceed when Gant bests their leader in a fight. Gant is later injured in a confrontation with gunrunner Isaac Q. Cumber (Donald Pleasance). In a secluded cave Cresta binds the soldier's wounds and the couple makes love. Anxious for Gant's recovery, Cresta rushes ahead to Fort Reunion where she learns that the cavalry is bound on a reprisal raid against the Cheyenne. Alarmed, she warns the tribe and discovers that Spotted Wolf is eager to make peace with the bluecoats. Ignoring Spotted Wolf's white flag, the cavalry savagely massacres the Indian encampment—raping the women, killing indiscriminately, and mutilating the dead. Gant, recently returned to the cavalry, is horrified at the destruction but powerless to stop it. Following the slaughter, he is hauled away in chains for insubordination while Cresta chooses to remain among the few surviving Cheyenne.

The climactic massacre of Cheyenne men, women, and children by American soldiers is what *Soldier Blue* is remembered for today, but this is as much a reputation that was deliberately crafted and promoted in 1970 as one acquired after the movie was released. At the time, the advertising for the film emphasized its graphic violence, clearly telling viewers what they were in for. One promotional poster declared *Soldier Blue* to be "THE MOST SAVAGE FILM IN HISTORY." Another alerted patrons to a screening policy of not allowing entry to the auditorium after the film had begun owing to its "controversial and devastating nature." As if those were too subtle, another poster asked moviegoers: "WHY? *Why* does 'SOLDIER BLUE' tell it like it was—and still is? *Why* does 'SOLDIER BLUE' show, in the most graphic way imaginable, the rape and savage slaughter of American Indians by American soldiers?" These questions were not rhetorical: "BECAUSE it's true . . . and now more than ever, is the time for truth."

The connection between violence and "truth" is also emphasized in a title crawl that opens the film. It begins, "In 5,000 years of recorded civilization mankind has written his history in blood," warns that the climax of the movie will show "specifically and graphically the horrors of battle," and concludes: "Brutal atrocities affect not only the warriors. But the innocent as well . . . the women and the children. The greatest horror of all is that it is true." In effect, the film justifies its presentation of violence on the grounds that it is an accurate representation of the brutalities of war. While it would be naïve not to see this strategy at least in part as a pragmatic response to the outcry over violence provoked by recent movies like *Bonnie and Clyde* and *The Wild Bunch,* Americans in 1970 were all too familiar with the atrocities of war.

The year before, horrific images of the mass murder of hundreds of unarmed civilians at the hands of U.S. servicemen in South Vietnam had flooded American newspapers, magazines, and television screens. In *Soldier Blue,* these images are brought to life and transposed to 1864. "The story they were afraid to talk about," as another promotional poster for the movie puts it, is really two analogous stories: the massacre of Cheyenne at Sand Creek and the mass murder of South Vietnamese at My Lai. Many shots from the movie's final massacre—piles of bodies, children cowering in the presence of American soldiers—deliberately mirror photographs of the My Lai massacre published in *Life* magazine.

By presenting moviegoers with the kinds of scenes that the Western had historically denied them but that were, in fact, part of the history of the American West, *Soldier Blue* equates the whitewashing of American history by the genre with the Army's cover-up of My Lai. The larger "truth" that *Soldier Blue* addresses is thus both that of the decimation of American Indians at the hands of whites and the subsequent decimation of other "native" peoples in the name of American imperialism.

In nearly every respect, then, *Soldier Blue* appears to be quintessentially revisionist. It offers a violent depiction of an ugly episode from American history; an indictment of the racism and imperialism that characterizes both frontier history and the movie Western; a sympathetic portrayal of Indians; a deflating depiction of traditional Western heroes; and a direct commentary on the Vietnam War. Yet, in spite of this long list of qualifications, the movie remains relegated to the bottom tier of the revisionist canon—frequently cited as evidence for the revisionist Western, but rarely examined in any detail. Why?

One possible reason: *Soldier Blue* does not have the same kind of authorial pedigree as the Westerns in the top two tiers of the canon. Nelson enjoyed a long and respectable career in film and television, but both

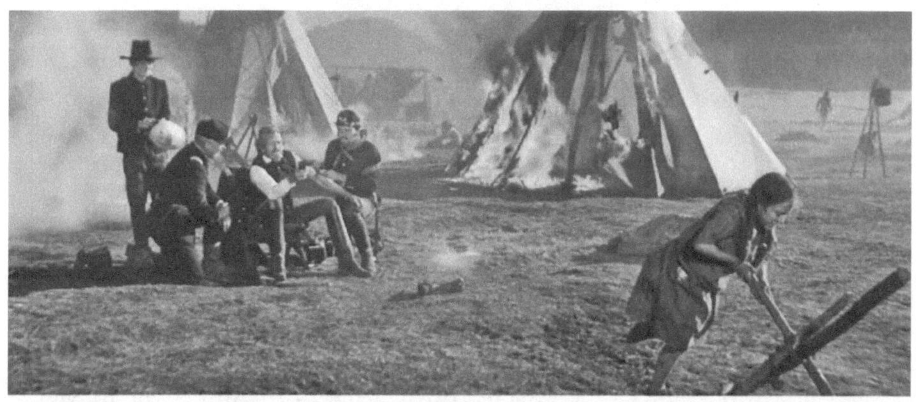

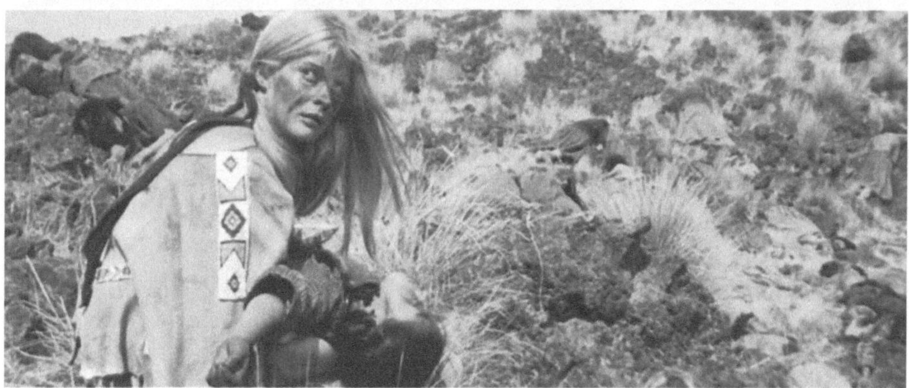

The climactic massacre in *Soldier Blue* (1970)

he and his work fall on the margins of cinema history. Reasons why are not as obvious as we may expect. Nelson was no hack. In the 1960s, he directed a number of successful pictures across a variety of genres, including *Requiem for a Heavyweight* (1962), which was nominated for an Academy Award, *Lilies of the Field* (1964), and *Charly* (1968). These and other movies like *Duel at Diablo* (1966), *Counterpoint* (1967), and *. . . tick . . . tick . . . tick . . .* (1970) deal directly with topical subject matter like race and the status of minorities—issues also at the center of *Soldier Blue*. Nelson's reputation was even invoked by the advertising for *Soldier Blue* ("*Why* did Ralph Nelson, after 'Lilies of the Field' and 'Charly,' film 'SOLDIER BLUE'?"). Yet neither Nelson nor his movies have been included in accounts of the Hollywood Renaissance. Although *Soldier Blue* was released in 1970, the peak of Nelson's career falls into something of a conceptual gap in the history of American cinema: between the end of Classical Hollywood, usually dated to around 1960, and the beginning of the Hollywood Renaissance in the late 1960s. Born in 1916, Nelson was also older than the roster of Renaissance auteurs born in the 1920s and 30s.

Whereas *Soldier Blue* has been classified as a revisionist Western, Nelson has not been classified as an auteur director—as much as it would be possible to trace an authorial signature across his diverse body of work. If Ralph Nelson is remembered today, it is for *Soldier Blue.* And the reason *Soldier Blue* is remembered today is its violence—specifically, the violence of the climactic massacre. This is what distinguishes the movie from other revisionist Westerns that arguably offer comparable critiques of American foreign policy, including *The Culpepper Cattle Co.*, *Ulzana's Raid*, and *Little Big Man.*

Even by contemporary standards, many of the images from *Soldier Blue's* concluding massacre are shocking—even if they do not, it must be acknowledged, fully capture the barbarity of the historical Sand Creek Massacre. A soldier is shown cutting into a woman's breast with a knife while he and other soldiers gang rape her. Children are killed indiscriminately. Babies are impaled on spears. Soldiers adorn their horses with the severed limbs and decapitated heads of the Cheyenne. Here, the movie more than lives up to its reputation. Yet what is curious about this final outburst of carnage is how anomalous it is in the context of the entirety of *Soldier Blue.*

The final battle is in fact not one but two sequences. The cavalry first engage the Cheyenne on horseback on the plains outside of their village. After defeating the Cheyenne's warriors, the soldiers *then* proceed to ransack the defenseless village. The first sequence mirrors the battle that opens the movie, where Gant's company is ambushed by Spotted Wolf's raiding party. In nearly all respects, these reciprocal skirmishes are strikingly *conventional*—composed of the type of competently staged horse-falls and cavalry charges that are the genre's stock-in-trade. There is also relatively little bloodshed. While there are several *Wild Bunch*–style, slow-motion bullet wounds—not uncommon for the period—maimed characters in these two battles are just as likely to clutch at bloodless, imaginary wounds and fall to the ground. This is a striking contrast to the graphic violence of the concluding massacre.

This conventionality also extends to the events these two skirmishes book-end. Whereas the two traditional battle sequences have some entertainment value, the remainder of the narrative alternates between uninspired tedium and soft-focus schmaltz. Scenarios in *Soldier Blue* such as the knife-fight between the white man and Indian brave and the encounter with the nefarious trader are ones Western moviegoers have seen many times before. The movie's love story, with Gant's concomitant enlightenment, is boilerplate, as is the manner in which the movie conveys the Indian point of view. It is not any of the Cheyenne but Cresta, the former white captive, who advocates the Indian cause. Since at least 1950, the dominant tactic of "pro-Indian" Westerns like *Broken Arrow, White Feather* (Robert D. Webb, 1955), and *Run of the Arrow* (Samuel Fuller, 1957) has been to feature a sympathetic Caucasian protagonist who serves as a mediator between the Indians and whites (including, by extension, those in the presumed audience). Making this protagonist a woman is not novel—Carroll Baker's Quaker missionary in John Ford's *Cheyenne Autumn* (1964) served the same function, as did Barbara Stanwyck's rescued captive in *Trooper Hook* (Charles Marquis Warren, 1957). Cresta's devotion to her captors and outright hostility to "her own people" is unusual—and, perhaps, revisionist—but she is not the first rescued female captive to come away with a greater sympathy toward Indians.

Like earlier pro-Indian Westerns that have been read as projecting onto historical Indian–white relations 1950s concerns about black–white relations, *Soldier Blue* is also arguably less about the plight of the American Indian than about a racial analogue: the South Vietnamese. Moreover, as was nearly always the case in earlier Westerns, the lead Indian in *Soldier Blue,* Spotted Wolf, is not played by an aboriginal actor but by one of another ethnicity (Jorge Rivero was Mexican). In fact, the picture spends very little time with its Cheyenne characters, relying instead on archetypal imagery of warriors on horseback and peaceful villagers. As a result, these characters are reduced to little more than stock victims. Even a positive evaluation of the movie by George N. Fenin and William K. Everson concludes that it is unfortunate the movie does not include "a deeper, more realistic portrayal of the Indians themselves as well as the events in which they were involved."[4]

What, then, are we to make of *Soldier Blue*'s claims about truth? It is apparent that the majority of *Soldier Blue* draws heavily upon—and does little to revise—ostensibly fictional conventions and scenarios that the Western had refined over the preceding thirty years. The movie's revisionist credentials, especially its purportedly corrective representation of aspects of American history, are based almost entirely on the strength of the movie's final, fifteen-minute-long massacre. Even if this were a deliberate juxtaposition of fiction and fact meant to jolt viewers out of a genre-induced haze, the lengthy lead up to the climax is far too uneven and laborious to achieve the desired effect. The finale is, again, shocking, but this shock lacks political or emotional weight. The cavalry get their revenge on the Cheyenne's warriors in the first part of the climax, in the battle on the plains outside the Indian village; the movie offers no motivation beyond blind racism for the slaughter of women and children that follows. As the entry for *Soldier Blue* in the *BFI Companion to the Western* puts it, "Too often the film lapses into cliché and stridency, and, most importantly, it lacks any real *explanation* for the final massacre, which it turns into a *mere* exercise in bloodletting of the kind it purports to condemn."[5] At the conclusion of the massacre, the cavalry soldiers dance wildly around in a circle, hooting and hollering—an image that deliberately parodies earlier cinematic depictions of "savage" Indians, yet offers just as little in the way of an explanation for the perpetration of violent acts.

In these ways, *Soldier Blue* is less complex than confused, a movie internally at odds with itself. While its reputation for violent revisionism is warranted on the strength of its brutal climax and conspicuous political parable, the resulting notoriety obscures how uninspired and prosaic the majority of the movie is. Because it is less concerned with correcting the Western's historical inaccuracies than presenting a Vietnam allegory, the picture ironically falls back on the very genre conventions which it aims to critique.

How much this contributes to the relegation of *Soldier Blue* to the bottom tier of the revisionist canon is an open question. Is the relative lack of attention paid to the movie an acknowledgement of its shortcomings or more a reflection of director Nelson's absence from larger narratives about moviemaking during the period? In my experience, many are aware of *Soldier Blue* but few have actually seen it. You could say that it is less the case that the movie has a reputation than that its reputation has a reputation—and not one that is likely to entice the average movie watcher, or even Western fan, to seek the film out. This reputation is, however, bound to the project of the revisionist Western: the movie's notorious violence is understood to be in service of the revisionist aims of historical accuracy and political critique.

Opposing Stereotypes

As noted above, other revisionist Westerns offer similar commentaries on armed conflict in foreign lands. *Ulzana's Raid,* another "Vietnam Western," also centers on a young soldier who undergoes a violent, emotional journey on the American frontier. Although not quite in the same league as the frenzied racial and sexual violence of the massacre in *Soldier Blue, Ulzana's Raid* does feature some very graphic depictions of brutal acts of cruelty. In one scene, three assailants disembowel a dead body and proceed to play with the entrails. In another, the smoldering, castrated body of a man is found staked to the ground with a dog's tail stuffed in its mouth. What may be surprising about these atrocities, however, is *who* is responsible.

These acts and others, including the rape of a white woman, are perpetrated by a band of renegade Apache Indians, led by the fierce Ulzana (Joaquin Martinez), who have escaped from the Indian Agency and embarked on a series of raids against the white homesteaders now occupying their lands. The Apaches are tracked by a group of U.S. cavalry soldiers, led by wily scout McIntosh (Burt Lancaster) and fresh-from-the-academy Lt. Garnett DeBuin (Bruce Davison).

The pairing of a wise veteran of the frontier with a young, idealistic counterpart is a common Western device. In many cases, each man ends up learning important lessons from the other. In *Ulzana's Raid,* however, the arc of enlightenment belongs solely to the young protagonist. The son of a respected Eastern minister, DeBuin arrives in the Arizona territory believing Christian compassion toward the Apache will earn their trust and respect—win their hearts and minds, you might say. DeBuin's commanding officer, Major Cartwright (Douglass Watson), has resigned himself to following the directives laid before him and does not share

DeBuin's youthful optimism. As the soldiers track Ulzana's band, going from horror to horror, DeBuin's feeling towards the Apache evolves first to hatred, then to a nihilistic understanding on par with McIntosh's.

Violence is understood in the film to be an essential facet of the Apache way of life, part of their natural and spiritual order. As McIntosh's Apache interpreter Ke-Ni-Tay (Jorge Luke) explains to DeBuin, for the Apache, life is about acquiring "power"—the power of others, by killing them. When McIntosh is later asked by DeBuin why he does not hate the Apaches in spite of their acts of barbarity, the scout replies that to do so would be like "hatin' the desert because there ain't no water in it."

Initially, this portrayal of the Apache appears decidedly—and perhaps offensively—out of tune with the liberal sensibilities on display in other Westerns of the period that depict Indian culture, as Philip French writes, "as a valid counterculture, a more organic, life-enhancing existence than white society, from which the central character in each film gains a new perspective on society and a new humanity."[6] From the early 1970s to the present, overviews of the Western's portrayal of Indians have described the releases of *A Man Called Horse, Soldier Blue*, and *Little Big Man* in 1970 as part of a process of moving beyond demeaning stereotypes of American Indians—stereotypes which *Ulzana's Raid* may seem guilty of reverting to—that began in 1950 with *Broken Arrow* and *Devil's Doorway* (Anthony Mann) and continued in subsequent Westerns like *Dances with Wolves* (Kevin Costner, 1990).[7] And yet, in the case of *Soldier Blue,* many of those stereotypes are revealed upon closer consideration to be remarkably persistent, even in the face of apparent condemnation. As much as Honus Gant does gain a new perspective and new humanity from Cresta, the Cheyenne are in the end little more than victims. Could the same be true of a similarly themed Western farther up the revisionist pyramid that enjoys a more privileged position in the prevailing, auteur-centered accounts of 1960s and 1970s American cinema? Or is it indeed the nature, or quality, of the revisionism of upper-tier pictures that distinguishes them from those below?

Little Big Man, based on the popular novel by Thomas Berger about an orphaned white boy raised by the Cheyenne who spends his life drifting back and forth between Indian and white civilizations, is a better movie than *Soldier Blue* in nearly every respect. Nevertheless, the two Westerns do have a number of features in common, including a romantic (and ultimately tragic) depiction of American Indians at the mercy of an encroaching, racist, white civilization.

Little Big Man's picaresque narrative has its hero, Jack Crabb (Dustin Hoffman), traverse back and forth across the American frontier, and while doing so he assumes a range of conventional Western personas, including pioneer, gunfighter, general store owner, town drunk (twice), hermit trapper, and Army scout. Each of Crabb's "periods" in white civilization proves short-lived, however, and he repeatedly returns, as if by fate, to his life as "Little Big Man" with the "human beings," as the Cheyenne refer to themselves. The movie spends a great deal of time with its Indian characters, developing them beyond the simplistic archetypes that *Soldier Blue* falls back on. Their depiction is not without problems, however. Good intentions aside, the movie risks replacing old stereotypes with new, politically correct ones. Buscombe observes that the Cheyenne "function as surrogate hippies, tolerant of homosexuality, kind to children, engaging in free love and conversations about the meaning of life."[8] Despite the emphasis on portraying the subtleties of the Cheyenne way of life, the end result is little different from what we observed in *Soldier Blue.* As Douglas Pye comments: "In creating the Cheyenne as he does, Penn effectively excludes any kind of specific social or political reference: the hippy dream, whatever its own social determinants, asserted itself as ahistorical and natural; in the film, it represents a retreat into sentimental fantasy, not, one feels, animated by conviction but essentially set up to be destroyed."[9]

Buscombe writes that the explicit violence of *Ulzana's Raid* "appears to be a deliberate refusal to 'sentimentalize' Indian behavior in the manner of such pro-Indian films of the early 1970s as *Little Big Man.*"[10] This is undoubtedly true. Although *Ulzana's Raid* follows the basic plot outlined by French, where the central character's outlook is dramatically altered by his interactions with Indians, the vision of Indian life is far from idyllic. In eschewing both sentimentality towards the plight of the Indian and a one-sided indictment of the actions of the U.S. Army, the movie paints a comparatively complex portrait of the central conflict between Indians and whites. Buscombe comments, "The film does not preach a policy of separate but equal, but it acknowledges that there is an irreducible difference, and it is careful to show at the same time that whites are also capable of vindictive violence when some soldiers mutilate the body of a dead

Apache, an act which, as the veteran scout MacIntosh, who has an Indian wife, wryly remarks, 'kind of confuses the issue, don't it?'"[11] Although it is surely the film's Vietnam War allegory, and not its representation of Indians, that qualifies *Ulzana's Raid* as a revisionist Western in the eyes of critics, those two aspects are in fact inseparable. The war between the Apache and U.S. Army is not fought out of conviction on either side. It is not, as in *Soldier Blue* or *Little Big Man,* a symptom of white racism. The clash is the inevitable result of diametrically opposed cultures trying to occupy the same space. *Ulzana's Raid,* then, is less a condemnation of the evils of imperialism than a commentary on the tragic futility of conflict. Unlike *Soldier Blue* and *Little Big Man,* the movie offers an explanation for violence—even if that explanation is unsavory.

In spite of its merits, the comparatively subtle commentary of *Ulzana's Raid* on the Vietnam War and the film's attendant, nuanced portrayal of the Apache are likely to come across as idiosyncratic in light of other popular depictions of Indians, both contemporary and more recent. On how cinematic representations of Indians changed from the 1970s onward, Paul Simpson writes: "In some ways, the Western had simply widened its repertoire of Native American clichés. In the bad old days, we had the crazed warrior lusting after white womanhood, the drunken dupe, noble savage, helpful scout and tortured half-breed. Now we have the Native American as pacifist environmental pioneer, New Age sage and Dalai Lama-like dispenser of spiritual truths."[12] This is a reasonable assessment, especially if we consider how Indians are portrayed in more recent popular movies like *Dances with Wolves,* Disney's *Pocahontas* (Mike Gabriel and Eric Goldbergh, 1995), *Dead Man* (Jim Jarmusch, 1995), or *The New World* (Terrence Malick, 2005), which opens with a scene in which Pocahontas offers a prayer to Mother Earth. As much as the new stereotypes are problematic, they may have been important to the survival of the Western. As Clint Eastwood remarked in a 1992 interview: "I thought *Dances with Wolves* was an admirable project, and the visuals were quite stunning. But it was kind of a contemporary guy out West who was interested in ecology and women's rights and Indian rights. If you did it like it was, people probably could've given a crap less about that in those days, but maybe that's what is needed to get a newer generation of moviegoers interested."[13] Given that a more sympathetic portrayal of Indians is held to be a key characteristic of the changes that took place in the revisionist Western, we may assume that pro-Indian revisionist Westerns like *Little Big Man* are responsible for popularizing the clichés described by Simpson, which remain in circulation today. This lineage is, however, just as much in need of reexamination as the representations of Indians in canonical revisionist Westerns.

Contrasting Pedigrees

For starters, stereotypes from the "bad old days" persist into the 1970s, most often in Western comedies. In *The Great Scout and Cathouse Thursday* (Don Taylor, 1976), drunken Indian Joe Knox (Oliver Reed) is on a "mission" to exterminate the white race by abducting "batches" of prostitutes and using his "badly battered sword of justice" to infect them with the clap. Advertising for the film featured an image of Knox proclaiming the picture "heap funny." In *Dirty Dingus Magee,* Dingus (Frank Sinatra) reluctantly trades his rifle for the daughter of Chief Crazy Blanket (Paul Fix). Says the Chief, "Me keep rifle! You take daughter! Go honeymoon. Crazy Blanket has spoken!" The Chief's scantily clad daughter, Anna Hot Water (Michele Carey), is a nymphomaniac who constantly wants to "make bim bam" with her new husband.

These kinds of crude caricatures are admittedly rare. In contrast, the majority of later Westerns that feature Indians portray them as serious and often noble characters. Yet, in their depictions of American Indians, these Westerns do share one conspicuous feature in common with the coarse comedies mentioned above: a lack of actual American Indians.

Soldier Blue, A Man Called Horse, and *Tell Them Willie Boy Is Here* all feature either white or Hispanic actors in the main Indian roles. The same is true of nearly every other Western released between 1969 and 1980. Moreover, it is not the case that such roles are always supporting parts for character actors. Leading Indian roles in a range of Westerns are played by actors who received top billing, ranging from Burt Reynolds in *100 Rifles* (Tom Gries, 1969) to Charles Bronson in *Chato's Land* (Michael Winner, 1972) to Desi Arnaz in *Billy Two Hats* (Ted Kotcheff, 1974). *Buck and the Preacher* (Sidney Poitier, 1972) features two of the leading African-American artists of the twentieth century in Sidney Poitier and Harry Belafonte, who were both active in the civil rights movement. The movie allies blacks with Indians, and equates the condition of the former under slavery with the plight of the latter under government treaties. Nevertheless, Indian actors do not play the lead Indian roles.

"Redface," then, was still a dominant, accepted practice in the 1970s.[14] How do we square this with notions about how the cultural upheavals and traumatic change of the 1960s somehow sheared the Western of its ideological baggage? Why did this practice not draw the ire of Western scholars like Cawelti and Kitses who, in spite of their admiration for the genre, were uneasy with some of its ethical implications?

The easy answer is to attribute this "oversight" to liberal hypocrisy. While that is undoubtedly part of it, scholarship on the Western is not unique in failing to grapple with some of the enduring contradictions in the representation of this aspect of American history. On the legacy of conquest in American culture, Patricia Nelson Limerick writes:

> The subject of slavery was the domain of serious scholars and the occasion for sober national reflection; the subject of conquest was the domain of lighthearted national escapism. An element of regret for "what we did to the Indians" had entered the picture, but the dominant feature of conquest remained "adventure." Children happily played "cowboys and Indians" but stopped short at "masters and slaves."[15]

The American Indian Movement, which staged a number of controversial, high-profile protests and occupations in the early 1970s, formed in the late 1960s out of frustration with the lack of gains made for Indians under the civil rights movement.[16]

This is not to say that the depiction of Indians in Westerns did not change over the course of the 1960s. It did, and the revisionist narrative does hold to a certain degree. In contrast to earlier decades, Westerns of the 1970s are nearly devoid of aboriginal villains. As in *Ulzana's Raid,* exceptions are qualified. *The Revengers* (Daniel Mann, 1972), for example, restages the traumatic massacre of a family homestead by a band of Comanche from *The Searchers,* but before the hero John Benedict (William Holden) sets out on his quest for vengeance he learns that the Indians were led in their raid by white men. In *Jeremiah Johnson* (Sydney Pollack, 1972), the title character (Robert Redford) sets out to kill any Crow he encounters after they murder his Indian wife and adopted son and burn his house. That massacre was in retaliation, however, for Johnson leading a cavalry patrol through a sacred Crow burial ground. In paying back kind with kind, Johnson enters into a vicious cycle of Indian violence that ultimately earns him the respect of Paints His Shirt Red (Joaquin Martinez), a great Crow warrior, and presumably a reprieve from the ceaseless fighting.

Like these two Westerns, *Ulzana's Raid* also draws upon *The Searchers,* recasting the earlier picture's hunt for a band of renegade Indians by a pair of white protagonists. The film clearly intends this parallel to be drawn. Early in their search for Ulzana, McIntosh explains Apache endurance to DeBuin: "Lieutenant, a horse will run so far, so fast, for so long, and then it will lie down on ya. When a horse lies down on an Apache, he puts a fire under its belly and gets him back on his feet. When the horse dies, he gets off, eats a bit of it, and steals another. Ain't no way you can better that." This exchange mirrors one in *The Searchers* between Ethan Edwards (John Wayne) and Brad Jorgensen (Harry Carey, Jr.) as they pursue the band of murderous Comanche.

> BRAD: They gotta stop sometime. If they're human men at all, they gotta stop.
>
> ETHAN: No, a human rides a horse until it dies, then he goes on afoot. Comanch comes along and gets that horse up, rides him twenty more miles, then eats him.

In *Arrowhead* (Charles Marquis Warren, 1953), a lesser-known Western released three years before *The Searchers,* scout Ed Bannon (Charlton Heston) offers a similar take on Indians: "Apaches don't like horses, Sergeant. They ride 'em until they drop, kill 'em and eat 'em and then steal some more."

The invocation in *Ulzana's Raid* of these earlier Westerns may rekindle concerns that the movie is, in fact, reverting to stereotypes long since discarded by the genre. *The Searchers,* unlike *Arrowhead,* is a sophisticated and challenging commentary on the issue of race and an excoriation of white racism, but it does not offer a redemptive view of Indians. It is important, therefore, to stress that McIntosh is no Ethan Edwards. His sagacity, and sanity, remain unquestioned throughout the movie; his role is to teach, not to learn. Yet even if his attitude toward the Indians is different than Ethan's—fatalism, rather than racism—his words are the same, implying that it is not the Indians who have changed but only attitudes about them. As it turns out, this "new" attitude is more common than most accounts of the period would have us believe.

The violence of the Apache in *Ulzana's Raid* is, again, certainly a riposte to the sentimental portrayals of Indians in *Little Big Man* and *Soldier Blue,* but McIntosh's attitude toward Indians is not new. As noted above, earlier Westerns sympathetic to the plight of the American Indian have been interpreted as allegories about post-war racial tensions. Richard Slotkin offers a standard reading: "The Western was a safe haven for liberals, because its identification with the heroic fable of American progress covered its practitioners with a presumption of patriotism. . . . Because it was safely 'in the past,' the tale of the White-Indian conflict and peace-making allowed filmmakers to raise questions of war and peace and to entertain the possibility of coexistence without the kind of scrutiny to which a film set in or near the present would have drawn."[17] Similarly, pro-Indian Westerns of the 1970s deal with contemporary social and political concerns like the war in Vietnam and the counterculture movement. If there is a lineage to be drawn from the 1950s to the 1970s (and beyond), though, we may wonder what happened in between these decades.

Hollywood's production of Westerns began to decline in the 1960s, and as a consequence fewer films of that era dealt with Indian subject matter. Many of those Westerns that did, however, arguably began to treat Indians less as proxies for other groups and to contend with them more directly, as distinct peoples with their own histories. The results are decidedly uneven. John Ford's *Cheyenne Autumn,* the most famous Indian Western of the decade, exemplifies both the potentials and perils of this approach.

Based on a historical incident in which a small band of Cheyenne set out to march 1,500 miles from a reservation in the Oklahoma territory to their former hunting ground in Yellowstone, the movie is a sincere attempt to represent the injustices suffered by American Indians at the hands of the United States government. (It is also, perhaps, an apology for Ford's own earlier cinematic treatments of Indians). *Cheyenne Autumn* is a better, more interesting movie than it is remembered to be. Whatever its merits, however, the picture is undeniably weakened by a lengthy running time, awkward plotting, and internal contradictions. The picture was filmed in Monument Valley, Ford's favorite Western location, and though the desert landscapes are undeniably majestic, they are quite unlike the actual terrain the Cheyenne would have traversed going from Oklahoma to present-day Wyoming. Non-Indians also play all of the principal Cheyenne roles. On this casting, Ford biographer Joseph McBride comments, "[G]iven its ostensible project of counteracting Hollywood clichés about Indian life, the film is seriously damaged by its lack of ethnic verisimilitude"—a remark that could just as easily apply to many later Westerns.[18] McBride writes that Ford initially wanted to cast nonprofessional Indian actors in the lead Cheyenne parts, and then, under advice from his producer son Pat that the movie's financiers would not accept unknowns in principle parts, intended to cast Anthony Quinn and Woody Strode, both of Indian descent. Warner Bros. "exercised its leverage," and Ford wound up with Mexican-born Ricardo Montalban and Gilbert Roland, and Italian-American Sal Mineo.[19]

Cheyenne Autumn also resembles later Westerns in another way. The movie includes the signing of a new treaty between the Cheyenne and the U.S. government (represented by enlightened white characters), but this is followed by a concluding act of violence incompatible with the values of American society. The young Red Shirt (Mineo), an impetuous Cheyenne brave whose actions have repeatedly endangered the band, faces off with Chief Little Wolf (Montalban), whose wife Red Shirt has stolen. Red Shirt is killed, and Little Wolf, having broken his vow never to kill another Cheyenne, goes into self-imposed exile. "The execution," writes Tak Fujiwara, "nails down that we don't yet understand the Cheyenne culture, that we don't have access to their 'insides,' that we should keep our respectful distance, and not judge them from our own values."[20]

What emerges in *Cheyenne Autumn* is a conception of Indian culture not unlike that in *Ulzana's Raid*: an irreducibly different, violent way of life that non-Indians cannot comprehend. This idea begins to take hold in the Western genre in the 1960s, including in other media. A description of the Cheyenne from Leigh Brackett's 1963 Western novel *Follow the Free Wind* conveys the same sentiment expressed nearly a decade later in *Ulzana's Raid*: "War in the white man's world was generally about something. Somebody won, somebody lost, something was decided and the war was over. Here war was its own cause and the idea of victory was unthinkable as a white man understood it. War was made because without it man would have nothing to do. . . . As well hate wind or lightening as the Cheyenne."[21] It is this more dispassionate understanding of Indians that prevails in Westerns of the 1970s: not free-spirited flower children or victimized Vietnamese peasants, but aliens, noble and moral in their own way but fundamentally different.

Consider the other pro-Indian Western released in 1970, *A Man Called Horse.* The picture concerns an English aristocrat, Lord John Morgan (Richard Harris), who is captured by Sioux in the Dakota Territory in the 1820s. After proving himself in battle, Morgan, dubbed "Horse," is accepted as a member of the tribe and eventually rises to become its leader.

Like *Soldier Blue,* the movie uses an opening title crawl to establish and foreground its relation to historical truth: thanking the American Museum of Natural History, the Library of Congress, and Smithsonian Institute, asserting that the dramatized rituals to follow are based on eyewitness documentation, and finally informing the audience that one of those rituals, the Vow to the Sun, was eventually forbidden by the U.S. government. Unlike *Soldier Blue,* however, *A Man Called Horse* is not a political allegory about Vietnam. The aim is instead to offer a historically authentic portrait of Indian customs and culture in the early 1800s. A Sioux historian, Clyde Dollar, was signed to serve as the film's technical advisor. Although the picture was filmed in Mexico, members of the Rosebud Sioux tribe from South Dakota were used as extras, and the Lakota language is used throughout the movie, without subtitles.[22] Nevertheless, Buffalo Cow Head, Morgan's adoptive Sioux mother, is played by white actress Dame Judith Anderson. It is also less Morgan's assumed Indian ways than his European savvy that is responsible for his—and by extension his tribe's—success against the rival Shoshone.

Although *A Man Called Horse* was a modest success, commentators pointed to numerous inaccuracies in the movie's purportedly authentic portrayal of the Sioux. Leaders of the American Indian Movement called the film racist, with historian Dollar singled out for particular castigation.[23] While the film's portrayal of the Sioux is not without fault, some of this criticism is unfair. As much as ideas about authorial expression are common in thinking about cinema, filmmaking is a collaborative enterprise, a compromise between competing interests. Dollar, who during production was presciently concerned that the movie's reputation would affect his own, repeatedly clashed with director Elliot Silverstein over the film's growing number of anachronisms and errors. Silverstein pressed ahead with many of his creative decisions, but in turn locked horns with the film's producers over what he felt was unwillingness on their part to show Indians as anything other than savages.[24] Singer and activist Buffy Sainte-Marie described *A Man Called Horse* as "the whitest of movies I've ever seen," but she evidently had no issue with the Mexican-led, stereotyped Cheyenne of *Soldier Blue*, for which she wrote and sang the title song.[25]

What distinguishes *A Man Called Horse* from every other contemporary Western about Indians—and, indeed, most other Westerns about Indians released before or since—is how the protagonist spends the duration of the movie immersed in Indian society. Because the Sioux of the 1820s are not yet in conflict with official American interests, Morgan does not have the conventional role of speaking on their behalf to white institutions or fighting on their behalf against white villains. He is initially held captive by the Sioux as a curiosity akin to a strange animal, but proves he is a man by killing two scouts from a Shoshone war party. Then, in order to become a full member of the tribe and marry the beautiful Running Deer (Corinna Tsopei), he must undergo a grueling rite of passage: the Vow to the Sun, the outlawed practice mentioned in the movie's opening titles. At the climax of the ceremony, Morgan is suspended from the ceiling by bone hooks imbedded in his pectorals and spun around until he passes out from the pain. This physical trial correlates to a spiritual awakening, as Morgan falls into a hallucinatory state in which he symbolically sheds his old self.

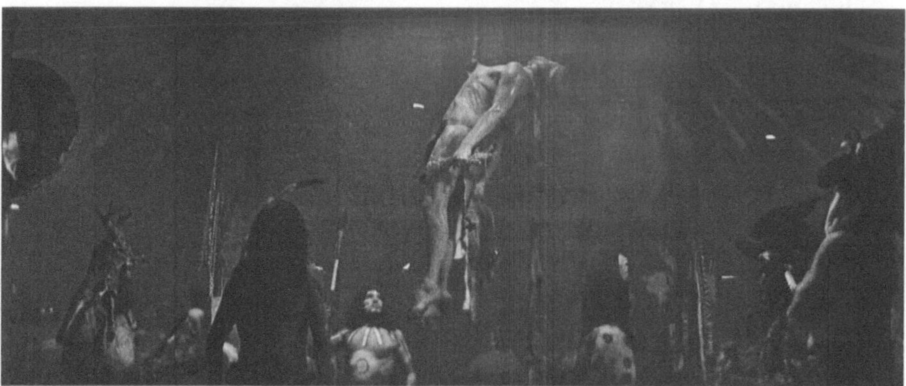

The Vow to the Sun ritual in *A Man Called Horse* (1970)

Deficiencies in historical accuracy aside, *A Man Called Horse* offers the most detailed and comprehensive portrait of an Indian culture counter to that of European America. But what is most significant about this portrayal, in terms of the Western's evolving cinematic depiction of Indians, is how membership in the Indian society is *predicated upon violence.*

Morgan's integration into Indian society proves tenuous. He remains with the Sioux after his pregnant wife is killed in a battle with the Shoshone, and is named chief when he agrees to become Buffalo Cow Head's son (to prevent her from being cast out of the tribe). When she dies, Morgan does finally leave the Sioux. Thus, like many Western heroes before him, Morgan leaves the Indians when his family ties with them are severed.[26] As in *Cheyenne Autumn* and *Ulzana's Raid,* then, the Indian way of life is ultimately irreconcilable with white society.

Cheyenne Autumn and *Ulzana's Raid* also point to another trend in the later Western. The prevailing strategy when dealing with the subject of Indians is to incorporate the antithetical conception of violent Indian culture into a "chase" narrative indebted to *The Searchers,* restaging that film's central pursuit of Indians by whites. In addition to *The Revengers* and *Jeremiah Johnson,* this plot is used in *Tell Them Willie Boy Is Here, Cry Blood Apache* (Jack Starrett, 1970), *Chato's Land, Alien Thunder* (Claude Fournier, 1974), and *Greyeagle* (Charles B. Pierce, 1977). It is also parodied, briefly, in both *Buffalo Bill and the Indians, or Sitting Bull's History Lesson,* when Buffalo Bill searches in vain for Sitting Bull after he and some of his braves "escape" from the Wild West Show, and *Little Big Man,* when Crabb searches (also in vain) for his wife Olga after she is kidnapped by Cheyenne.

What we see emerging is an alternative genealogy to that proposed in the dominant accounts of the revisionist Western. Instead of the genre moving lockstep with progressive American culture towards tolerance and inclusivity, we find antiquated elements from the "imperial mainstream" to which pro-Indian and other counter-traditional Westerns began to offer an alternative in the 1950s. *The Searchers* is the type of Western that is supposed to go away, but it clearly does not. Many other later Westerns that do not feature Indians also employ a chase narrative where, as in *The Searchers,* a character seeks vengeance after a violent assault on his or her family. Examples include *True Grit, Hannie Caulder,*

Big Jake, *The Hunting Party* (Don Medford, 1971), *Santee* (Gary Nelson, 1973), *The Deadly Trackers* (Barry Shear, 1973), *The Last Hard Men* (Andrew V. McLaglen, 1976), and *Kid Vengeance* (Joseph Manduke, 1977).

Anyone distressed by these observations can still take heart in the fact that the portrayal of violent Indians from *A Man Called Horse* and *Ulzana's Raid* does not persist beyond the 1970s. As Simpson notes above, contemporary Indian stereotypes emphasize qualities like spirituality and environmentalism. This seems much more like the "surrogate hippies" of *Little Big Man*—a Western that also stars an Indian actor in the lead Cheyenne role.

If the portrayal of Indians in *Little Big Man* is, as it appears, in fact a minority position, then the continued presence of the stereotypes identified by Simpson may be evidence of the enduring influence of the movie's representation of Indians. *Little Big Man* was hailed shortly after its release as "a milestone in the history of the Western, beyond any doubt the most advanced document in the process of re-evaluating its sacred myths, a work of art in the cause of peace and understanding."[27] In an article that accompanied a 2010 showing of the movie on Turner Classic Movies as part of a series on "Native American Images on Film," Kimberly Lindbergs writes that it "changed the way that audiences viewed Native Americans and . . . helped to broaden our understanding and interpretation of American history."[28] Is this true? Did *Little Big Man* really alter popular perceptions of Indians at the time?

As detailed above, the representation of Indians in *Little Big Man* does suffer from flaws similar to those of *Soldier Blue*. Furthermore, as a result of Crabb's wandering ways the movie's portrayal of Cheyenne society never achieves the same level of detail as the Sioux in *A Man Called Horse*. But even if the Cheyenne of *Little Big Man* are, as Pye charges, ultimately little more than an ahistorical sentimental fantasy, the film's treatment of them is nonetheless sympathetic and nuanced. The picture also features the most fully developed and interesting Indian character of the period: Crabb's adoptive Cheyenne grandfather, Old Lodge Skins. The role was allegedly turned down by a number of other actors, including Marlon Brando, before it was improbably offered to Dan George, a 70-year former chief of the Tsleil-Waututh Nation of North Vancouver, who had been acting for less than a decade, and only on television. George's performance was widely acclaimed, earning him an Academy

Award nomination, and he worked steadily in film and television for the remainder of the decade, always playing virtuous Indian characters.

It is the guru-like Old Lodge Skins who articulates Cheyenne values and beliefs throughout *Little Big Man.* When Crabb asks his grandfather whether he hates the white man after soldiers have attacked the Cheyenne, Old Lodge Skins gestures to a white scalp and says:

> Do you see this fine thing? Do you admire the humanity of it? Because the human beings, my son, they believe everything is alive. Not only man and animals, but also water, earth, stone. And also the things from them . . . like that hair. The man from whom this hair came, he's bald on the other side, because I now own his scalp! That is the way things are. But the white man, they believe *everything* is dead. Stone, earth, animals. And people! Even their own people! If things keep trying to live, white man will rub them out. That is the difference.

Little Big Man also distinguishes itself from other Indian Westerns in another, crucial way: popularity. In contrast to *Soldier Blue, Ulzana's Raid,* and nearly all other 1960s and 1970s Westerns mentioned in this chapter, *Little Big Man* was a significant box office success. It earned $15 million in rentals domestically, making it the seventh-highest-earning picture of 1970.

Given this success, and given that the film's representation of Indians is epitomized in a popular performance by an Indian actor, it is likely that *Little Big Man* did have some impact on popular perceptions of American Indians at the time. How to measure that wider impact is another matter. What *is* clear is that the movie's influence on subsequent Westerns was negligible. In spite of its success and acclaim, *Little Big Man,* as evidenced in the quotation above from Old Lodge Skins, did not move the genre away from the conception that emerged in the Western in the 1960s of Indians and whites as irreducibly different. Furthermore, it is not the movie's countercultural representation of Indians, but rather its manifestation of contemporary cultural anxieties, that it is remembered for. Consider the following comment from David A. Cook: "[T]here has probably never been another time in the history of American cinema when a 150-minute film that bitterly indicts American imperialism and depicts the U.S. military waging genocidal war could become a popular hit."[29]

Like *Soldier Blue, Little Big Man* features a violent sequence in which a village of Cheyenne is decimated by the United States cavalry. Here, the historical reference is the Battle of Washita, in which, on the morning of November 27, 1869, George Armstrong Custer, then a colonel, led his 7th Calvary Regiment against a large encampment of Cheyenne along the Washita River in Oklahoma. Unlike the Sand Creek Massacre, there is wide disagreement about the nature of the battle, including the number of the causalities and how many were women and children.[30]

Regardless of this historical uncertainly, in *Little Big Man* the clash is presented as an outright slaughter of women, children, and ponies led by the megalomaniacal Indian-hating Custer (George Mulligan). As Penn told interviewers in 1971, "Custer was engaged in the battle of the Washita River in Oklahoma where he gave the order to massacre the inhabitants of the village, just as we've been doing in Vietnam."[31] Mentions of *Little Big Man* nearly always make reference to its Vietnam War allegory. As Lindbergs remarks, "Today . . . when the movie is written about or mentioned it can't seem to escape the shadow of the Vietnam war."[32] What is more, the movie is often coupled, conceptually, with *Soldier Blue.*

> Once "revisionist" films like Little Big Man and Soldier Blue began to appear in 1970, mainly as a sop to mounting protest of the Vietnam War, previously glorified martial figures like Custer began to lose their allure.[33]

> Such acerbic condemnations of white America as Ralph Nelson's *Soldier Blue* (1970) and Arthur Penn's *Little Big Man* (1970) debunk hitherto dominant mythologies of regenerative violence, substituting them with radical notions of genocidal impulses amongst the ruling elite.[34]

These associations are unfortunate in several respects. They tie *Little Big Man* not only to an inferior film, but also to a specific, historical event with limited significance in the broader scope of American history—in contrast to, say, "the winning of the West." Penn appears to recognize this in later interviews, where he often claims that *Little Big Man* is less about the Vietnam War specifically than about the history of genocide. When asked in 2004 how much Vietnam was on his mind while making *Little Big Man,* the director responded:

> Well, it was not so much Vietnam, although, when it comes to wars of genocide, or genocidal attempts, they tend to resemble each other. I was really, in my mind, carrying the Holocaust. You know? Because it was such indiscriminate killing, based on some kind of societal definition of humans who can be dispensed with. And that impulse, it's happening today. It's happening everywhere. It happened in the Second World War, it happened in Vietnam, it's happening in Iraq, in war after war. They're mostly ethnic or religious genocidal wars.[35]

Little Big Man's depiction of the Battle of Washita patently invokes imagery from Vietnam: burning tepees, woman and children fleeing soldiers, the ground strewn with bodies. The indictment of American imperialism is clear, although most of the burden falls on the unstable Custer, who is equally consumed by delusions of grandeur, lust for power, and hatred of Indians. Unlike *Soldier Blue,* the massacre of Indians is not the climax of the film; the narrative instead builds towards Custer's fabled last stand at the Battle of Little Big Horn, where the Indians get their revenge on the General and his soldiers. The movie also importantly lacks the promotional campaign and title crawl calling attention to its allegory that were used in *Soldier Blue,* although it does share in common a director—in this case, a highly regarded one—willing to pontificate to receptive reporters.

The two massacres also differ in other significant ways. The main protagonist of *Soldier Blue* is Private Gant, and it is from his perspective that we experience the majority of the movie's events, including the climactic massacre. Aside from his romance with Cresta, he has no association with the Cheyenne (to whom, again, the film devotes very little screen time). During the final slaughter, the film intends to portray Gant as traumatized and powerless in the face of the chaos that surrounds him, but because he has no more than a superficial connection to the Cheyenne his personal investment is actually quite minimal. Cresta's survival is all but guaranteed because she is white. Gant's experience of the final slaughter—and

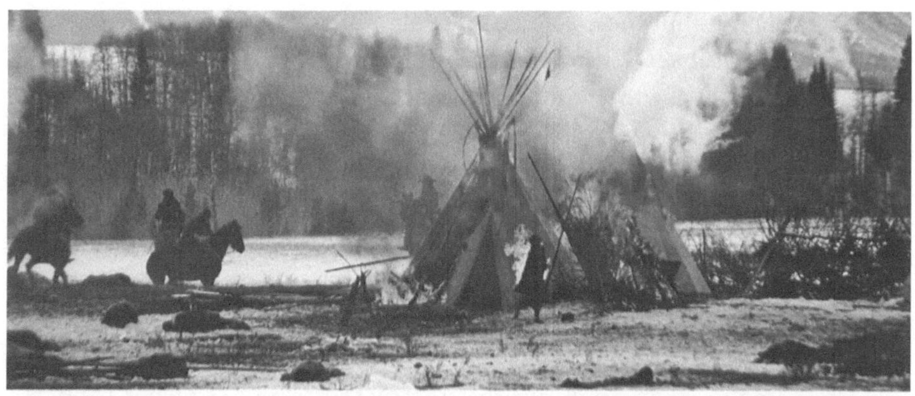

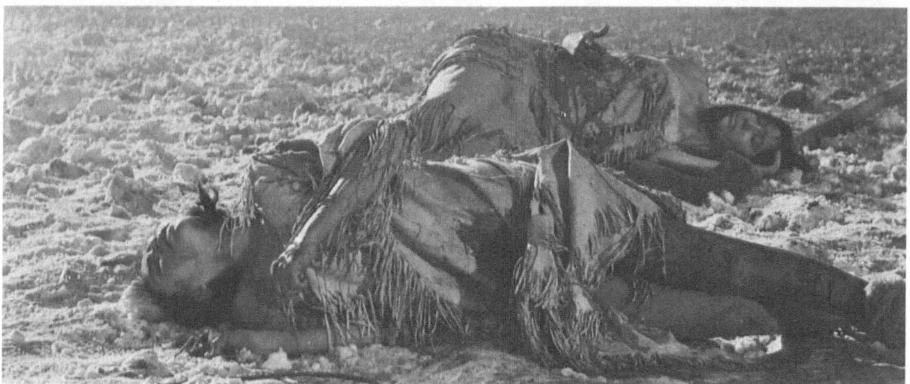

The Battle of Washita in *Little Big Man* (1970)

thus the audience's—is one of confusion and revulsion, certainly, but it is also emotionally detached. Jack Crabb, by contrast, has much *personally* at stake in the massacre at Washita. His Cheyenne grandfather, wife, and newborn son are all in the encampment. Because the film has developed its Cheyenne characters beyond clichés—particularly through Crabb's relationships with his wife Sunshine (Amy Eccles) and grandfather Old Lodge Skins—our investment in the scene mirrors Crabb's. Crabb first ushers Old Lodge Skins to safety after convincing him that he is invisible to the soldiers. Running back to the village, Crabb is unable to rescue his wife and child, and is forced to watch from a distance as they are shot dead. Contrasts in the presentation of these two events serve to heighten the tragedy of the latter. The rescue of Old Lodge Skins is comedic, with the old man grinning throughout and Crabb remarking in voice over, "I can't explain it, but those soldiers didn't lay a hand on us . . . maybe we really was invisible!" When he returns, the music of the cavalry's flute and drum fades, along with most other diegetic noises. The scene cuts rapidly back and forth between Crabb on the outskirts of the fracas, yelling for his wife, and Sunshine running out of her burning tepee and towards her husband, child strapped on her back. The scale of the alternating shots increases, a formal proximity that belies the actual physical distance between the couple. Loud gunshots ring out, and Sunshine falls. Crabb screams in agony. The cavalry music fades back in, and the sequence is over.

It is important to point out that the success of this sequence is not the result of any formal or technical innovation. It is violent, but not so graphic as to warrant an R rating from the Motion Picture Association of America. The movie instead relies on a competent use of classical Hollywood storytelling techniques to imbue the sequence with emotional resonance. Moreover, any political commentary present is arguably more potent because the audience is invested in the proceedings—although we should bear in mind that simply because a filmmaker says his work is symbolic does not mean it will be received that way. One could easily argue that *Little Big Man* was well received in spite of its Vietnam allegory.

The contrast between comedy and tragedy in the Washita massacre is representative of *Little Big Man* as a whole. The movie repeatedly punctuates lengthy comic episodes with moments of loss or sorrow. On balance, though, the movie *is* a comedy—a fact obscured by critical discourse focused on symptomatic interpretation. As Crabb goes through his various "periods," *Little Big Man* parodies nearly every kind of Western picture, including, if only by virtue of its running time, the epic. The film was also promoted as a comedy, with advertising that proclaimed "Little Big Man was either the most neglected hero in history or a liar of insane proportion!"

Although *Little Big Man* may be atypical relative to other contemporary Westerns in its representation of Indians, it is in keeping with another trend in the genre. Many of the most popular Westerns of the 1960s and 1970s were comedies intended for wide audiences, including *Cat Ballou, Paint Your Wagon* (Joshua Logan, 1969), *Support Your Local Sheriff!* (Burt Kennedy, 1969), and *Blazing Saddles.* Humor was also a large part of the appeal of other popular Westerns, including *Butch Cassidy and the Sundance Kid, True Grit,* and *The Life and Times of Judge Roy Bean.*[36]

While the notion of contrasting Western pedigrees—*Broken Arrow–Little Big Man–Dances with Wolves* on the one hand, *The Searchers–Cheyenne Autumn–Ulzana's Raid* on the other—may be conceptually useful in pointing to shortcomings in existing accounts of the Western, we see that the reality is much more complex. This has always been the case. As with other films included in the Western counter-tradition proposed by Kitses, many earlier pro-Indian Westerns were just as "mainstream" as *The Searchers*—if not more so, in certain respects. As Buscombe observes, a character like Ethan Edwards is a rare exception to the rule that "familiarity with Indian ways brings not contempt but sympathy and even admiration."[37]

It is difficult to say to what degree contemporary audiences "read into" the symbolism of 1950s pro-Indian Westerns. It is doubtful, however, that they did so with the same enthusiasm as later critics and scholars. Given that Hollywood filmmakers, like artists in every other storytelling medium, have always displaced contemporary events and concerns onto past (or future) events, it is entirely possible that the declining number of Westerns that dealt with Indians was due, in part, to the initial gains made for African Americans by the civil rights movement, or to the end of Hollywood's "red scare." If this were the case, however, it would still reflect the unwillingness identified by Limerick to engage directly, and seriously, with the history of American Indians.

Cawelti sees Hollywood's renewed interest in Indians as a reflection of wider societal tendencies. On the 1970s cycle of pro-Indian Westerns, he writes: "This new Indian western is clearly a response to that complex new fascination with traditional Indian culture, particularly among the young, that Leslie Fiedler analyzes."[38] Beginning with Fiedler's 1968 study, *The Return of the Vanishing American,* cultural critics observed a renewed interest in Indian culture, especially among young Americans. Slotkin writes that, from the mid-1960s, "Native Americans and their culture had become important symbols of rebellion in the so-called 'counter culture' of college-age White Americans. The connection had been recognized (and propagated) by the mass media since the Woodstock festival in the summer of 1969."[39]

From a financial standpoint, it makes sense for Hollywood studios to craft movies that will appeal to the younger viewers who, then as now, make up the bulk of the audience for their products. As such, it is entirely possible that the appearance of *Little Big Man* and other so-called revisionist Westerns was to some degree a calculated response to the revived enthusiasm for Indian culture detected by critics and reported in the media. Of course, we have also seen how the appearance of the same (small number of) films is explained as a response to another element of the counterculture movement: opposition to the war in Vietnam. Moreover, as much as the general idea of Indian society as antithetical to hegemonic American society may be in sympathy with aspects of the counterculture movement, more specific features of the contemporary cinematic depiction of Indians, like culturally innate violence and resignation to a doomed existence, are certainly not.

The Crying Indian

Through all of this investigation, one question remains unanswered. If the legacy of *Little Big Man* is, rightly or wrongly, its Vietnam allegory, and Indians in the 1970s Western continued to be portrayed as culturally irreconcilable with whites, where do the more modern Indian stereotypes come from—in particular, the association of Indians with environmentalism? As it turns out, these stereotypes do come to prominence around the same time as the Westerns under examination, but owe their propagation to other cultural factors.

While the theme of concern for the stewardship of the land does surface occasionally in Westerns, often in relation to the decline of "traditional" Indian ways of life, environmental issues are almost entirely absent from Westerns of the 1960s and 1970s. Rather than deriving from any contemporary cinematic representations, new Indian stereotypes can be attributed to the renewed interest in Indian culture being co-opted by the ecological movement, which in turn used *traditional* Hollywood imagery to promote its agenda. The genesis of this new Indian cliché is a landmark television public service announcement produced by the Ad Council for the Keep American Beautiful foundation, which first aired on Earth Day in March of 1971.

The commercial begins with an Indian in a canoe on a scenic woodland river. He is dressed in "traditional" beaded buckskins, with his long hair in braids. As he paddles, the landscape quickly changes. Flotsam appears in the water; factories with bellowing smokestacks line the riverbank. The Indian brings his canoe ashore on a rubbish-stream beach, heads inland and emerges on the side of a busy freeway. "Some people have a deep, abiding respect for the natural beauty that was this country," intones the announcer. "And some people don't." A motorist carelessly tosses a bag of trash from his vehicle, which explodes at the Indian's moccasins. The commercial cuts to a shot of the Indian's face, and quickly zooms in on a solitary tear streaming down his cheek. "People start pollution. People can stop it."

The public service announcement won two Clios, awards given annually to honor the best in advertising and design, and was followed by a print campaign featuring the Indian's crying visage that entreated Americans to "Get Involved Now. Pollution Hurts All of Us." Three years later, the "Crying Indian" returned in a follow-up commercial, riding horseback through a recuperated botanical garden in California. "The first American people loved the land," states the announcer. "They held it in simple reverence." Once again, the Indian in the end arrives teary-eyed at a littered roadside.

The Ad Council credits this advertising campaign with embedding the cause of pollution prevention in American culture, leading to "hundreds of other environmental messages through the years."[40] The campaign also ranked number 50 in a list of the top 100 advertising campaigns of the twentieth century compiled by Ad Age Magazine.[41] Without discrediting the campaign's intentions or outcomes, though, its lasting influence is less a reduction in pollution—especially if we go by the need for hundreds of subsequent anti-pollution advertisements—than the association of American Indians in popular culture with environmental causes.

As stereotypes go, hugger of trees may be preferable to scalper of whites, but it is similarly removed from the realities of American Indian life. Historically, Indians were not the environmental custodians they are often made out to be. In more modern times, Indian tribes have fought for the right to self-determination, not to protect Mother Earth.

Complicating matters further is the particular Indian featured in the advertisement. The Crying Indian is played by Iron Eyes Cody, an actor familiar to Western fans from his numerous appearances in movies from the 1920s onward, including *A Man Called Horse.* Up to his death in 1999, Cody claimed to have been born of a Cree mother and Cherokee father. It was revealed in 1996, however, that his Indian heritage was a fabrication. As one commentator succinctly puts it, Cody's "asserted ancestry was just as artificial as the tear running down his cheek in that television spot—the tear was glycerin, and the 'Indian' was a second-generation Italian-American."[42]

That Cody was a fake Indian did not prevent Keep America Beautiful from reviving the Indian campaign in 1998, where the image of Cody's crying face was brought "back by popular neglect." The image continues to be used today by Keep America Beautiful, which also gives out an annual award in Cody's honor to "outstanding male volunteers for exceptional leadership in raising public awareness about litter prevention, roadside and community beautification, solid waste issues, and the need for citizens to participate in activities that preserve and enhance natural resources and public lands." Buscombe notes that even official bodies like the American Indian Registry for the Performing Arts defend Cody's status as essentially Indian on the grounds that the actor lived as one and advocated Indian causes. He observes, "It's a testament to the overwhelming power of our preoccupations about Indians, our need to believe in the myths we have created, that someone who was not Indian at all can be seen as even more Indian than the real thing."[43]

Although the association of Indians with environmental causes that emerges in the 1970s is far removed from prevailing contemporary cinematic portrayals, the new stereotype still draws upon cinema's traditional Indian archetypes. In doing so, it falls prey to the most problematic, paradoxical tendency in popular representations of American Indians: an absence of American Indians.

It must be said that the fatalistic attitude that prevails in the Western in the 1960s and 1970s has its own shortcomings. In as much as later Westerns work to challenge the genre's conventional representations of Indians, they are, as we have seen, still shaped by those representations, as well as by changing norms of cinematic verisimilitude—in particular, increasing violence. The Vow to the Sun ceremony in *A Man Called Horse,* for example, was promoted in much the same way as the climactic massacre of *Soldier Blue.* In addition to an opening title crawl that heralds the event, promotional materials for the movie were designed to highlight the ceremony, calling it "the most electrifying ritual ever seen!" What these new representations risk, then, is an exoticization of the "other" predicated on the graphic depiction of violent Indian customs and practices.

In other respects, however, these representations are a step forward, because they acknowledge some of the unfortunate realities of the American Indian experience: the Indians lost, and there is no possibility of Indian–white integration in the manner of black–white integration. This attitude is not limited to the Western. Films from other genres, like *The Savage Innocents* (Nicholas Ray, 1960) and *Island of the Blue Dolphins* (James B. Clark, 1964), also convey the message that there is no future for traditional indigenous cultures. Even *Little Big Man,* which concludes with a Cheyenne victory, acknowledges this. As Old Lodge Skins tells his adopted grandson, "There is an endless supply of white men. There has always been a limited number of human beings."

4

Legends in Changing Times

Cowboys, Lawmen, Outlaws, and Fools

> My intention was just to take a more honest look—satirical or not—at some of our myths, to see what they are. . . . We like to think of Cody as a brave man, a great buffalo hunter, an Indian scout. Well, he shot a lot of buffaloes. But lots of guys who lived in the West at that time got jobs as scouts; that's like saying you worked on the railroad.
>
> —Robert Altman, 1976

What does it mean when heroes become villains? If the hero is of the historical variety and not a fictional character who can change his stripes at a writer's whim, there are a limited number of possible explanations. It could be that the hero was not as heroic as was once thought; that new research has uncovered historical details, unsavory truths, or outright falsehoods, perhaps propagated to some end or other by earlier generations of historians and storytellers. Or it could be that the hero is a victim of changing times—that the values and abilities that once made one a hero are now looked upon less favorably, or even derisively.

A combination of these factors is said to be responsible for one of the central features of the revisionist Western: a depreciation of the courage and valor displayed by the heroes of earlier Westerns, many of whom were based (to varying degrees) on famous frontier personalities. This implies, however, that earlier representations of heroism were relatively stable, and not subject to the same inspection. Many 1970s Westerns are undeniably critical of—if not cynical about—the genre's heroes. Yet they are not the first films to offer reappraisals of them.

The Culpepper Cattle Co.

The Culpepper Cattle Co. lacks both the intra- and extra-textual touches of *Soldier Blue.* The picture was promoted principally as a vehicle for actor Gary Grimes, fresh from his breakout success in *Summer of '42* (Robert Mulligan, 1971), rather than a socially conscious exercise in genre revisionism. It also lacks the violence of *Solider Blue* and *Ulzana's Raid.* Yet both the critique of genre convention and the political allegory are there for anyone who wishes to see them.

At the conclusion of the movie, the young protagonist Ben Mockridge (Grimes) leaves a cattle drive in order to defend a sect of religious pacifists from ruthless land baron Thornton Pierce, in whose valley the sect has been "guided" to settle. Four gun-savvy range-hands, upset at the drive's leader, Frank Culpepper, for refusing to stand up to Pierce during an earlier confrontation, ride back to help Ben. In the ensuing shoot-out, Ben watches helplessly as his four friends are gunned down, taking Pierce and all of his men with them. Afterward, the innocent members of the sect prove to be just as self-serving as Culpepper or Pierce. With no one left to protect them, the group's leader proclaims the land "soiled with blood" and elects to move on. "God never meant for us to stay," he says. "He was only testing us." Ben angrily demands the would-be settlers help bury his friends. After they are laid to rest, he discards his own pistol and rides away alone.

The movie deliberately plays off a familiar Western scenario, the "ride to the rescue," even presenting shots of the four riders, rifles in hand, galloping purposefully towards the camera, all set to triumphant music. That these riders meet an untimely demise is not, in and of itself, much of a revision. From each version of Custer's "last stand" or the siege of the Alamo up to *The Wild Bunch* and *Butch Cassidy and the Sundance Kid,* innumerable Western heroes have faced up to incalculable odds and died in a blaze of gunfire. *The Culpepper Cattle Co.* stages this same heroic action, but then subverts it. The pious pacifists, unwilling to fight for their land, are also unable to stomach the measures needed to defend it for them. Ben's friends have died in vain.

Or have they?

The ending of *The Culpepper Cattle Co.* is meant to be a strong rebuke of the myth of heroic action. The leader of the cattle train, trail boss Culpepper, chooses to leave rather than stay and fight. The cowboys who do stay not only die, but their deaths are senseless and without glory because they do not alter the course of history. Read in light of the war in Vietnam, this rebuke certainly has allegorical resonance. At the same time, how the movie engineers its reproach of Western convention—the contrivance of the craven religious group—is in fact highly conventional. Change the setting from a verdant basin to a frontier town, replace the pious pacifists with cowardly citizens, and what do you get? *High Noon,* the 1952 Western about a town that refuses to come to the aid of its embattled marshal when threatened by the return of an old villain and his gang. As we saw in chapter 2, *High Noon* is among the most influential Westerns of all time in terms of establishing a basic scenario that is reworked time and again in later movies. Although *The Culpepper Cattle Co.* is more selective in its citations than most Westerns that draw upon *High Noon,* these references are nevertheless specific.

At the conclusion of *High Noon,* after Marshal Will Kane (Gary Cooper) has bested Frank Miller and his gang, he prepares to ride out of town once and for all with his new bride (Grace Kelly). Townsfolk gather around their buggy. Kane surveys the crowd, steely eyed. Without a word, he removes his badge and casts it to the ground. The camera quickly tilts downward, framing the discarded badge in the dirt at Kane's feet. Kane then climbs into his buggy and he and his wife ride away.

These actions are precisely mirrored at the end of *The Culpepper Cattle Co.,* down to the staging and camera movement when Ben drops his pistol to the ground.

In contrast to *The Culpepper Cattle Co.*'s subversion of the archetypal Western ride to the rescue, this invocation of *High Noon* is not a critique. Like Kane, Ben symbolically renounces the way of the gun in the presence of those he had vowed to protect. There are important differences: unlike Ben, who is paralyzed by chaotic gunplay, Kane shoots it out with the villains and survives to pass judgment on the people who had forsaken him. But that Ben is unable to partake in the violence is a reflection not of cowardice but inexperience. Like most Westerns about cattle drives, *The Culpepper Cattle Co.* revolves around a young tenderfoot who sees in the promise of the open trail an escape from his mundane, domestic way of life. Although the movie departs from its cattle-drive narrative in the third act, incorporating aspects of other traditional Western scenarios, the plot, not unlike in *Soldier Blue* or *Ulzana's Raid,* remains centered on the young hero's emotional journey. The final lesson that Ben learns, about the grim reality of bloodshed, is one that youths in Westerns have been absorbing for decades—from at least *The Gunfighter* up to *Unforgiven.* Thus, while *The Culpepper Cattle Co.*'s concluding censure of the romantic notion that valiant outsiders can ride, guns blazing, into a trouble spot and automatically expect gratitude and loyalty, may seem especially apposite in light of current events, it is anything but original. It actually speaks to the fundamental paradox that marks the Westerner as a tragic figure: his association with violence bars him from integrating into the community he uses that violence to protect. This is why he often chooses to leave town when the dust settles, rather than remain and settle with it. If he does elect to stay and become the town's permanent lawman, we may get the scenario that unfolds in *High Noon*, where the once-beloved lawman learns he has few friends in the community he has risked his life to defend.

Kane is not any less a hero for staying, however. That he refuses to leave even after friends and neighbors have abandoned him is not a sign of weakness but of his devotion to the greater good. In *The Culpepper Cattle Co.,* Ben is treated much the same way. The movie does not question the rightness of his decision to leave the cattle drive. Pierce is unambiguously a villain. The members of the religious group, prior to the shoot-out and their opportunistic change of heart, are presented as virtuous. Although they are unable to bear arms, their leader is defiant when Pierce demands the flock leave his land or face the consequences. What ultimately distinguishes Ben's predicament from Marshal Kane's is a lack of alternatives. Kane rides away with his bride to begin a new life. Ben rides away alone, to an unknown, uncertain future. He has renounced violence, but for what? The life of the single-minded Culpepper, concerned with nothing but getting his cattle to market, is not a laudable alternative. Neither is that of the vicious land baron Pierce or the gutless religious pacifists.

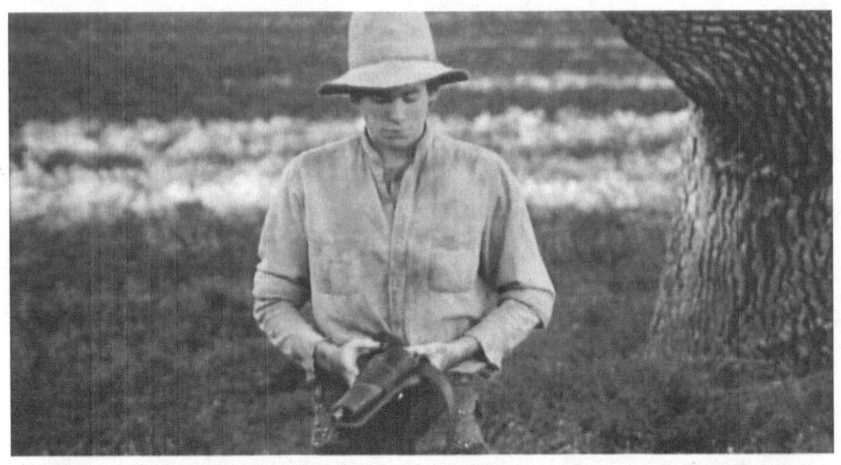

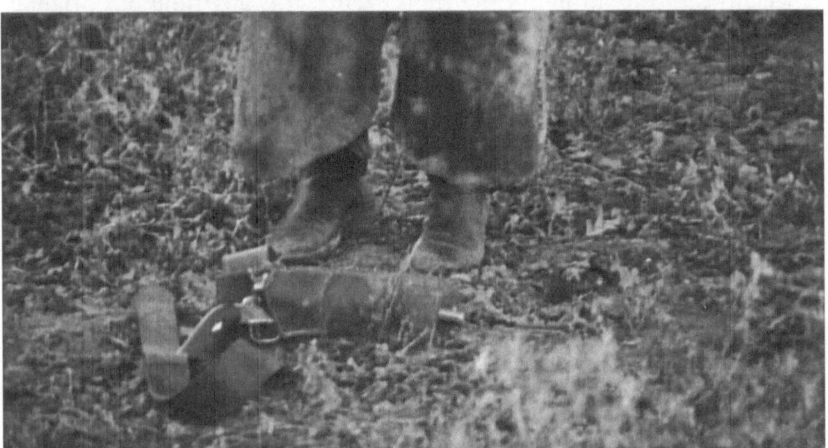

Ben drops his pistol to the ground (*above*) at the end of *The Culpepper Cattle Co.* (1972), mirroring the conclusion of *High Noon* (1952) (*opposite*)

The ending of *The Culpepper Cattle Co.* is intended to be purposely ambiguous rather than indecisive, and some critics see it that way, commenting that the picture's conclusion "smacks not of evasion but of genuine and satisfying ambiguity."[1] Moreover, a downbeat ending that leaves open more questions than it answers could be taken as a response to the over-engineered, unrealistic conclusions allegedly found in earlier Westerns (and earlier Hollywood movies, generally). As much as *The Culpepper Cattle Co.* invokes a variety of traditional Western scenarios,

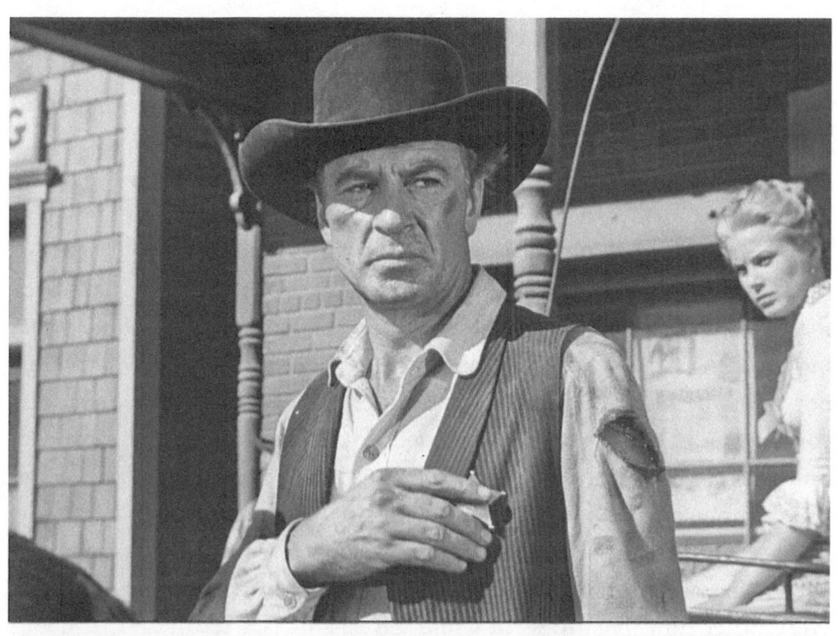

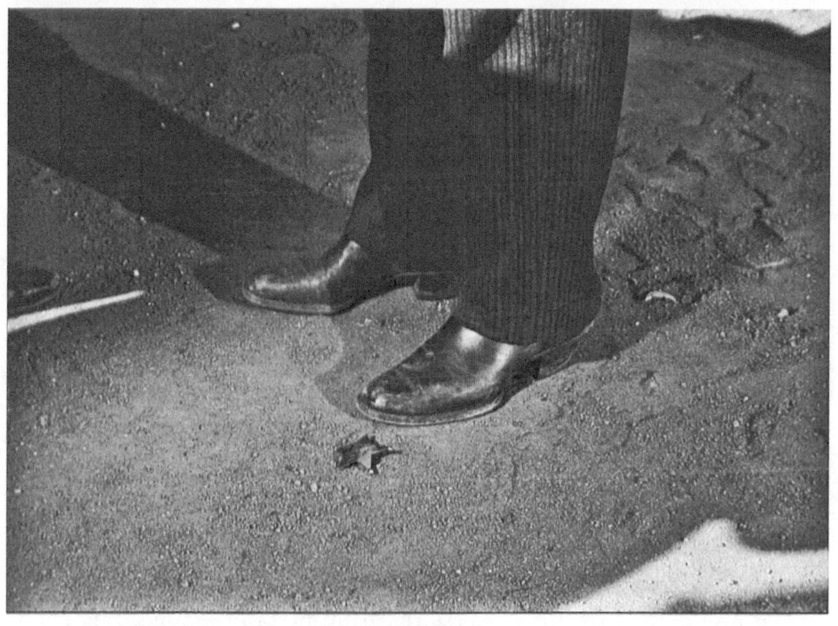

it is intently concerned with offering a far more authentic portrayal of cowboy life—especially the hardships and unpleasantries.

Along with some other Westerns of the 1970s, like *The Great Northfield Minnesota Raid, Doc,* and the aptly titled *Dirty Little Billy, The Culpepper Cattle Co.* presents a decidedly unglamorous view of life in the latter half of the nineteenth century. In contrast to the clear vistas and pristine towns of earlier Westerns, where folks often appear to be dressed in their Sunday-go-to-meeting clothes every day of the week, the worlds of these Westerns are dirty, overcast, and populated by ugly people wearing ill-fitting clothing. The question to entertain, however, is whether or not this type of representation of frontier life points to revisionist self-consciousness. Are these pictures deliberately critiquing the sanitized, unhistorical depictions of frontier life seen in earlier Westerns, or are they simply evidence of changing norms of verisimilitude? Certainly, many Westerns of the 1970s feature a degree of period detail not present in the same fashion in the 1940s or 1950s, but this is true of almost every other film, regardless of genre. "Realism" is a set of aesthetic and thematic standards and practices that change over time. What was "realistic" to audiences of the 1950s seemed highly artificial to audiences of the 1970s, but the same was true of audiences of the 1990s looking back on Westerns of the 1970s, with their abundance of fashionable sideburns and bell-bottom trousers.

Is, then, the perceived ambiguity at the conclusion of *The Culpepper Cattle Co.* part of a larger concern with authenticity, or could it be something else? Consider, again, how the movie arrives at its uncertain ending: a hurried and somewhat uneasy synthesis of several conventional Western scenarios. In his 1972 review of the movie, *New York Times* critic Roger Greenspun commented favorably on the attention to period detail, but concluded that the movie "seems mostly vacant behind its facade of atmospheric realism."[2] With this in mind, we may question whether the intended thoughtful equivocation of the finale is not really indecision, signaling a lack of depth symptomatic of the movie's overwhelming concern with surface detail.

Not unlike the pro-Indian Westerns examined in the preceding chapter, a consideration of how *The Culpepper Cattle Co.* unevenly inspects and upholds traditional Western elements brings into focus tensions within the movie. Although it is far more committed to crafting a new narrative out of archetypal Western stories than is *Soldier Blue,* the picture's reliance on convention similarly outweighs, and even confuses, the criticisms of the genre it is trying to make.

Ersatz Earps and a Dirty Doc

The critique of heroism in *The Culpepper Cattle Co.* does differ from that in some other canonical revisionist Westerns in one significant way: it is not directed at a particular frontier hero. Countless Westerns are based upon the lives and legends of a select list of American historical figures associated with the annexation, migration, and expansion west of the Mississippi River that followed the conclusion of the American Civil War in 1865. This fraternity of frontier heroes includes names like Jesse James, Billy the Kid, General Custer, and Wyatt Earp. Each of these men was a subject of great interest and notoriety in the popular press of his day—or slightly after his day, in some cases—and their exploits, factual and otherwise, were memorialized in innumerable newspaper stories, biographies, and dime novels. The contentious legacies of these and other heroes of the American West have also been a subject of ongoing debate for well over a hundred years, as generations of researchers and writers have repeatedly combed the shifting sands between myth and history, looking for something approaching truth.

Drawing upon, entering into, and influencing this dialogue, American cinema has provided us with multiple renditions and iterations of each man's story. By most accounts, however, the nature of these narratives follows a set progression as we move from the classic to revisionist Western: from celebratory commemoration to scathing indictment.

As a central aspect of popular culture, heroes—and the representations thereof—give us at least an indication of what values and attributes the public esteems at a particular moment in history. If those values and attributes fall out of favor or fashion over time, it stands to reason that the hero will experience a similar diminution in status. The decline of the Western as a popular movie genre beginning in the 1960s is often explained in this way. In light of race riots at home and the growing conflict in Vietnam, the "imperialist" ideology that appeared to be exemplified by the Western genre's mythical frontier heroes seemed increasingly archaic, even dangerous—so the baby boomers "traded in their toy pistols, chaps, spurs, cowboy hats, and coonskin caps for long hair, bell-bottoms, beads, and protest placards."[3] The genre then began to reflect this thinking, as frontier legends became "handy whipping boy[s] for political and social commentators."[4] Yet evolving values alone cannot account for the changes we can observe in the representation of Western heroes.

As ostensibly historical figures, Western heroes like Earp and Custer cannot as easily be "updated" to reflect contemporary concerns (and combat contemporary villains and evils) as can fictional characters like comic book superheroes. Instead, historical heroes are subject to an ongoing process of reinterpretation. Christopher D. Geist and Jack Nachbar observe that "traditional" heroes became increasingly sparse in the popular culture of the 1970s, and attribute this decline in part to a trend in historical studies to critically reexamine conventional interpretations of events in America's past. This resulted in "the discovery that many of our past heroes had all-too-human faults."[5] The revisionism experienced by the Western in the 1960s and 1970s is often equated with this historical revisionism. Marsden and Nachbar state that the emergence of the anti-Western, which uses the genre as a vehicle for social critique, was "influenced by revisionist history popular on college campuses."[6] The onscreen diminution in status experienced by Wyatt Earp from the 1940s and 1950s to the 1960s and 1970s, for example, corresponds to a critical revision of the famed lawman's history.

For nearly 30 years, Stuart N. Lake's 1931 biography *Wyatt Earp: Frontier Marshal* stood as the authoritative account of the events of Earp's life, including the famous gunfight at the O.K. Corral in Tombstone, Arizona. Written with Earp's collaboration, and including numerous quotations from the marshal, the biography served as the official sourcebook for *Frontier Marshal* (Alan Dwan, 1939) and *My Darling Clementine*, and the unofficial one for countless other Westerns about Earp and his exploits, including *Wichita* (Jacques Tourneur, 1955) and *Gunfight at the O.K. Corral.* Lake also served as a consultant on the first season of the television series *The Life and Legend of Wyatt Earp* (1955–1961).

While the portrayal of Earp in these films ranged from relaxed to stoic, the character always embodied the qualities of the prototypical frontier movie lawman: virtuous, cool-headed, humble, intelligent. Beginning in 1960, however, popular perceptions of Earp began to change. That year saw the release of *The Earp Brothers of Tombstone* by Frank Waters. Based on the recollections of Virgil Earp's third wife and Waters's own research, this revisionist biography revealed Lake's account to be largely fabricated and the famous lawman to be anything but virtuous. In the introductory chapter, Waters sets the tone by offering a decidedly unsavory description of Earp: "Wyatt was an itinerant saloonkeeper, cardsharp, gunman, bigamist, church deacon, policeman, bunco artist, and a supreme confidence man. A lifelong exhibitionist ridiculed alike by members of his own family, neighbors, contemporaries, and the public press, he lived his last years in poverty, still vainly trying to find someone to publicize his life, and died two years before his fictitious biography recast him in the role of America's most famous frontier marshal."[7] Subsequently, cinematic depictions of Earp began to change. Both John Ford and John Sturges revisited the character in the 1960s, in *Cheyenne Autumn* and *Hour of the Gun* (1967), respectively. In the former, James Stewart plays the character for laughs in the picture's infamous Dodge City interlude. Quite unlike Henry Fonda's compassionate Earp in *My Darling Clementine,* Stewart's white-clad, cynical Earp is more interested in cards than anything else, including the threat to the public's safety posed by "renegade" Indians. The latter movie opens with a title asserting, "This picture is based on fact. This is the way it happened." From there, the film quickly proceeds to the shootout at the O.K. Corral, which, unlike the climactic confrontation in Sturges's earlier Western, is an awkward affair lasting all of fifteen seconds. The remainder of the picture concerns Earp's merciless pursuit of the surviving members of the Clanton gang and his growing alienation from his allies.

These cinematic "revisions" of the Earp legend certainly augur the kinds of reassessments of traditional frontier heroes we encounter in the revisionist canon. But before pursuing that line of inquiry, it is important to note that we need not wait until the 1960s or 1970s to find narratives that offer alternatives to, if not outright critiques of, the representations of frontier valor supposedly found in Westerns from the 1930s and 1940s. We do need to know where to look, though.

The exact number of films each heroic figure named above has appeared in is harder to gauge than we may expect, owing to a number of factors. These include the less than perfect record of movies made during cinema's early and transitional periods, as well as the contentious issue of movies that feature fictional characters modeled on historical personages. "Based on" is a slippery concept. It can encompass implicit variations like "obviously based on," "loosely based on," "arguably based on," and so on. Henry Fonda's character in *Fort Apache* (John Ford, 1948), an arrogant lieutenant colonel from the East with a blind hatred of Indians, who leads his men on a suicidal charge that wipes out him and his entire force, is clearly modeled on Custer and the battle of Little Big Horn. The movie's criticism of Custer does not approach the level of *Little Big Man,* where the general is portrayed as a "genocidal maniac," but it is a criticism nonetheless. *Fort Apache*'s displacement of both the historical figure and his fabled last stand onto an ostensibly fictional scenario is understood as the filmmakers not wanting to outright villainize a man then popularly regarded as a national hero—a concern, we shall see, that is not entirely absent in later decades.

For every Custer-by-another-name, there are at least a half-dozen ersatz Earps: shootists of repute who ride into gunplay-ridden towns and only don the sheriff's or marshal's badge as a means of avenging a personal loss. Notable examples include *Dodge City* (Michael Curtiz, 1939), with Errol Flynn as a gunman charged with getting the riffraff out of Dodge, and *Law and Order* (Nathan Juran, 1953), a solid programmer featuring Ronald Reagan as a lawman facing the prospect of yet another town to clean up. Other examples include the films examined in chapter 2: *Man with the Gun,* starring Robert Mitchum as the gun-for-hire; *Warlock,* a re-working of the Earp myth with Henry Fonda as the gun-for-hire and Anthony Quinn as his gambler right-hand man; *Young Billy Young,* with Mitchum again in the gunslinger role; and *Lawman,* starring Burt Lancaster as a determined marshal in pursuit of a gang of cowboys.

Many of these movies offer less flattering views of both the burgeoning frontier community and the gunman that community enlists to eradicate its more undesirable elements. In *Man with the Gun,* the citizens of Sheridan City, though living under constant threat of violence, are at first reluctant to engage the services of the notorious "town tamer" Clint Tollinger, and quickly turn on him when his violent methods prove more than they can stomach. The citizens' committee of *Warlock* is at odds over hiring Clay Blaisdell, a renowned gunman, to combat a group of violent cowmen that threaten their town. The hero of the picture is not the dispassionate, materialistic Blaisdell but Johnny Gannon (Richard Widmark), a reformed member of the villain's gang who accepts the job of deputy sheriff.

As much as these Westerns do interrogate aspects of the Earp legend, they nevertheless portray the hero as a tragic figure. Unlike the historical Earp, whose occupations ranged from stage driver to buffalo hunter to faro dealer, his stand-ins like Tollinger and Blaisdell know no trade but marshalling, so are trapped by it. As *Warlock* in particular makes clear, the lawman's skill with a gun curses him to a life of aimless wandering.

Around the same time as these two Westerns were offering veiled criticisms of the Wyatt Earp legend, both *Wichita* and *Gunfight at the O.K. Corral* featured heroic Earps. Even *Hour of the Gun,* which directly questions the lawfulness of Earp's vengeful actions—both the movie's promotional poster and theatrical trailer asked moviegoers if Earp was a "hero with a badge or a cold-blooded killer"—redeems him in the end. After Wyatt finally kills Ike Clanton (Robert Ryan), he visits "Doc" Holliday. Near death, Holliday ostensibly forgives his old friend. Earp's final, symbolic act before riding away is removing his pistol and gun belt and stowing them in his saddlebag. "I'm a Westerner myself, and I can tell you I don't go for that Stuart Lake baloney," Sturges said in 1962, but his second crack at the Earp legend did not take him that far away from his first, albeit glossier rendering.[8]

It is not without some merit, then, that 1971's *Doc* claimed to offer the first truly oppositional portrayal of Wyatt Earp—and, in this case, his associates Holliday and Katie Elder. As the film's poster declared: "For the Past 90 Years These Three People Have Been Heroes. Until Now!"

In contrast to earlier Westerns that offered tempered criticisms of Earp's violent ways, the Wyatt Earp of *Doc* (played by Harris Yulin) has not resigned himself to, but instead *embraced,* the way of the gun, for reasons that quickly become apparent. A megalomaniacal political operator, here the famed lawman doesn't want the job of sheriff of Tombstone out of a sense of justice, or to avenge a personal loss. He is after power—power his current post of marshal does not allow him. "Sheriff's got the power," he tells Holliday. "Marshal's got no jurisdiction in town."

The nature of Earp's conflict with the Clanton family is also changed. Unlike in *My Darling Clementine* or *Gunfight at the O.K. Corral,* where members of the gang are responsible for the murder of one of Earp's brothers, in *Doc* the motivation for the initial antagonism is not clear. Unlike their sinister cinematic forbearers, here the Clantons and their associates are an uncouth but hardly threatening group. In the movie's first scene, Holliday (Stacy Keach) is able to win the prostitute Katie Elder (Faye Dunaway) from Ike Clanton (Michael Witney) in a poker game and then intimidate the sore loser and his partners to flee. The next time we see the Clantons, Katie delivers a swift knee to Ike's groin in front a saloon full of amused onlookers. That Earp perceives the Clantons to be the only substantive obstacle to his ascension is an early mark of both his paranoia and his impotence.

When Holliday first asks Earp about the Clantons, Earp describes them as "bad people." But later in the same conversation, after Earp details his plan for taking over the "wide open" Tombstone—Earp will run the law, Holliday will run the gambling—Doc says to his friend, "We sound like bad people, Wyatt." Seemingly unaware of the parallel Holliday is drawing, Earp replies, "We are."

In an earlier exchange in the saloon, where the marshal goads Ike by pushing him out of his way, Ike has to be restrained by his gang from physically attacking Earp. "Forget it, Ike!" his brother Billy says. "He's packin' and you ain't." This brief encounter is an inversion of a scenario commonly found in movies about Wyatt Earp, where the lawman confronts an adversary without his pistols. In *My Darling Clementine,* Earp's initial act of heroism is incapacitating a rowdy, hopped-up Indian without the use of his gun. "What kind of a town is this, anyway?" asks Earp. "Selling liquor to Indians!" (a line that Fonda would later regret). Later, in his first meeting with Holliday, the gambler attempts to provoke Earp into a confrontation. The resolute Earp reveals that he is unarmed, and then refuses when he is offered a weapon. Early in *Wichita,* a disarmed Earp thoroughly thrashes an assailant in a bare-knuckle fight. As such, when Earp assumes the post of marshal and passes an ordinance banning guns from town—a common plot device in the Western—we know he is acting nobly, because he has already proven himself to be the better of any man even without his sidearm. In contrast, the Earp of *Doc* is increasingly fixated on his weapon: "You'd be surprised what you can solve with a bullet," he says. Not surprisingly, when Earp finally agrees to unbuckle his gun belt and face Ike man-to-man, he comes out the loser. "Ain't much without them guns, are you Earp?" Ike yells after he has beaten the marshal bloody and senseless.

Other Westerns of the period offer similar rebukes of the gallant unarmed lawman. In *The Deadly Trackers,* a pacifist sheriff (Richard Harris) is unable to prevent the murder of his wife and child by a band of marauding outlaws. In *There Was a Crooked Man* (Joseph L. Mankiewicz, 1970), the unarmed Sheriff Lopeman (Henry Fonda) attempts to disarm a rowdy bar patron but is jumped from behind and knocked out. What distinguishes *Doc* from these other Westerns, though, is the symbolic dimension of the critique. Earp's overcompensatory obsession with his sidearm is one of the least subtle touches in a generally unsubtle film. The marshal becomes increasingly unstable after Holliday, suffering from tuberculosis, spurns his offer to help take over Tombstone for a prospective life of relative comfort with Kate. Yulin reportedly refused to explicitly characterize Earp's relationship with Holliday as homosexual, but the suggestion is obvious and critics have read it as such.[9]

The aim of *Doc* is clearly the critique of earlier representations of Wyatt Earp, and the film evidences a good familiarity with the character traits and scenarios those films have elaborated. But is the aim here corrective—that is, to provide a more accurate depiction of the historical events in question—or is it to offer a portrayal more in keeping with contemporary sensibilities? A line from *Variety*'s review of the movie is instructive: "Earp . . . emerges as a shifty politician of flexible motivation, by today's cynical standards a model pragmatic man of public life."[10] No longer even a lawman whose sense of justice has been distorted by thirst for revenge, in *Doc* Earp is the lowest of the low: a scheming politician with delusions of grandeur. Journalist Pete Hamill, who wrote the movie's screenplay, claimed that *Doc* was an indictment of America's delusional political leaders.

> I went to Vietnam in 1966, and it was evident to almost everyone except the military that the war was wrong, but that we were continuing to fight because of some peculiar notions of national macho pride, self-righteousness and the missionary spirit. I started to realize that within Lyndon Johnson there was a western unspooling. In that western the world was broken down into White Hats and Black Hats. Indochina was Dodge City, and the Americans were some collective version of Wyatt Earp.[11]

Doc is certainly a cynical film. Whatever Hamill's intentions, however, *Doc* makes no obvious references to contemporary political events, and the character of Earp is not equated with a contemporary politician like Richard Nixon—in contrast to a later Western like *Posse* (Kirk Douglas, 1975), which does both. Jon Tuska writes that director Perry's intention may have been to tell the story of the gunfight as it "really happened," but the resulting picture was "neither more truthful nor less ridiculous" than any earlier screen treatment.[12] Tuska overstates his case only slightly, but, more importantly, his comment points to the ultimately *fictional*—or unhistorical—nature of the picture. Other contemporary reviews of *Doc* note how the movie's aim of "debunking" the mythology of the gunfight at the O.K. Corral is at odds with its invocation of genre conventions. In the *New York Times,* Howard Thompson writes: "[T]he climax, when [Earp and Holliday] serenely slaughter a clan of seven . . . is a pious, gory jolt that yanks the rug from under the whole picture. What realistic history book yielded this incident?"[13]

Revisionist histories of Wyatt Earp published from the 1960s onward largely discredited Lake's heroic accounts of the man and his exploits. The confrontation between the Earps and the Clantons at the O.K. Corral on October 26, 1881, was less a gunfight than an ambush by the Earps, lasting mere seconds, in which three men—not seven—were killed. Yet no Earp Western has yet to deprive audiences of a dramatic shoot-out, including the most recent cinematic treatments of the legend, the entertaining *Tombstone* (George P. Cosmatos, 1993) and the lumbering *Wyatt Earp* (Lawrence Kasdan, 1994).[14] In a 1972 review, Peter Buckley writes: "[Y]es, one can tell that *Doc* is a '70s film because it's full of bareass and 'bullshit,' but that hardly qualifies it as a first-class myth-cleanser. It just looks like a snappy, well meaning remake, which is in fact all that it is."[15] In order to offer a critique of earlier representations of the character, the movie must draw upon those very same representations. Yet in doing so it is also shaped, even carried away by them.

The Bad Man from Missouri and Other Last Rebels

The revisionism of *Doc* boils down to making Earp into a villain, but not all frontier heroes are heroic in the conventional sense of upholding the values of society against forces that threaten it. Some are by definition criminals—so are *already* villains, in a sense. The general narrative of

Jesse James, for example, is one of an innocent man driven to banditry in response to the oppression of his people by a corrupt and unscrupulous establishment. Stripped of its nineteenth century trappings, this story is pure Robin Hood. But Missouri is a long way away from Sherwood Forest. The real Jesse James—to risk such an expression—was far from a hero. He did not rob from the rich and give to the poor. He robbed from everyone, for no one but himself, and killed many of those who found themselves in his path.

In 1864, seventeen-year-old Jesse and his older brother Frank joined a group of Confederate irregulars under the command of the infamous William "Bloody Bill" Anderson, who had been one of William Clark Quantrill's Raiders and participated in the infamous massacre of Lawrence, Kansas. Guerilla warfare was a prominent feature of the Civil War, practiced by both North and South with equal barbarism. It was in this irregular context—and not that of conventional warfare—that Jesse and Frank acquired the skills that would serve them in their outlaw careers. Anderson was killed in the autumn of 1864. Jesse James's career as an outlaw began on February 13, 1866, when he allegedly participated in the daylight robbery of a bank at Liberty, Missouri. This was followed, again allegedly, by a number of other robberies over the course of the next two years. The question of whether or not the James brothers participated in these early crimes remains open to debate, as in nearly all cases their involvement was affirmed only retrospectively, after the brothers had achieved a degree of notoriety. What is certain is that the brothers joined with Cole Younger and his two brothers in 1868, forming what would become known as the James–Younger Gang. Jesse achieved his first degree of real celebrity following a bank robbery in Gallatin, Missouri, in 1869, when he killed the bank's cashier, mistakenly believing him to be the Union officer responsible for the death of "Bloody" Bill. These initial flames of fame were fanned by *Kansas City Times* editor John Edwards, whose admiring editorials cast the James–Younger gang as oppressed Southerners fighting an ongoing Civil War. The *Times* also published numerous letters from James. In the years that followed, the gang carried out a sensational series of holdups and robberies, stretching from the East Coast to as far west as Kansas, and from Texas north to Iowa. It should be noted that the gang did not carry out their first train robbery until 1873—thus dispelling the popular notion that the gang's actions were retribution against land-grabbing railroad men from the East. In fact, James mostly operated not out of the West but the East, making him less a manifestation of the frontier than an unfortunate testament to the bitter legacy of the American Civil War.

The question of how Jesse James was viewed—his reputation—both during his life and afterward is a complicated one. The lines between those who regarded him as a hero and those who regarded him as a villain are not always clear. The short answer is that James meant, and continues to mean, different things to different people. This is perhaps not a wholly satisfying answer, but it is at least a realistic one.

As we may expect, the cinematic chronicles of the bandit's life vary quite a bit over the years, especially in terms of how James is portrayed. It is not difficult to make sense of these variations using a revisionist model. As a means of illustration, we can contrast a scene from *Jesse James* (Henry King, 1939) with one from *The Missouri Breaks.* Both present one of the most famous scenarios in the Western genre: the train robbery.

In *Jesse James,* this criminal act is one of vengeance against the corrupt railroad that has been unjustly displacing Missouri farmers. The moonlight boarding of the train by James (Tyrone Power) is an impressive physical feat, where he is able to transition smoothly from horseback to the top of the moving train car—traversing, as it were, a symbolic boundary with ease. He is also able to single-handedly bring the entire train to a halt. When he arrives alone, gun drawn, in the locomotive, the engineer asks, "What you aimin' to do, partner?" "I ain't aimin' to do nothin,'" James replies. "I'm doin' it. I'm holding up this train." When his gang boards the train, they work with methodical precision. Although they do steal from the passengers, they are exceedingly polite, asking only for cash so that the passengers can be reimbursed by the railroad. The only piece of jewelry taken is the stickpin of the picture's villain, and it is taken by Bob Ford (John Carradine), one of the brothers who ultimately betray James.

In contrast, the motivation for the train robbery in *The Missouri Breaks* is purely personal gain. Tom Logan (Jack Nicholson) boards the train not through impressive horsemanship, but by sheepish subterfuge, hiding beneath the hay in the livestock car. From there he proceeds uneasily, not toward the engine but *backwards,* toward the mail car. There, his gunpoint instructions to the mail clerk, Nelson, are followed with indifference, and his boasts are met with skepticism. "You get through this, Nelson, and you can tell folks you met Jesse James!" says Tom. "You aren't Jesse James," Nelson replies as he hands Tom the money from the safe. Yet, despite having to ultimately collect the money from a river, the robbery is successful. In spite of—or perhaps because of—Tom's decidedly amateur status, his plan displays a remarkable degree of common sense. Hiding on the train is certainly easier than jumping onto it from a galloping horse. Disconnecting the mail car is an efficient way of not having to deal with the conductor and the passengers. And robbing the safe is likely to yield significantly more money in less time. All of which just goes to show that you don't need to be Jesse James to rob a train.

With all of that said, you may think that the Jesse James of 1939 would not lower himself to hiding in the hay. But you would be wrong, as he does just that in order to elude capture later in the film following a failed bank robbery.

Tag Gallagher has argued that the reflexivity attributed to Westerns made during the 1960s and 1970s should not lead us to forget that the supposed naïveté that is now detected in earlier Westerns "disguises a play of allusions, a recycling of conventions, characters and motifs that are consciously revisiting not only the old West, but older Westerns." Even though they may be invisible to contemporary viewers, the presence of generic elements in these movies was undoubtedly perceived by spectators in 1939, who were closer to, and more familiar with, Westerns of the silent era.[16]

Peter Stanfield has detailed how early Hollywood had in fact made a number of attempts at adapting the story of Jesse James for the screen, all of which proved to be controversial. The first, *The James Boys of Missouri,* released by Essanay in 1909, was met with strong disapproval from the trade press: "The notorious James brothers murdered, robbed and set fire to buildings . . . one can wish heartily that the effort [of making the film] had produced something elevating, or at least harmless, instead of the seeming realism of bloodshed, crime and brutality."[17] It is important to bear in mind that this was only twenty years after James was killed. The next film about James would not come until 1915, followed in 1921 by two pictures starring James's son, Jesse Jr. The 1927 Paramount release *Jesse James* prompted scores of letters to the Studio Relations Committee, particularly from filmgoers in the South, censoring the company for supporting outlaws and warning against making a criminal into a hero.[18]

The challenge facing Twentieth Century-Fox in its attempt to bring the legendary outlaw to the Technicolor screen in 1939 was how to negotiate the exploitable value of the name "Jesse James" alongside the recognition that his legendary status was based on banditry. The solution, which was no secret, was to present a version of James that was quite obviously far better than the real man ever was. As director Henry King told the New York Times in 1939: "What we were trying to do was create a Jesse James who would be worthy of the legend, for we knew that no matter what we or any other creators of fiction did now, the legend would persist. Our effort was to make the legend a better one, morally as well as dramatically."[19]

This emphasis on mediating the truth manifests in varying ways in the adaptations of James's life story that were to follow. *The True Story of Jesse James* (1957), as its title implies, purports to offer a more accurate portrayal of the bandit's life. According to its theatrical trailer, Nicholas Ray's film offers the story of Jesse James "stripped of all fiction, lies and legend." Yet, in a classic example of Hollywood doublespeak, the trailer's concluding titles tell us that this story is "as seen through the eyes and hearts of the people who loved him"—the eyes and heart being two of our less reliably objective organs. This is not a case of false advertising, however, as the majority of the film is told through the flashbacks of Jesse's friends and family. Near the beginning of the film, a newspaper editor expresses his frustration at not knowing "who is Jesse James." Over the course of the movie, the recollections of the other characters provide us—but not the editor—with the answer.

The film does expand its purview to include the Civil War, and introduces the reflexive device of Jesse's awareness that a measure of his fame owes to exaggerated, dime novel accounts of his exploits. Yet, despite claims to being the "true story" of Jesse James, the movie's screenplay is based not on any historical account but on Nunnally Johnson's screenplay for the 1939 film. Johnson claimed to have extensively researched the 1939 project, but Jo Frances James, granddaughter of Jesse, said of the resulting picture: "about the only connection which it had with fact was there was once a man called James and he did ride a horse."[20] What's more, *The True Story of Jesse James* incorporates entire sequences from its predecessor, all cropped to the Cinemascope aspect ratio. The three action set pieces of the 1939 film thus become the three action set pieces of the 1957 film. These are the train robbery; a segment of the gang's escape after their ill-fated raid in Northfield, Minnesota, that has them crash their horses through a shop window and ride through the store to the rear exit; and an infamous shot of Jesse and Frank riding their horses off a cliff into the water below.

Subsequent screen versions of the life and times of Jesse James would continue to make various claims to authenticity and veracity. The advertising for *The Great Northfield Minnesota Raid* made a variety of declarations about its truthful representation of outlaws Jesse James and Cole Younger. The movie offered the "Real Story of Legendary Outlaw Jesse James' Most Daring Bank Robbery" and a depiction of what outlaws Younger and James were "really like." As if that were not enough, the same advertising also promised that the movie would show "the West the way it really was!"

At the start of the picture, a voice-over narration tells us:

> Even before the wounds of the Civil War had healed in Missouri, the railroads came swarming in to steal the land. Everywhere, men from the railroads were driving poor, defenseless families from their homes. And that's when a fresh wind suddenly began to blow. It was other Clay County farmers, the James and Younger boys, coming to the rescue. They tarred and feathered the railroad men and drove them from the land. From that moment onward, they were outlaws. But the people of Missouri would never forget what the boys had done for them.

In addition to the ill-fated bank raid of the title, the movie also stages other famous episodes from the James mythology, including him giving mortgage money to an aging widow only to steal it back from the landlord.

Although lighter in tone than *Doc, The Great Northfield Minnesota Raid* uses a comparable strategy to debunk the mythic heroism of its legendary figure: a traditional supporting character is made the central protagonist. Philip Kaufman's take on the legend is structured around the opposition between the psychotic James (Robert Duvall) and the thoughtful Cole Younger (Cliff Robertson), the central conceit being that James continually gets the credit for Younger's ideas and exploits. Jesse is regarded as having invented train robbery, and credited as the first to carry out a bank robbery in broad daylight, although the truth—in the movie, at least—is that Cole was the innovator of both. The plan for the raid on the First National Bank of Northfield was a scheme that Cole discarded to the outhouse for use as toilet paper, but that Jesse later claims came to him in a vision.

Other ironies abound in the movie. Cole's fascination with mechanical marvels leads him to repair a calliope located on the street outside the First National Bank of Northfield—music from which, through an unfortunate series of events, will later play a crucial role in the foiling of the bank robbery. Frank and Jesse escape the final melee, and as they ride away—with Jesse disguised as the aging widow he helped earlier in the movie, and has now murdered for her clothes—Jesse muses about forming a new gang that will include Bob Ford.

What distinguishes *The Great Minnesota Raid* from most other contemporary Westerns that set out to discredit the legacies of America's frontier heroes is an acknowledgment, even embrace, of the inescapability of myth. The devil may be in the details, and that is where screenwriter–director Kaufman directs the movie's energies, but the storybook Jesse James narrative is not displaced. Circumstances and motivations are changed, but, paradoxically, outcomes are not. When James asserts that he can't think of a single honest man his gang has ever robbed, his brother replies, "'Cause we robbed the robbers, that's why. Just the railroads, the banks, all the damned plughats." Although *The Great Minnesota Raid* does present a less flattering view of Jesse James, it is one still based on the myth of Jesse as the "last rebel of the Civil War," fighting to avenge the wrongs wrought upon the South by the Yankee nation.

Not unlike Wyatt Earp, the Jesse James myth has inspired cinematic tales of "other" last rebels. These include one of the best Westerns of the 1970s, Clint Eastwood's *The Outlaw Josey Wales* (1976). Eastwood stars as a Missouri farmer whose wife and son are killed and home destroyed in a savage raid by a band of "Red Leg" Yankee guerillas during the Civil War. Wales joins up with a company of Rebels and sets out to combat the Northerners. Refusing to surrender at the conclusion of the War, Wales is hunted by the Union Army as he makes his way westward. His pursuers include the soldiers who murdered his family. He is unable to turn and fight, however, because he continually finds himself in the company of those who need his protection.[21]

In his 1993 study *Clint Eastwood: A Cultural Production,* Paul Smith argues that Eastwood's post-Leone Westerns begin a process of restoration that saw the merging of his "Man with No Name" persona with the narrative scenarios and moral order of the classical Hollywood Western. While perhaps an oversimplification, this is still a suggestive and productive idea. Certainly, all of Eastwood's later Westerns work through the material of earlier Westerns, albeit in varying ways. While *Pale Rider* (1985) is the most explicit example—with a narrative about a mysterious gunman who protects locals against an insidious mining operation, which recalls the scenario of *Shane*—each of Eastwood's Hollywood Westerns displays a high degree of awareness of the genre's history.

Revenge is a recurring theme in the Western, but in many of Eastwood's movies the trope is often working on two levels: at the level of an individual film's narrative, where revenge motivates the hero's actions, and also in a transtextual fashion, where the protagonist is avenging wrongs from earlier Western movies. To use Smith's idea: we find out what would have happened if the Man with No Name had been in the place of earlier, less fortunate Western characters. The opening scene of *Hang 'Em High* (Ted Post, 1968), where Jed Cooper (Eastwood) is wrongly accused of murder and stealing cattle, recalls *The Ox-Bow Incident.* But rather than the movie devoting the entire narrative to deliberating over the accused man's fate, Cooper is promptly hanged—only to survive and seek retribution against the members of the lynch mob. Similarly, in *High Plains Drifter* (Clint Eastwood, 1973), the cowardly townsfolk who abandoned their lawman in his time of need—as in *High Noon*—receive a grotesque comeuppance at the hands of a supernatural avenger.

The Outlaw Josey Wales is a complex film, both in its portrait of a wronged hero and its engagement with Western conventions. Like the historical Jesse James, Wales initially joins a group of Confederate irregulars under the command of "Bloody Bill" Anderson (John Russell). In a stylized, gray-tinted montage sequence, the band is shown riding and shooting their way across the land, hanging Red Leg Yankees where they find them. Midway through this sequence, Wales is shown administering to a fatally wounded Anderson. The relationship between Wales and Anderson is not developed beyond a brief exchange when the Rebels first find Wales, and a few simple gestures at the scene of Anderson's death, but these moments contrast sharply with the earlier brutality of the Union officers.

Even though the Western genre is generally sympathetic to the South—slavery crucially excepted—it is exceedingly odd to find in a Western a sympathetic portrayal of irregular military elements from either side of the Mason–Dixon line. In the Civil War, guerilla warfare was one of the ugliest aspects of an already ugly conflict, and it engaged some of the War's most unsavory personalities, including Quantrill and Anderson. Historian Geoffrey C. Ward has described Anderson as follows:

> [He was] already fond of killing before his sister died in Union custody, and afterward apparently psychotic, riding into battle with a necklace of Union scalps around his horse's neck, laughing as he helped gun down unarmed Yankee captives, then encouraging his men to scalp their corpses. "If you proclaim to be in arms against the guerillas, I will kill you," Anderson wrote to one newspaper. "I will hunt you down like wolves and murder you. You cannot escape."[22]

As detailed above, James held Anderson in high enough regard to murder a man he mistakenly believed was responsible for Anderson's death.

In Westerns like *Quantrill's Raiders* (Edward Bernds, 1958) and *The Desperados* (Henry Levin, 1969), Confederate raiders are depicted unambiguously as villains. *Kansas Raiders* (Ray Enright, 1950), one of the few Westerns to dramatize Jesse James's participation in the Civil War, negotiates James's mythical persona as the Robin Hood of the Ozarks with his earlier involvement with Confederates guerillas. Jesse and Frank James, along with Cole and James Younger and Kit Dalton, join Quantrill's Raiders seeking revenge against the Red Leg Yankees who killed their parents, only to find themselves participating in even worse atrocities against innocent Northerners. *The Outlaw Josey Wales* devotes little time to the Confederate guerillas, but this is not an evasion of contentious subject matter. Instead, it is emblematic of the movie's larger concern. The film is not about the Civil War; it is about Josey Wales.

As in *The Searchers,* the movie's action is inaugurated by a traumatic massacre of the hero's family. In *High Plains Drifter,* flashbacks by other characters are used to link the death of the town's old sheriff with the mysterious stranger's subsequent desecration of the town. In *The Outlaw Josey Wales,* by contrast, images from the murder of Wales's family come to the hero in his own dreams. Although vengeance clearly motivates his decision to join up with the army, Wales is not consumed by a desire for retribution. Instead, he is more haunted by the memory of the massacre and, implicitly, his inability to aid his wife and son. As such, he sets out to protect those who fall into his company rather than abandon them and hunt down his pursuers. In this way, clichés about "the past catching up to you" do not do the film justice. When Wales ultimately confronts Terrill (Bill McKinney), the Union captain responsible for leading the massacre of his family, Eastwood gives the scene the silent treatment. Both out of bullets, Wales and the captain are reduced to a wordless physical clash.

The cause Wales fights for is not that of a government, or a country, or a people. This is exemplified in a powerful exchange between the outlaw and Comanche chief Ten Bears (Will Sampson), who has taken two of Wales's group hostage and whose band threatens the safety of the others in Wales's company. Recognizing Wales as the "gray rider" who refused to surrender to the "blue coats," Ten Bears tells Wales that he may go in peace. In this gesture is the indication of an affinity between American Indians and the Confederacy, based on a common enemy. This kinship has been explored in earlier Westerns, most notably Samuel Fuller's *Run of the Arrow,* in which a resentful Rebel continues his war against the Union as a member of the Sioux. Here, however, Wales rejects the offer, and in doing so reinforces that his cause is not the Confederacy. Wales is, as the movie's promotional poster puts it, "an army of one." He instead offers to exchange with the chief life for life, or death for death, in the hope that "men can live together without butcherin' one another." Ten Bears replies, "It's sad that governments are chiefed by the double tongues. There is iron in your words of death for all Comanche to see, and so there is iron in your words of life. No signed paper can hold the iron. It must come from men. The words of Ten Bears carries the same iron of life and death. It is good that warriors such as we meet in the struggle of life . . . or death. It shall be life."

Without discounting the degree to which Eastwood, as star and filmmaker, is consciously invoking the conventions and traditions of the

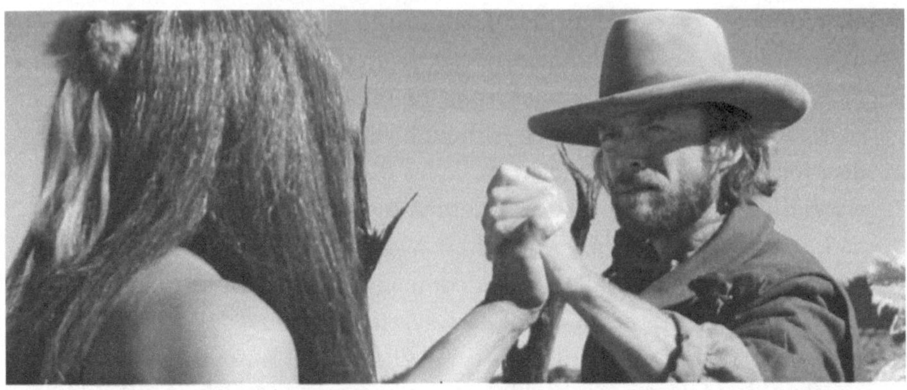

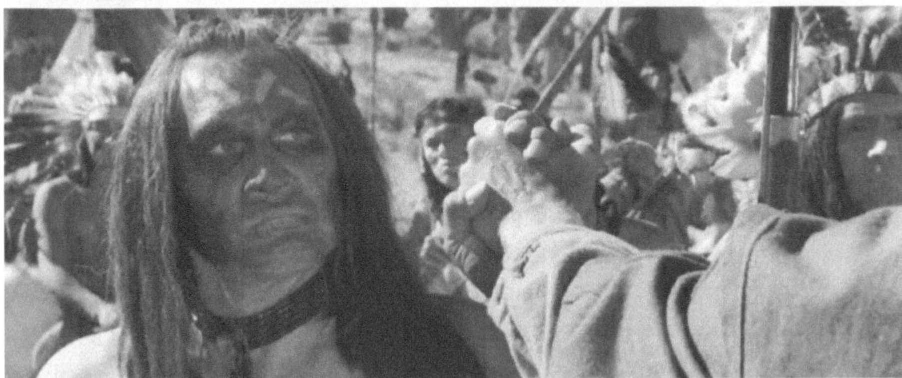

Josey Wales and Ten Bears in *The Outlaw Josey Wales* (1976)

Western genre in a sophisticated way, there is always a risk in this kind of criticism of overstating an individual artist's idiosyncrasy or directorial agency. Take, for instance, a filmmaker closely associated with Eastwood's Westerns: Sergio Leone, the Italian filmmaker who used his encyclopedic knowledge of Hollywood Westerns to turn the genre on its head, contorting conventional iconography and scenarios into perverse, overblown spectacles of gunplay and death—the man who made Henry Fonda, with his famous baby-blue eyes, into a child killer.

The problem with this variety of auteurist, quasi-evolutionary criticism is that it tends to overlook the diversity of the genre. Leone's putative subversion of Fonda's heroic persona in *Once Upon a Time in the West* would not have been much of a shock to either moviegoers familiar with the actor's career or those who frequented Westerns. Fonda certainly played his share of heroes, but he also made a clear, concerted effort over the course of his career to select roles that offered him the opportunity to question the standard of frontier valor his character displayed in *My Darling Clementine.* This trend in Fonda's career began shortly after Ford's take on the Earp legend, and continued in the wake of Leone's Western opus. We have already encountered three such Westerns—*Fort Apache, Warlock,* and *There Was a Crooked Man*—and others include *The Tin Star* (Anthony Mann, 1957), *Fire Creek* (Vincent McEveety, 1968), and a later Italian Western, *My Name Is Nobody* (Tonino Valerii, 1973).

Similarly, an earlier example of the "wrongly accused" scenario than *The Ox-Bow Incident* appears in William Wyler's *The Westerner* (1940). In this Western, the hero Cole Harden (Gary Cooper) cleverly maneuvers his way out of a lynching at the hands of notorious "Judge" Roy Bean (Walter Brennan) by exploiting Bean's love of British singer Lily Langtry. This is not unlike the referencing in *Ulzana's Raid* of dialogue from *The Searchers*—dialogue which echoed that of an even earlier Western, *Arrowhead.*

The general point to be emphasized here is that this cyclical play of repetition and variation is less the product of individual filmmakers than a key characteristic of the genre. According to most conceptions of the Western's development, the only reason a genre looks back is to critique, and then only after the genre has reached a point of self-consciousness or exhaustion. This is wide of the mark, even in the work of the most idiosyncratic of filmmakers.

Altman's Useful Idiots

Buffalo Bill and the Indians, or Sitting Bull's History Lesson, Robert Altman's second crack at the Western following *McCabe & Mrs. Miller,* is an obvious and forceful attempt at debunking—or destroying, really—the very idea of the Western hero. In this case, the titular hero, "Buffalo Bill" Cody (Paul Newman), is unmasked as a fraud: the product of a writer's imagination who lives in a fantasy world which he is unable to recognize, and thus unable to escape. The film's opening establishes this conceit very effectively. A slow tracking shot moves across a distant mountain range, finally settling on a frontier homestead. A voice-over asserts the veracity of the events that are about to transpire. The small cottage is presently attacked by a band of Indians. The nondiegetic music that begins to play is notable for its incongruity with the scene: it is circus music. The attack is soon revealed as only for show—a rehearsal. As technicians and stagehands rush in, the camera zooms out, and we see that the "homestead" is but one of several artificial scenes and man-made structures that comprise the compound of Buffalo Bill's Wild West Show.

How this sequence is filmed points to the most interesting aspect of the movie: the manner in which its formal operations reinforce Cody's entrapment within his own myth. We—or, more specifically, the camera—never leave the Wild West compound at any point during the movie. As such, our knowledge of events taking place outside it—from Sitting Bull's mysterious river crossing to Cody's failed pursuit of Bull and his band after they "escape"—is limited to what could be seen looking out from behind the high walls of the compound (and, of course, to what characters *say* happened in the outside world). This is an effective, subtle touch that contrasts sharply with the movie's other, more blatant attempts to subvert Cody's mythic heroism.

In the 1970s, one of director Robert Altman's aims was the deconstruction of many of the classic Hollywood genres, from the backstage musical to the war film to the detective mystery to the Western. "[I] see it only after the fact, and then I say to myself, Well, there I go again," explained Altman in a 1976 interview. "I think what happens is that I research these subjects and discover so much bullshit that it just comes out that way."[23] Not unlike *Nashville*'s cynical look at the world of country music, however, *Buffalo Bill and the Indians* often feels like a movie that does not completely understand what it is trying to criticize. The "cowboy showman" is actually a recurring figure in the Western genre, used many times in earlier, better movies to call into question the legendary nature of the prototypical frontier hero. In *Ride the High Country,* washed-up cowboy Gil Westrum (Randolph Scott) is revealed to be using buckshot in his sharpshooting exhibition—a gag replayed with Cody in *Buffalo Bill and the Indians.* Even 1935's *Annie Oakley* (George Sherman) poked fun at aspects of Cody's "constructed" stage persona.

Rather than turn the hero into a villain, the main debunking tactic of *Buffalo Bill and the Indians,* as in Altman's first Western *McCabe & Mrs. Miller,* is to make the mythical hero an idiot. Each movie's disposition towards these heroes is less contempt than pity, however. Their idiocy results from being ordinary, naïve individuals trapped within legends not of their own making. To its credit, *McCabe & Mrs. Miller* handles this conceit with far greater subtlety than *Buffalo Bill and the Indians* (which at times feels as though someone told Altman what a revisionist Western was supposed to be, and he set out to follow those instructions—which is entirely possible, given the film's comparatively late release date of 1976).

As opposed to being literally confined within a mythical façade, John McCabe (Warren Beatty) brings the exaggerated reputation of a gunfighter with him to the muddy, ramshackle town of Presbyterian Church in America's Pacific Northwest. McCabe is far from the first gunman of repute to wander into a nascent frontier community, but the response to his arrival is different. As Gerard Plecki observes, "The very basis of McCabe's appeal in Presbyterian Church is that he killed a man; murder is respectable."[24] McCabe's reputation endears him to the locals, giving him the foothold he needs to set up his saloon, but it also leads to his downfall at the hands of a powerful mining operation. Ironically, McCabe in the end lives up to his reputation. He does away with three gunmen hired by the mining company to kill him, but is fatally wounded in the process. Meanwhile, the residents of Presbyterian Church have rallied together to extinguish a fire that threatens to consume the town's half-built church—a church none of them will ever attend. McCabe dies alone in the snow, a strong rebuke of mythic frontier heroism.

As with most of the other revisionist Westerns examined thus far, realism is a significant component of *McCabe & Mrs. Miller*'s critical cachet. The cinematographic image was manipulated using flashing and fog lenses to achieve a look that critic Aljean Harmetz describes as having "the archaic feel of an old photograph left for too many years in somebody's attic."[25] In a 2002 interview, cinematographer Vilmos Zsigmond recalled Altman's direction to make the film look like a faded photograph: "I was doing everything I could to destroy the clarity of the film, including using a heavy number three fog filter. I wanted it to have that antique, historical look."[26] The aim of this tinkering was to complement the detailed mise-en-scène and, in Altman's words, "make the audience see the film as more real."[27] The only exception is the final, snow-bound sequence where the three gunmen pursue McCabe through the town. The degree to which the film stock was flashed was incrementally reduced over the course of the movie, to the point where there was no flashing in the final sequence, where fog filters were also abandoned, because Altman "wanted to increase the reality of the 'moment of truth' with as harsh a black-and-white effect as possible."[28] As in *Buffalo Bill and the Indians,* then, formal elements of *McCabe & Mrs. Miller* are used in an intelligent way to achieve thematic ends. As Robert T. Self enthuses in his monograph on the movie: "The look of the film asks to be understood not literally but metaphorically; it ceases merely to ground the reality of the story with a photographic realism and serves less as a literal presentation than it serves as a figurative representation of its significance."[29]

The discourse about the movie's manipulated images provides a good example of the highly subjective nature of both what constitutes realism and auteurist criticism. Altman essentially contends that in order to make the movie seem "real"—both visually and, one assumes, thematically—he deliberately resorted to representational clichés. This is not the paradox it may appear to be. Altman's admission that in order to make something appear authentic he needed to fake it confirms that "realism" is a set of aesthetic standards. The use of flashing and fogging is a novel approach that imparts on the movie a unique visual look. Moreover, it is entirely possible that some moviegoers did find *McCabe & Mrs. Miller* more authentic because it conformed to widely held visual norms that signal an image is old.

Critics, however, have conspicuously turned a blind eye to a comparatively crude element of the movie's visuals. Snowfall is added to the majority of the exterior shots in the final sequence using a post-production optical effect. The effect is not at all convincing. Depthless, opaque globules circulate on the screen, obviously superimposed over the photographed image, sliding back and forth across people and buildings in concert with the movements of the frame.

Self notes that that the antiquated look of *McCabe & Mrs. Miller* was "widely noted at the time by reviewers and continually praised by film critics since."[30] Given this attention to the movie's visuals, it is odd that no evaluation of the movie (as far as I have found) has pointed out the obvious artificiality of the snowfall. The use of this optical effect is indicative of the technical limitations of the time, but it nevertheless compromises the intended stark look of the movie's climax.

How do we account for this oversight? It is possible that this is a case of moviegoers—reviewers and critics included—simply being willing to suspend disbelief, or forgive shoddy effects? As much as the crude snowfall may undermine some of the thematic aims of the sequence, it does not detract from its dramatic drive. The sequence is very suspenseful. A second, more suggestive possibility is that critics have noted the limitations of the sequence but have chosen not to comment on it, perhaps in deference to the director. In the preceding chapter, we saw how comments made by filmmakers about their artistic intentions can help shape critical discourse. Commentary on *McCabe & Mrs. Miller* takes up where Altman leaves off, imputing, as Self's comments illustrate, a deeper philosophical significance to aesthetic decisions.

As we have seen in other Westerns from the revisionist canon, claims of realism and historical truth can be misleading. What passes for historical revisionism is often a mixture of generic continuity obscured by changing aesthetic and social norms no more "historical" than the representations of frontier life found in earlier Westerns. Furthermore, the open assertions of authenticity made by various 1970s Westerns should not be taken as an indication that these issues were of little or no interest to earlier generations of moviemakers. As the case of Jesse James makes particularly clear, Westerns have always been in the business of "truth telling"—an enterprise that includes revisiting, time and again, seminal events from America's past as part of a cyclical process of regeneration. Indeed, claims to truth are common to the vast majority of movies that have a biographical or historical component, regardless of genre. We have seen repeatedly how the representation of that truth will always be subject to multiple determinants—generic, industrial, cultural, and otherwise.

While the aim of certain 1970s Westerns was a critique of previous representations of the purported heroes of the American frontier, this has always happened. The legends have been under constant "revision."

PART III

Popularity and Preponderance

5

The Duke & Co.

PLAYBOY: Like *Stagecoach*, most of the 204 pictures you've made—including your latest, *Rio Lobo*—have been Westerns. Don't the plots all start to seem the same?

WAYNE: *Rio Lobo* certainly wasn't any different from most of my Westerns. Nor was *Chisum*, the one before that. But there still seems to be a very hearty public appetite for this kind of film—what some writers call a typical John Wayne Western. That's a label they use disparagingly.

PLAYBOY: Does that bother you?

WAYNE: Nope. If I depended on the critics' judgment and recognition, I'd never have gone into the motion-picture business.

—John Wayne, interview with *Playboy* magazine, 1971

Given their repeated designation as "traditional," we should expect John Wayne's later Westerns to invoke the genre's conventions in a straightforward fashion. We have seen, however, that the Western's conventions are continually being updated and reworked in a cyclical play of repetition and variation. Upon close examination, we find that the later Wayne Westerns are drawing on both traditional *and* contemporary iterations of the genre's conventions in order to engage in a dialogue centered on the question of the Western's future. Rather than using the genre to allegorize contemporary politics or deconstruct the myth of the frontier hero, these films argue for the enduring relevance of the values embodied by that hero—while acknowledging that, in changing times, if those values are to survive they must be successfully passed on to a subsequent generation. The aim is not revision in the sense of self-criticism or self-destruction, but regeneration.

Chisum

John Wayne's first feature of the 1970s was *Chisum,* released in June of 1970. Directed by Andrew V. McLaglen—who first worked with Wayne on *McLintock!* (1963) and had helmed his preceding two pictures, *Hellfighters* (1968) and *The Undefeated* (1969)—the movie is a loose adaptation of the events of New Mexico's 1878 Lincoln County War, which famously involved Pat Garrett and Billy the Kid. Wayne stars as John Chisum, a self-made cattle king who leads a group of ranchers in the fight to protect their land from scheming, monopolistic developer Lawrence G. Murphy (Forrest Tucker). Chisum and neighboring rancher Henry Tunstall (Patrick Knowles) first try to contend with Murphy through commerce, opening their own rival bank and general store—much to the frustration of Chisum's longtime friend Pepper (Ben Johnson), who would rather they answer Murphy's misconduct with their Winchester rifles. But after Tunstall is murdered, and appeals to the law prove useless, Chisum leads his allies against Murphy's gang in a final confrontation in the streets of Lincoln.

The film opens with a striking four-minute credit sequence. A series of amber-hued paintings by Western artist Russ Vickers pass before the camera, set to a forceful musical theme by composer Dominic Frontiere. After an opening shot of the Kinney National–era Warner Bros. logo, the music swells over rapidly cut shots of men on horseback and painted cattle, the first credit announcing Wayne as the film's (only) top-billed star. The musical theme then erupts into a sweeping harmony at the presentation of the film's title. An accompanying chorus of baritone voices further emphasizes the title, bellowing: *"Chisum! John Chisum! Weary! Saddle-worn!"* The song goes on to alternate between the sung chorus and spoken verses telling of the trials Chisum faced moving his herd of cattle westward from Texas to New Mexico, eventually establishing his "*empire 'neath the sun.*"

This use of song and painting draws on two artistic traditions complementary to the Western film genre. Vickers's paintings are part of a practice that originated with painter and sculptor Frederic Remington at the turn of the century. Remington's depictions of stoic cowboys and heroic cavalry officers set against the sweeping vistas and natural landscapes of the American West captured the public's imagination at the time, and influenced a generation of artists and, significantly, filmmakers. Looked at today, Remington works like *Fired On* (1907) and *A Cold Morning on the Range* (1905) resemble stills from classic Western films. As director John Ford described the look of his Technicolor *She Wore a Yellow Ribbon* (1948): "I tried to copy the Remington style there. You can't copy him one hundred per cent, but you can get the color and the movement."[1]

In *Chisum,* paint and celluloid merge as Wayne's character is introduced. As the opening credits draw to a close, we are shown a painting of a ranch house, still under construction, situated at the base of an expansive valley. The camera pans rightward across this painted scene, coming to rest on a solitary cowboy. He is on horseback beneath a large pine tree, overlooking the valley below. The frame seamlessly switches from canvas to film, and the camera zooms in on the lone cowboy: it is Chisum. Cut to the original view of the valley: the large ranch house is now complete, and as the camera pans we see herds of cattle grazing on the valley floor.

The song that accompanies the opening credits, "The Ballad of John Chisum," had a more recent progenitor than Vickers's canvases. While country and folk music have always figured prominently in Western films, the popular success of Frankie Lane's rendition of "High Noon (Do Not Forsake Me, Oh My Darlin')" in 1952—sung in the film by Tex

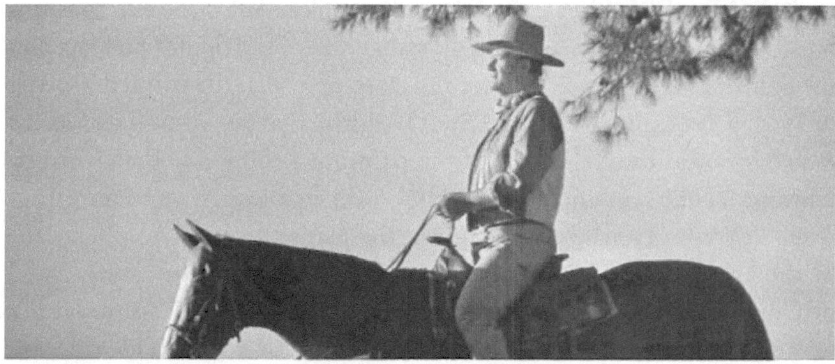

John Chisum surveys his spread in the opening of *Chisum* (1970)

Ritter—made the addition of a lonesome ballad to a Western's opening credits a common—though not always welcomed—practice.[2]

In the opening credits of *Chisum,* the paintings and title song function as devices that narrate Chisum's backstory. After the title credit, the camera moves over a painted scene of cattle being driven across a river. A close-up draws our attention to a cowboy on horseback perched on a hill high above the herd. Wearing a tan vest, he and another rider direct the ranch hands and herd below. Over these shots the first verse is spoken:

> They say that you can't make it
> Will you hark to what they've said?
> Or will you move your beeves to Texas
> Across the River Red?
> They say that you can't make it
> But you've bet your life they're wrong
> So keep moving t'ward the Pecos
> To find where you belong

The story then continues as we are shown subsequent events from Chisum's cattle drive, culminating in the sweep across the painting depicting him overlooking his spread and incomplete ranch house. As the camera focuses on the ranch house, the verse states that, even after winning "a hundred battles," for Chisum the "fight keeps goin' on." As we pan across the valley, the final line of the song asks: "Chisum! John Chisum! Can you still keep goin' on? Can you still keep . . . going on?"

In some instances, we are able to fill in parts of the story depicted in the credits with information learned later in the film. As a basic example, it is possible that a viewer may not gather that one of the figures portrayed in the paintings is Chisum. Despite the close-up shots, the painted likeness of Wayne is admittedly rough. But the distinctive tan vest—seen on the lone cowboy as the credits shift from painting to film, and then worn by Chisum for the remainder of the film—will enable viewers to retrospectively figure him as the protagonist of the painted scenes. Another scene in the credits depicts a battle between Chisum's company and a band of Comanche Indians. Alternating close-ups juxtapose Chisum with a Comanche in a white feather headdress. We are later able to identify this character as Comanche chief White Buffalo, a respected rival now "pent up on a piece of desert the government calls a reservation." "That's the end of his way of life," Chisum tells his niece, adding: "Pretty good way, too"—his remarks recalling similar ones made by Wayne's character at the end of *Hondo* (John Farrow, 1953).

In addition to drawing on the traditions of Western painting and song to narrate the title character's history, another generic element is apparent in *Chisum*'s opening credits. Watching and listening to the sequence, viewers familiar with the genre are likely to think of *Red River,* Howard Hawks's 1948 Western about a troubled cattle drive from Texas to Missouri. As R. Philip Loy notes in *Westerns in a Changing America: 1955–2000* (2004), *Chisum* could be viewed as either an alternative to *Red River,* where the hero heads further West for a fresh start rather than east to Missouri, or as *Red River*'s ultimate ending, with the hero moving his herd to New Mexico when the market in Texas goes bust.[3]

Other connections between *Chisum* and earlier Wayne Westerns are made as the film progresses. We learn that, like his character Tom Dunson in *Red River,* Wayne's Chisum left a girl behind in Texas. Like Ethan Edwards in *The Searchers,* that girl married the hero's brother. What are we to make of these references? Do they simply confirm the charges of Michael Coyne and others that by the 1970s Wayne had resorted to acting out the same old stories over and over again?

There is, again, a strong tendency in genre criticism—and in particular criticism of the Western—to try to "read" films for underlying meaning, and the latter movies of John Wayne are no exception. Of those critics who do comment on Wayne's 1970s Westerns, few are able to get past the possible implications of his mere presence in a picture—as if the physical "monumentality" of Wayne described by Deborah Thomas has grown beyond the bounds of the screen, taking on an extra-filmic dimension.[4] Wayne's well-known political conservatism produces an artistic conservatism, which in turn affects (or infects) every aspect of the production of his movies, from the choice of scripts to the selection of directors. In this way, the Wayne films are actually appraised in a manner similar to how the revisionist Western is interpreted. While the intended ends are certainly different—proving irrelevance rather than relevance—social and cultural factors external to the films proper still act as the critical barometer. This approach has the (surely unintended) effect of affording Wayne the status of a powerful auteur.

To cite a more specific example: in the sparse writing—critical and otherwise—that does exist on *Chisum,* American President Richard Nixon's admiration for the film is mentioned repeatedly—often as an underhanded way of criticizing the movie. Today, this anecdote is often relayed without any citation, its meaning thought to be obvious. Accounts that do provide more detail about Nixon's purported admiration for the film, like those of Philip French or Stephen Tatum, include a number of errors, and still also lack context.[5]

Nixon mentioned *Chisum* publicly on only one occasion, at the Federal Building in Denver, Colorado, on August 3, 1970. Nixon was in Denver to meet with representatives from the Law Enforcement Assistance Administration. His remarks, on the subject of law enforcement, were given before the press—not, as it is often reported, at a conference held by the American Bar Association. The reference to *Chisum* came toward the end of his remarks. He praised Wayne's performance and assessed the film as "far better than average movies, better than average Westerns." The President continued:

> [Watching the film] I wondered why it is that the Western survives year after year after year. A good Western will outdraw some of the other subjects. Perhaps one of the reasons—in addition to the excitement, the gun play, and the rest, which perhaps is part of it, but they can get that in other kinds of movies—but one of the reasons is, perhaps—and this may be a square observation—is that the good guys come out ahead in the Westerns; the bad guys lose.[6]

Nixon's commentary on Wayne's latest picture was a prelude to a broader, concluding message about the role of the law in a civil society and the President's concern at that time with the media's glorification of criminals and its effect on America's youth. The criminal Nixon had in mind was Charles Manson, whom the President unwisely referred to as "a man who was guilty, directly or indirectly, of eight murders without reason." This comment was interpreted as the President pronouncing Manson guilty before his trial had concluded, and White House Press Secretary Ronald L. Ziegler gave a statement clarifying the President's position later that same day.

Taking into account John Wayne's announced conservative political position and Nixon's invocation and advocacy of the traditional moral order on display in *Chisum,* Tatum concludes, "it is difficult to deny that for many audiences *Chisum* displaced contemporary problems about the generation gap, the use of violence, and the erosion of respect for law and order into [its] legendary New Mexican story."[7] This is a reasonable assessment. Nixon was a shrewd politician, and his Denver remarks, in their candidly "square" emphasis on the need for the traditional values of civility and order in the face of changing times, are in many ways typical of his appeals to the "silent majority" of socially conservative Americans thought to have voted him into the White House in 1968 and who would usher him to a landslide reelection victory over George McGovern in 1972. But given his specific remarks on the Western genre, at first one might question how familiar the President was with the contemporary movie scene. Nixon's identification of moral certainty as the essential reason for the Western's enduring success may seem questionable in light of the direction the genre had taken in the late 1960s and early 1970s. Rather than "good guys coming out ahead," as they do in *Chisum,* we have seen that many Westerns of the time showed their protagonists being violently gunned down at film's end, or portrayed traditional Western heroes as villains.

In actual fact, Nixon was an avid movie watcher, screening over *five hundred* films during his six years in office. While his taste did favor classical Hollywood films, and Westerns, in particular, Nixon frequently viewed newer releases, including *Dirty Harry* (Don Siegel, 1971), *Funny Girl* (William Wyler, 1968), and *Butch Cassidy and the Sundance Kid* (but not *Little Big Man, Soldier Blue*, or *The Wild Bunch*—though he did screen *The Professionals*). Records kept by the Secret Service show that *Chisum* was one of the few films Nixon watched twice: first on July 31, 1970, and then again on August 31.[8]

It is also important to emphasize that the Nixon of 1970 was not the morally problematic figure he would be revealed to be in 1974, especially in terms of public perception. When critics note how "Nixon liked *Chisum*," it is the criminal, paranoid, profane Nixon exposed in subpoenaed White House audio tapes that automatically comes to mind. As unpalatable as it may seem in light of the events of Watergate, the Nixon of 1970 was a President who, while still a polarizing figure, enjoyed high approval ratings and a connection, however improbable, with a majority of the American people. This was also the Nixon who would go on to the second-largest presidential victory in American history in 1972.

Under scrutiny, then, what was initially an attempt to color a film by associating it with a politically charged historical figure results in the opposite of the desired effect. This should not, however, be seen as an affirmation of a reflectionist approach to genre criticism where, once we get the facts straight, the causal relationship between films and society becomes clear—in this case, that a successful Nixon (somehow) meant a successful *Chisum.* On the contrary, that *Chisum* could find success in the same year that Westerns as diverse as *Little Big Man*, *Two Mules for Sister Sara*, and *The Cheyenne Social Club* (Gene Kelly) also met with audience approval points to the multifaceted nature of the Western genre at this time. Nachbar has observed how the early 1970s were a time when Westerns such as *McCabe & Mrs. Miller* and *The Wild Bunch* were being acclaimed as classics at the same time millions of dollars were being spent making epic Westerns starring Wayne.[9] Moreover, in 1970 an individual viewer may have seen each of that year's popular Westerns—or only one, or none at all, for a variety of possible reasons.

And he (or she) may or may not have been a Republican.

With all of that said, Nixon's comments might still provide a valuable insight into *Chisum,* in particular the movie's relationship with the Western genre. Given the voracious appetite for Hollywood films he displayed during his years in the White House, Nixon had likely seen hundreds of Westerns in his lifetime. His "square observation" that, in Westerns, the good guys usually win the day is a basic but important point. As noted above, at this time many other Western movies of note did not conclude in such an upright, affirming fashion. What Nixon is identifying, then, is a part of the genre's tradition—a tradition that is carried on in *Chisum.* Here a clear trend begins to emerge.

From its opening credits onward, *Chisum* clearly (and repeatedly) invites audiences to view it not in the context of Wayne's politics, or even as a reflection of societal tendencies, but in relation to earlier Westerns—and not only those starring Wayne, as *Red River* certainly holds no monopoly on cinematic cattle drives. In this and subsequent Wayne Westerns, we find a systematic effort to tie these films to the established traditions and conventions of the genre. As such, criticizing the conventional elements found in these (or any) films without examining the *function* those elements serve within their respective works is an exercise of dubious critical value.

Rather than being seen as invocations of the genre's rich cadre of conventions, the conventional elements that appear in later Wayne Westerns are instead often interpreted as acts of self-consciousness: essentially, as Wayne making deliberate references to his past acting achievements. Wayne's longevity as a Hollywood leading man, and his equally lengthy association with the Western genre, are unique in this regard, as both he and the characters he played are bound up with the genre's history. Difficult as it may be, it is important to examine not the man but the characters. Douglas Pye has argued that, after *Red River,* characters like Wayne's Tom Dunson became increasingly common in the genre, "anachronistic, morally problematic figures stranded in some sense by historical change, whose assertions of identity are increasingly undermined."[10]

Disapproving of Wayne's 1970s Westerns on the grounds of generic self-referentiality is also odd in light of other recent developments in the genre. In the rather limited Western oeuvres of both Peckinpah and Leone, for example, we find many of the same themes played out time and again. Clint Eastwood also managed to escape censure despite his numerous variations on the "Man with No Name" persona in the 1960s and 1970s.

As we have seen, appeals to a genre's traditions for purposes other than deconstruction are often viewed as knee-jerk reactions against change and progress. Yet, in the later Wayne Westerns, these aspects clearly demonstrate not only a high degree of knowledgeability of the genre's history, but also an awareness of its more recent developments.

One of the villains of *Chisum* is a "half-crazy bounty hunter" named Dan Nodeen (Christopher George), a merciless killer with a pronounced limp that resulted from a wound inflicted by Billy the Kid (Geoffrey Deuel). In appearance and demeanor, Nodeen is an obvious play on the "Man with No Name" persona—by this point in time, a character type familiar to Western audiences, through not only Leone's films but also countless imitations in other Italian Westerns. Perpetually sporting two days' growth and holding a steely eyed glare, Nodeen squints frequently and rarely speaks more than three sentences at a time. After bringing in a wanted man dead rather than alive, Sheriff Brady (Bruce Cabot) says to Nodeen, "You just had to kill him, huh?" Nodeen replies: "No. Less trouble that way."

The prospect of exacting revenge against Billy prompts Nodeen to accept an offer from Murphy to install him as the new Lincoln town sheriff. Ultimately, Nodeen is revealed to be a coward. At the end of the film, after Chisum and his allies have defeated Murphy's gang in a lengthy shoot-out on Lincoln's main street, Nodeen throws away his badge. "I resign," he says as he rides away. "No more paydays around here." That Nodeen not only survives the final melee but also gets away suggests that *Chisum* is very much aware of the continuous presence in the genre of the "Man With No Name" character. Yet he is but one conventional Western character among many others, most of whom have been around for significantly longer—as illustrated by the opening credit sequence. In this way, the film explicitly refers to other contemporary genre trends as both existing and rhetorically useful, but those trends are situated within the much larger tradition of the Western.

From its opening credits, where Western painting and song are used to give the main character a history that links him to past heroes of the Western genre, *Chisum* draws on elements and conventions of the Western genre from both past and present to fashion a new narrative. Which is, of course, one of the primary ways movies genres function.

Godfather of the West

The issue of regeneration is central to genre filmmaking. A particular genre's viability—financial and otherwise—often depends on how well its constituent films are able to counterbalance convention with innovation, using elements from an established canon to fashion a new-yet-familiar narrative. Given how genre practice would seem to be one big Catch-22, this is no small feat. That the Western was able to endure as a popular film genre for well over thirty years indicates its ability to negotiate the "paradox of genre" more successfully than some other, more short-lived genres and cycles. This also calls attention to the problematic designation of most Westerns of the 1970s as "revisionist." While the term as it is generally understood—as a description of Westerns that adopt an overtly critical stance towards the genre's conventions and their attendant cultural and ideological aspects—is arguably suitable for a numerically small but critically privileged group of movies, it has the unfortunate side effect of mischaracterizing earlier Westerns as a unified, unchanging mass—a thirty-year-long "classical" phase of the genre's "evolution." Furthermore, later Westerns that are not seen to explicitly scrutinize the genre's conventions are either neglected altogether or dismissed as relics of an earlier stage of the Western's development. This is particularly so with the later Westerns of John Wayne.

At a time when the production of Westerns as a proportion of Hollywood's annual output was declining rapidly, Wayne's movies did only a little more—and sometimes less—than other Westerns of the time to forestall the genre's falling off with audiences. *True Grit* was a critical and financial hit, and his subsequent features *Chisum, Big Jake, The Cowboys*, and *Rooster Cogburn* all achieved modest box office success. Other movies fared worse. *Rio Lobo,* released in December of 1970, generated only $4.25 million in rentals, just enough to exceed production costs.[11] By contrast, *Little Big Man* made $15 million that same year. Of course, that sum is still a far cry from 1970's top earners *Love Story* and *Airport,* which netted $48.7 million and $45.22 million, respectively. No matter how in tune they may have been with the zeitgeist, the revisionist Western did not stave off the genre's decline.

What, then, can be said about the 1970s Wayne Westerns? While they invoke the genre's conventions in a much different way than other Westerns of the time, what do they say about the genre's *future?*

Given that a sexagenarian actor of considerable girth and with a history of cancer headlines the films in question, the prospects for regeneration—of any kind—might not strike us as encouraging. What is more, the movies make no secret of Wayne's aging. In a scene midway through *Rio Lobo,* Wayne's character McNally awakens to find the nubile Shasta (Jennifer O'Neill) sleeping next to him at their campsite, having chosen to warm herself next to him rather than alongside the considerably younger Cordona (Jorge Rivero).

McNally: How did she get here?
Cordona: Why don't you ask her?
McNally: Hey, you! How'd you get here?
Shasta: What? Oh. When you were asleep. It was cold.

McNally: Well, why me? Why don't you pick on him?
Shasta: Well, he's young and . . . well, you're older. You're comfortable.
McNally: Comfortable? Been called a lot of things, but "comfortable" . . .

Similarly, in *The Train Robbers* Wayne's character Lane rejects the advances of Ann-Margaret by remarking that he has a saddle older than she is.

This recognition that things have inevitably changed with time is not unique to Wayne's later Westerns. Recall that Nachbar argues that the common, prevailing theme for *all* of Westerns of the late 1960s and 1970s is "time as a traitor to Western legends," replacing the epic moment of confrontation between civilization and wilderness. Nachbar nevertheless confines Wayne to the "traditional" variant of later Western, a classification echoed in Cawelti's second genre trend, which he terms the "return of the rugged individual." Noting that these films "dominantly" star Wayne, he describes them as "generally attempts to restate the traditional western themes in a slightly new fashion."[12]

The prospect that the passage of time has betrayed the heroes of the American West is certainly present in the later Wayne pictures, but these films do not show their old-fashioned heroes being mowed down by machine gun fire, or claim "historical accuracy" that depicts officers of the U.S. Cavalry as raping, pillaging rogues. Instead, the films contend that their Western heroes, while perhaps out of place, are decidedly *not* irrelevant. Whether or not this contention for the continuing significance of the genre's traditions imbues the films with any sense of regeneration remains to be seen.

The "return of the rugged individual" is certainly an apt description of Wayne's third Western of the 1970s, *Big Jake.* The first of four pictures Wayne made in quick succession after wrapping up *Rio Lobo* in June of 1970, *Big Jake* was filmed under the direction of George Sherman between October and December of that year and released in May of 1971. Wayne stars as Jacob "Big Jake" McCandles, a Texas rancher who sets out with two of his estranged sons and an Indian scout to deliver a $1,000,000 ransom for the safe return of a kidnapped grandson he has never laid eyes on.

Following the disappointing response to *Rio Lobo, Big Jake* proved to be a modest success, earning $7.5 million in rentals and turning a healthy profit.[13] Today, the film is considered by some to be a minor, neglected classic. Wills considers *Big Jake* to be the best of Wayne's post–*True Grit* pictures, and Simpson, in *The Rough Guide to Westerns,* enthusiastically remarks, "It's hard to believe a Western this good can be so neglected." Science fiction fans will also recognize *Big Jake* as the inspiration for elements of John Carpenter's *Escape from New York* (1981).[14]

The movie begins with the presentation of a series of black and white photographs, bordered in purple in the center of the frame, depicting, as a matter-of-fact voice-over narration tells us, the "genteel civilization" that had by 1909 firmly established itself in the eastern United States—including the wonders of both science (the telephone, automobile, airplane) and culture (Caruso, Toscanini, the Barrymores). The tenor of the credits then shifts dramatically. A view of Florenz Ziegfeld's chorus girls smiling amiably at the camera is followed by a picture of a large crowd of men posed beneath a lynched man who hangs from a tall tree. "1909 in the western part of the forty-six United States was not so refined," we are told.

The sequence continues in this way, contrasting the mannerly East with the still-rugged West. Whereas in the East a lady could purchase maxis and boots and "live in style," out West "they didn't care about style, just living"; the team of the East was Notre Dame's football squad, led by Knute Rockne, while the team of the West was the rangers of the Arizona territory, "busy just trying to keep the peace"; eastern empires like those of the Vanderbilts and Carnegies are contrasted with the cattle empires of the West, such as "the great McCandles ranch"—the well-being of which depended on having enough men and guns for protection. The music that accompanies the images and voice-over narration also serves to underscore the dichotomy. The strains of classical violin that accompanied Russian ballerina Anna Pavlova as she performed in *Swan Lake* are contrasted with the lively piano that went with the dancehall girl of the Klondike gold rush saloon.

In its final example of the opposition between East and West, the sequence takes on a self-reflexive character. "By 1909, still photographs had come to life. Motion pictures had been born with *The Great Train Robbery.*" We are shown a still image from Edwin S. Porter's 1903 film, which "comes to life" as a train passenger flees a group of bandits, only to be mercilessly shot down.[15] The scene cuts to a (moving) shot of a group of riders crossing a river. As the image expands in size to fill the entire frame, we are told that "[w]hile that make-believe drama was on the movie screens, nine men crossed the Rio Bravo into Texas. The turbulent years between the Civil War and the turn of the century brought out the best in some people, but in others it brought out the worst." The voice-over narration proceeds to introduce the riders one by one, ultimately revealing them as the group led by "sometimes solider and bounty hunter" John Fain (Richard Boone) that were responsible for carrying out the "infamous McCandles raid."

The illustration in the credit sequence of the dichotomy between East and West is certainly forceful enough to bring to mind the structural models of critical analysis that had sprung up in the years prior to *Big Jake*'s release to account for the Western's formal operations and enduring appeal. But while it is naïve to think that filmmakers are unaware of happenings in academic circles, viewing the opening credits as an invitation to simply apply existing interpretive schemata to the film would be imprudent. Instead, their function needs to be examined within the context of the movie as a whole.

"Traditional" is a loaded term, and in times of change films designated as such are likely to be seen as reactionary. The label of traditional applied to Wayne's later Westerns could be seen as implying that the films can be analyzed in "traditional" ways—were they not so often dismissed outright beforehand. In the case of *Big Jake,* the credits are clearly designed to establish the fact that, even as late as 1909, the western part of the United States was still wild—which is to say that the West was still *the West.* And if the West was still *the West*, you can have a Western. In this way, the credits establish one of the film's central premises, assuring viewers that although *Big Jake* is set nearly twenty years after the frontier was officially declared closed by the United States Census Bureau, they can still expect Indians, rangers, ranches, hangings, guns and, of course, dancehall girls.

Also, to see the integrity of the west's identity as dependent on its difference—or deviancy—from a refined, eastern "other" is to ignore the irony that underlies the juxtaposition as presented in the credits (and, perhaps, in the Western genre in general): that, for all its trappings of sophistication and innovation, the East was really no more "advanced" than the West.

While the meanings ascribed to films by contemporary audiences are the hardest to recover, it is fair to assume that, even in the comparative context within which they are presented, the "wonders of the modern age" shown in the credits would have struck viewers as neither wonders nor modern. But this is only part of the point. By and large, the developments cited as examples of progress are, in fact, associated with frivolity and passivity: "genteel" civility, shopping, opera, the ballet. Even undeniable technological achievements like the automobile and airplane tend to pale in comparison to the more transcendent values embodied in the concerns for "just living" and "keeping the peace."

The final comparison made in the credits, ostensibly between *The Great Train Robbery* and *Big Jake,* raises a question, however. Is the contrast between the "make-believe" drama of the former and the supposedly concurrent, "real" action depicted in the latter a claim to authenticity, or historical accuracy, on the part of the film, in the manner we have encountered in revisionist Westerns like *Soldier Blue* and *A Man Called Horse*? It would be easy to read it as such, especially given that a concern for historical fidelity is a large component of the critical cachet afforded to many revisionist Westerns. Yet such an interpretation relies on considering the brief comparison in isolation from the rest of the film. In keeping with the theme of the credit sequence, the final comparison in fact indicates that, to many in 1909, the violent acts depicted in moving pictures like *The Great Train Robbery* seemed the stuff of make-believe. This motivates the lack of preparedness of the residents of the McCandles ranch for the onslaught about to befall them.

Shortly after the conclusion of the opening credits and the introduction of Fain's gang, McCandle's wife Martha (Maureen O'Hara), conversing with her foreman, expresses disbelief that there could be any threat to her ranch: "Bert, this is nineteen hundred and nine. There . . . there just can't be rustlers." "Can be, Mrs. McCandles," Bert replies. "I'm forty-two years old, and I fought in the Lincoln County War. It's just not that long ago that . . . why it's just fifteen years ago, himself, Mr. McCandles hung. . . ." At the mention of her estranged husband's name, Martha gives Bert a stern look and he looks down apologetically. Martha ultimately agrees to consider Bert's request for more protection, and, as she looks out off the porch, notices something in the distance. A shot from behind Martha and Bert shows the riders approaching. The camera quickly zooms in on the riders to the degree that Martha and Bert are no longer in frame.

This is the second emphatic camera effect that punctuates the otherwise placid and mundane morning at the McCandles ranch. Earlier, we are shown a scene of a young, well-dressed boy playing the piano under the watchful eye of an instructor. The ranch maid, Delilah, enters the lavishly appointed room and opens the window. She, too, notices the riders in the distance, and the same quick zoom effectively transports us from inside the house to the field where the riders approach. Delilah proceeds upstairs, where one of Martha's sons, Jeff (Bobby Vinton), refuses to get out of bed despite it being mid-morning. Outside, ranch hands struggle with a stubborn horse. Servants pick flowers.

On the whole, the ranch is decidedly lacking in both men and guns.

In the violent raid that follows, most of the ranch staff are killed, Jeff is wounded, and the boy—Jeff's son "Little" Jake—is kidnapped. In the next scene, both the U.S. Army and the Texas Rangers offer to deliver the $1,000,000 ransom to the kidnappers in Mexico. Martha declines both proposals. "It is, I think, going to be a very harsh and unpleasant kind of business," she says, "and will, I think, require an extremely hard and unpleasant kind of man to see to it."

Cut to an extreme close-up of Jacob McCandles—looking straight at us down the barrel of a rifle. The next shot reveals his target: a man on horseback with a rope around his neck, about to be hung by three other riders. McCandles raises his weapon, saying to his aptly named dog, "Dog," that he had learned long ago not to go butting into anyone else's business.

Formally, the first shot of Jacob evokes countless other images of Western characters taking aim "at the audience." Examples are found in Westerns ranging from *The Wild Bunch* all the way back to the original, iconic image of a cowboy firing his six-shooter at the unsuspecting viewer at the end of *The Great Train Robbery.* The scene's setup, with Jacob perched high on a ridge far away from the hanging, is also likely to bring to mind the hangman scenario exploited by Blondie and Tuco in Leone's *The Good, the Bad and the Ugly.* Rather than using his rifle

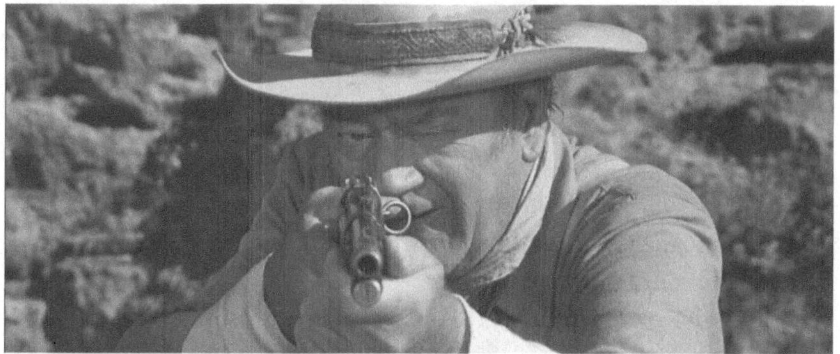

Jacob McCandles is introduced in *Big Jake* (1971)

to free the hanged man from afar, however, Jacob first turns away. But when the riders begin to beat the hanging man's son, Jacob decides to ride down to confront them in person—a decision both principled and, as it turns out, practical. We later learn that Jacob's eyesight is beginning to fail him (and for that reason he now favors a Greener shotgun over a rifle or pistol).

Aside from the striking image of Wayne taking aim at the audience, the introduction of Jacob is notable for the fact that it comes more than nineteen minutes into the picture. While this duration reinforces the physical and emotional distance between Martha and Jacob, their separation is an inversion from the scenarios of Wayne and O'Hara's previous Western film pairings, *Rio Grande* (John Ford, 1950) and *McClintock!*. In those films separation between their characters is the result of O'Hara leaving Wayne, only to return and reconcile with him by each film's conclusion. In *Big Jake,* there is no such reconciliation between the former couple. Instead, the focus is on the growing camaraderie between Jacob and his two sons, James (Patrick Wayne) and Michael (Christopher Mitchum), as they endeavor to rescue Little Jake.

Wills notes that *Big Jake* contains "echoes" of earlier Wayne Westerns *Red River*, *The Searchers*, *The Man Who Shot Liberty Valance*, and, somewhat curiously, *Fort Apache.* The aim of these echoes is to present Jacob "as the remnant of some older order, brought back for a limited mission in 'modern' times." Yet, according to Wills, this return is only a partial one. Jacob is called upon to "revive a bit of the old savagery," but only to the end of doing away with an even *older* savagery.[16] Similarly, Cawelti argues that the rugged individual's return is limited in scope, consisting of only "one more heroic quest or battle."[17]

In the film, Jacob's reappearance is actually presented as something more otherworldly. When he confronts the small mob about to lynch the fourth man, who is revealed to be a sheep farmer, Jacob demands they release him. After learning Jacob's identity, the hangmen comply immediately—but only after one of them remarks, "Oh, I uh . . . I thought you were dead, Mr. McCandles." This line becomes a running gag throughout the film.

That Martha must "resurrect" her estranged husband from the wilderness after a ten-year absence is, like the comparisons presented in the film's opening credits, certainly suggestive that a structural opposition between civilization and wilderness may be at work in the film. Although Wills seems to do so more explicitly, both he and Cawelti draw on this traditional model for their criticism. They both conceive of the Western hero as still emerging from the desert to purge the garden of evil so that it may grow and flourish, and in the process help to forge a community in which the hero has no place. Only now the hero is much older—a proximity to death that figures prominently in criticisms of the traditional Western.

Out of all of Wayne's 1970s pictures, perhaps the strongest articulation of the *need* for regeneration came in his next film, *The Cowboys,* released in January of 1972. Directed by Mark Rydell, the movie tells the story of Wil Andersen, a 60-year-old rancher who hires on eleven young boys, ranging in age from nine to fifteen years, to help him drive 1,500 head of beef from Montana to Belle Fourche, South Dakota, along the Bozeman Trail. While not dealing with the onset of "wonders of the modern age" like Jacob McCandles, Andersen is still a man in changing times. The boys are Andersen's last resort after his hired hands, wanting to get in on a nearby gold strike, quit on him. "A fool comes to town with a fist full'a gold dust and every jackass in fifty miles around lights out after him," Andersen laments to his wife, Martha. "In my day a man'd stay with you on a handshake." "It's a different day, Wil," she replies.

In the picture, the boys are able to demonstrate the determination necessary to gain Andersen's reluctant confidence. Like James and Michael in *Big Jake,* it is less a question of having ability than acquiring skill. Initially, Andersen takes a hard hand to the boys' frontier education. "Now you'll show up at my place first Monday, first Monday after school's out at 5 A.M.," he tells them after hiring them on. "And come with grit teeth, 'cause gentlemen, that's when school really begins." On the trail, the boys are roused each morning at 3 A.M. to the sound of Andersen yelling, "Let's go! We're burning daylight!" Over the course of the cattle drive Andersen teaches the boys tough lessons about the values of hard work, sacrifice, and bravery. As the boys earn Andersen's respect, he begins to see them more as sons than employees. One evening he tells his cook, Nightlinger (Roscoe Lee Browne), that he lost two sons.

ANDERSEN: Went bad on me. Or I went bad on them. I don't know. I can't figure it out.
NIGHTLINGER: You've got another chance.
ANDERSEN: They're not mine.
NIGHTLINGER: They could be.

The Cowboys is one of the few films in which Wayne's character dies on screen. What is particularly notable about this case is that Andersen's death comes not at the film's climax, but three-quarters of the way through. When a group of rustlers try to take his herd, Andersen bests their leader Longhair (Bruce Dern) in a bloody fistfight. Enraged at losing to a man twice his age, Longhair pulls his pistol and guns Andersen down. After burying Andersen in the prairie that, as Nightlinger eulogizes, was like a mother to him, the boys exact justice against Longhair and his gang. With help from Nightlinger, they kill the rustlers and deliver Andersen's beeves to market in Belle Fourche. As they drive the cattle through the town's streets to the stockyard, adults stare in silence as children, no older than the cowboys themselves, run and skip alongside the slow-moving herd.

In the movie's final scene, the boys and Nightlinger return to mark Andersen's grave with a proper tombstone ("Wil Andersen: Beloved Husband and Father"), but are unable to locate the burial site, his temporary grave having vanished. "Boys," says Nightlinger, "I think it's close enough." "Well, come on," says Slim, the eldest cowboy. "We're burnin' daylight." While the Biblical overtones of this scene—with Andersen as the Christ of the frontier and the cowboys as his apostles—are rather forced, the point is made clear that the heroic legacy of the Western hero has been successful passed on to a new generation.

Like *Big Jake* before it, *The Cowboys* proved to be a minor success. Released in January of 1972, the film went on to earn $7.5 million in rentals. Such success did not, however, allay the concerns of all critics about the genre's prospects. Nachbar, for one, is skeptical of the regeneration depicted in *The Cowboys.* Acknowledging that the film is intended as "a message of hope for lovers of old Westerns," he instead finds most significant the acknowledgement in the film of Wayne's advancing years in a scene where Andersen tells Martha that he is "sixty years old": "It is a shocking admission. As we hear Wayne say it we become fully aware that he *is* getting old. If this greatest of all Western heroes can age and die, so, obviously, can all others. Time has therefore finally caught up to and is destroying the Western myth of the eternally recurring moment of heroic action."[18] Nachbar's skepticism of the potential for regeneration in the later Wayne Westerns is not based on the films or their characters, then, but on Wayne himself.

It is Wayne, the man, who often acts as the critical lens through which his films are interpreted. Rather than analyze the films as aesthetic works or examine their relationship to the Western genre, a prevailing critical tendency is to read the movies symptomatically, either as expressions of Wayne's political personality or for biographical resonance. We can find examples of both routes in the limited writing that exists on Wayne's sixth picture of the 1970s, *Cahill: United States Marshal.* Released in July of 1973, the film was Wayne's fifth and final collaboration with director Andrew V. McLaglen. Wayne stars as widower J. D. Cahill, a U.S. Marshal whose professional success has come at the expense of his relationship with his sons, seventeen-year-old Danny (Gary Grimes) and eleven-year-old Billy Joe (Clay O'Brien). In their father's absence, the boys rebel and fall in with a group of bank robbers. When the robbery goes wrong and two men are killed, Billy Joe hides the money. After four men are wrongly accused of carrying out the robbery, the two sons must decide whether to tell their father or turn the money over the bank robbers.

R. Phillip Loy reads *Cahill: United States Marshal* as an example of Wayne's social activism. Loy argues that "[a]s he neared the end of his career and his life, John Wayne was doing more than protesting changes in American culture that he abhorred; he also wanted to ingrain in younger cohorts a respect for the values around which he had built his public persona."[19] *Cahill* becomes, for Loy, a social commentary on the consequences of parents not spending time with their children. At stake, then, is not the regeneration of the genre but the regeneration of a way of life.

McLaglen adopts a similar view in his commentary track for the film's DVD release, stating that *Cahill* was the "first film where Wayne had to deal with a modern subject, taking care of your children while they were young." While McLaglen asserts that Wayne was an "attentive father," he speculates nonetheless that the question of "whether I spent enough time with my children" might have passed through Wayne's mind and motivated his decision to make the picture. Biographers Randy Roberts and James S. Olson are less equivocal about Wayne being an absentee father. In their view, it was through his films that Wayne expressed his feelings for his children, *Cahill* being "very close to autobiographical" in its depiction of a father whose devotion to his work means time away from his family.[20]

In an otherwise well-researched biography, these claims stand out as highly questionable. To argue that Wayne's choice of scripts was determined principally by their thematic resemblance to his personal life—as opposed to, say, choosing projects that were within the financial capabilities of his Batjac production company and could be filmed in favored locations like Durango, Mexico—is to rely on speculation, rather than analysis of the films in question or knowledge of their production circumstance. Likewise, to question the possibility of regeneration in these films because Wayne, in real life, was nearing death is to ignore what the films are saying. On the subject of *Cahill: United States Marshal,* we might ask what is more productive: considering the film to be a vehicle selected by Wayne through which he could make a personal statement on a modern subject that would resonate with both contemporary audiences and his own children, or examining it as a variation on the theme of regeneration detected in preceding later Wayne Westerns? Or, more specifically, as a variation on the depiction of relations between fathers and sons found in some of those films? Choosing the second path, we could note how *Cahill* takes the convention a step further by having those sons actually cross over to the wrong side of the law. Depictions of the Western hero as father are actually rather rare in the genre. Instead, we more often find the hero acting as a surrogate father. That Jacob McCandles's sons stayed on the straight and narrow is likely due to the influence of their mother (as was the case with Yorke's son in *Rio Grande*). In *Cahill*, however, Danny and Billy Joe's mother has passed away, leaving them in the intermittent care of their father, who is continually called away on official duty. This dedication is construed by Cahill's sons—Danny, especially—as a preference for work over family, which leads to the boys' rebellion. Like Wil Andersen, whose boys also "went bad" on him, Cahill is offered a chance at redemption. After Danny is deputized and accompanies his father on the search for the bank robbers, he and his father come to a new understanding. Observing his father on the job, Danny gains a new appreciation for his father's integrity and principles. At the same time, Cahill acknowledges that his commitment to his job has cost him his relationship with his sons, which he resolves to rebuild.

The biographical interpretation of Wayne's films can be understood in relation to the tendency toward symptomatic interpretation that dominates criticism of the Western genre. As we have seen, Wayne's later Westerns are actually explained in a manner similar to other Westerns of the time: by appealing to factors beyond the films proper. In this case, the difference detected by critics between revisionist and traditional Western of the 1970s is attributable to Wayne. The explanation for the appearance of these films is still an auteur figure who is able to use the Western's conventions to shape the films to his personal vision, only in this case the resulting pictures do not reflect prevailing social and cultural tendencies.

A problem with this approach—even more so than in appraisals of the filmmakers of the Hollywood Renaissance—is that it is largely ahistorical, neglecting more concrete aspects of the films in question in favor of conjecture and interpretation. As much as Wayne made his personal politics known, after his much-maligned (but financially successful) *The Green Berets* (John Wayne, 1968) the actor seldom commented on matters of artistic intention or motivation. We can never know exactly what motivated him to make this or that picture, but we can closely examine his movies to determine how they convey meaning and relate to the Western genre. Biographical interpretation, by contrast, presumes to know the former while largely ignoring the latter, effectively placing the critical apparatus before the object of study. This is not intended as a repudiation of the value of star-based studies, or of the value of analyzing the relationship between films and culture, but rather as a caution against ascribing meanings to films based on abstractions. Even if these movies do tell us something about Wayne the man, that does not mean that Wayne the construct can tell us something about the movies.

Wills's observations of similarities between *Big Jake* and earlier Wayne Westerns are mostly valid, but he sees these references functioning in an extra-textual fashion: instead of attempts to draw on genre tradition to say something new, they are deliberate attempts to date the film. When Wills notes that *Big Jake* is like *The Man Who Shot Liberty Valance* because both feature protagonists whose archaic frontier ruthlessness is needed to kill off an even older savagery, the point is that Wayne's hero is doing the same thing in 1971 that he was doing in 1962. Without discounting the degree to which moviegoers may make these kinds of connections, it is debatable whether Jacob's status as "belonging to an older order" is due more to *Big Jake*'s similarities to older Wayne pictures than to the movie's more tangible formal and thematic features, from the hero's delayed introduction to the portrayal of strained family relations resulting from Jacob's ten-year absence.

For his part, Cawelti—without abandoning the savagery/civilization schema—has thought out the implications of the rugged, aging hero more thoroughly. On the later Wayne Westerns, he writes: "In none of these films is there much question of group regeneration associated with the hero's purging action."[21] Because society in these movies is portrayed as frail and corrupt, and thus unable to protect the innocent, the only solution lies in the private action of a strong leader—one who is able to overcome both society's deficiencies and the villain's iniquity through his own superior force. It is in this respect, Cawelti argues, that "return of the rugged individual" Westerns resemble the new form of gangster movie typified in Francis Ford Coppolla's *The Godfather*. He writes:

> Because society has failed to extend its protection and order to an adequate degree, the little man is constantly threatened by violence against which he cannot protect himself.
>
> The fantasied solution is to fall back on the Godfather—or, in the case of the western, on the grandfather, Big Jake—and to create under his absolute authority a close-knit, small group, like a family, which in return for absolute loyalty will protect its members.[22]

Problems with chronology aside (*The Godfather* was not released until 1972, after *Big Jake*), it is easy to find examples from the later Wayne Westerns that would seem to prove Cawelti's point. The residents of Lincoln are faced with corruption stretching from the town sheriff to the governor's mansion . . . until John Chisum finally leads his allies into battle. The town of Rio Lobo is under the rule of a mysterious moneyman and his bought law . . . until Cord McNally rides into town. In *Big Jake,* when James rails against his father's domineering nature, Jacob's Indian guide Sam Sharpnose (Bruce Cabot) rebukes him: "You do what he tells you, every time he tells you and we might come through this alive! Might even save the boy. Otherwise you're gonna get yourself killed. Don't matter to me. But you'll probably get him [Jacob] killed too, and that does." What Cawelti fails to take into consideration, however, is the nature of the action in these films—specifically, how it is *group* action. As in *Chisum* and *Rio Lobo,* victory in *Big Jake* results not from the actions of a heroic individual but from cooperation and coordination among a company of heroes made up of members both young and old. Over the course of the narrative, talents are revealed in characters that come into play in the movie's finale. Jacob initially ridicules James for his use of a gas-operated Bergman handgun: "I'll bet you could almost get that fancy gun out of that fancy holster before some fast gentleman with an old-fashioned six-gun blew a hole in ya!" But James is later able to best two men in a fair fight in a saloon and then, in the final shoot-out, outdraw the kidnappers' fastest gun. James's brother Michael turns out to be a deadeye shot with a rifle, which enables him to pick off the enemy gang's own sharpshooter during the climactic standoff.

Although Cawelti does not explicitly say so, the inference to be drawn from his criticism of the traditional Western is that a reliance on an aging hero—in this case, one who is for many intents and purposes already dead—will lead to society's downfall. Yet this concern for regeneration would seem to imply that, even after the hero has completed his final mission and purged the garden of evil, the specter of future malevolence remains—otherwise, what does it matter if a new hero fails to take Wayne's place? Cawelti's disparagement of society's portrayal as weak in these films is also a curious criticism. On a purely practical level, society must be portrayed in Westerns—and, indeed, nearly all movies—as at least somewhat vulnerable to the forces of evil. Otherwise there would be nothing for heroes to do.

While not the point Cawelti intends to make, that the qualities of the Western hero will always be needed is a major theme of the later Wayne Westerns. The films are replete with instances that purposefully problematize fixed conceptual boundaries between East and West, wilderness and civilization, and even past and present. Concomitant with this focus on transcending symbolic demarcations is an emphasis on the passing down of knowledge from Wayne's characters to a younger generation. As Lusted has observed, in most of Wayne's final films, "the issue becomes more one of learning from, rather than protecting, the memory. The central conflict in [these Westerns] is the struggle between honouring traditions and the figures that embody them whilst also recognizing the need to move on."[23] In *Chisum,* it is Pat Garrett who emerges as Chisum's successor and suitor to his niece because he understands what Billy the Kid does not: the difference between vengeance and justice. Cordona and Tuscarora represent the future of heroic action in *Rio Lobo,* not the "comfortable" McNally. In *Big Jake,* the skills of Michael and James are needed to make up for Jacob's deficiencies (not only his failing eyesight, but also the suggestion that he is not as quick on the draw as he once was). It is only after they earn the respect of their father, however, and learn the values of humility and bravery, that the two sons are able to put those talents to work in rescuing their nephew. Rather than returning one final time to rid society of savagery—an act purportedly carried out countless times by the hero's predecessors, but with less finality—the hero instead returns to assert the timeless nature of the values he embodies, and pass those values on to his successors. *Big Jake* concludes with an emphatic statement to this effect. After defeating Fain's gang and rescuing Little Jake, three generations of McCandles are assembled for the first time. James says to his father, "Let's go home." Jacob looks to his sons, then down at his grandson, and replies, "Good idea."

"The Last Shootist, Extant"

Like many other Hollywood icons of the classical era, John Wayne is today largely remembered less for the specific roles he played than for a more general collection of ideals and images that make up his "star persona." The inevitable result of this selective condensation is an often-confusing conflation between stars and their roles. As an example of this, we can look to a line of officially licensed John Wayne giftware produced by the Lyon Company of Salt Lake City, Utah. Items ranging from a cigar box to a mechanical alarm clock are each adorned with Wayne's image and, in many cases, a quotation. A sixteen-ounce coffee mug, for example, features the quote: "A man's got to have a code, a creed to live by." While it is entirely possible that Wayne may have uttered this line at some point in his life, it just so happens that his character John Bernard Books says nearly the exact same thing in *The Shootist.*

A star persona could be seen as forming a kind of concentric circle around the specific, smaller-scale components of an actor's life and work. To get to those interior circles—be they individual films or biographical details—means having to pass through the outer layers, and once we arrive it can be difficult to discern where the star persona ends and the person, character, or film begins. In some respects—commercially, for example—this is actually the desired result, and so it comes as no surprise that the quotation on the coffee mug is attributed to Wayne and not his character. Suffice it to say that most folks are likely more inclined to purchase a "John Wayne" mug than a "J. B. Books" mug. In other respects, however, the value of the premise that Wayne was in effect "playing himself" in his films is questionable, especially when used as a critical lens through which to interpret his work. If the goal is to learn about these movies, then it is more productive to begin one's analysis *there,* at the source, rather than in the outlying regions of star persona or other explanatory models.

If there were, however, a case to be made *for* the symptomatic interpretation of the Wayne's films, it would likely be found in *The Shootist.* Directed by Don Siegel, *The Shootist* concerns the final days of aging gunfighter John Bernard Books. In January of 1901, Books rides out of the mountains and into Carson City, Nevada, the site of a past skirmish, to visit his old friend Doc Hostetler (James Stewart). After an examination, Hostetler offers a grim diagnosis: "You have a cancer, advanced." Books, who already suspected as much, resolves to live out his final days in solitude in a boarding house run by the widow Bond Rogers (Lauren Bacall) and her teenage son Gillom (Ron Howard). But word of Books's presence in the town, and of his looming death, soon spreads, and he must contend with a series of unwanted visitors. Attempts are made on his life; a prying newspaperman offers to write a series of "factual" stories about his exploits; even an old girlfriend appears, hoping that a quick marriage will allow her to live off Books's name. During a subsequent visit to Hostetler, the doctor describes the agonizing experience that awaits Books as he draws closer to death.

> HOSTETLER: There's . . . there's one more thing I'd say. Both of us have had a lot to do with death. I'm not a brave man, but you must be.
> BOOKS: Aw . . .
> HOSTETLER: Now . . . now this is not advice. It's not even a suggestion. It's just something for you to reflect on while your mind's still clear.
> BOOKS: What?
> HOSTETLER: I would not die a death like I just described.
> BOOKS: No?
> HOSTETLER: Not if I had your courage.

His determination to die on his own terms renewed, Books kindles relationships with both Bond and Gillom Rogers, and begins to orchestrate the scene of his demise.

As *The Shootist* is Wayne's final film, there is a tendency to read it as a kind of final statement—about Wayne's career, or the Western genre, or both. That Wayne would pass away from cancer three years after the film's release makes such assessments come across as all the more apposite. Criticism of the film is marked by observations about an air of finality or how Wayne had at last accepted his age and fate—redemptive acts in the eyes of some of his detractors. Michael Coyne, who had before dismissed Wayne's later pictures as politically conservative derivatives of his early work, is highly complimentary of *The Shootist* and devotes part of the final chapter of his book *The Crowded Prairie* to a discussion of the film. Unlike the other Westerns he examines, however, it is exempted from cultural interpretation owing to its focus on Wayne's legacy. Coyne explains: "*The Shootist*, however, is primarily concerned with a particular American personality rather than U.S. national identity."[24]

Most appraisals like these are made in retrospect, with the knowledge that Wayne's own cancer was returning and that he would die shortly after the film's release. Just as J. B. Books is the "last shootist, extant," Wayne was the last remaining Western star. And both were dying. Yet the correlation between Wayne and his character is not so straightforward. Lusted, for example, writes that Wayne was "suffering from the same cancer as the character he portrays in the film,"[25] but this is not exactly true. Although not stated explicitly in the film, the suggestion is that Books is dying of prostate cancer, whereas Wayne's cancer afflicted his lungs. In making a rhetorical point about how Wayne's characters reflected his personal circumstance, Lusted unintentionally does the opposite: positing Wayne as the reflection of his character. Wayne had, in fact, beaten cancer in the 1960s—a fact he boasted about frequently—but in truth his health had been in decline for over a decade. As such, we might wonder how any of Wayne's other films from the 1970s might be remembered were they to have been his last, regardless of the degree to which they apparently evoked his real life situation.

Through all of this, one thing remains clear: whatever illness Wayne was battling off-screen did little to curtail his brisk production schedule. It would certainly be difficult to accuse an actor who had made ten films in six years of slowing down, let alone of giving any indication that the sun would soon set on his career. The clear sense is that Wayne, who began working as an uncredited extra in silent Westerns in the late 1920s, intended to continue making movies for as long as possible.

An emphatic reminder of this cinematic longevity opens *The Shootist*. First, the Paramount Pictures emblem is presented not in color but in shades of gray. As the music begins, we cut to a black and white shot that pans rightward across a range of snow-capped mountains. The camera stops as a solitary rider comes into frame in the distance, riding away from the sierra. The credit sequence then cuts to a series of clips from a number of Wayne's earlier Westerns. Shots of his characters in *Red River, Hondo, Rio Bravo*, and *El Dorado* are appropriated to represent successive stages of Books's frontier career, narrated by Gillom Rogers. Even though the latter three films were color productions, they are presented in the credits in black and white (in contrast to the remainder of *The Shootist,* which is also in color). Gillom's voice says that Books was not an outlaw but a lawman, and that he lived by a strict creed: "I won't be wronged,

I won't be insulted, I won't be laid a hand on. I don't do these things to other people, and I require the same from them."

Not unlike the painted credits of *Chisum,* the opening sequence of *The Shootist* draws on elements from earlier Wayne Westerns to help fashion a backstory for its protagonist. Yet John Chisum's long journey to New Mexico is not represented using actual images from earlier films, even though there would have been plenty of examples to choose from. When *Chisum* invokes Western conventions like cattle drives and battles with Indian tribes in order to construct the movie's story, it gives those conventions *new* representations: the painted scenes we see in the credit sequence. What *The Shootist* does instead is take images of Wayne in earlier roles and *re-present* them in a new context, asking the viewer to see existing representations as standing in for the history of one (new) character.

Contrary to what we may expect based on "revisionist" accounts of the period, the vast majority of Westerns made during late 1960s and 1970s do not actively advance themselves as corrective (in order to appeal to the counterculture or what have you). Instead, films were often promoted as being part of an ongoing genre tradition, either by drawing in their advertising upon traditional Western imagery, or by explicitly positioning themselves as part of a tradition of great Western movies—this being one of Hollywood's oldest marketing strategies. *Bite the Bullet,* largely forgotten today, was marketed as "a new Western classic" in "the tradition of *Shane* and *High Noon.*" Even the promotion for an openly critical film like *Doc* attempted to associate the movie with a list of other Western hits while at the same time distinguishing itself from that tradition.

The theatrical trailer for *The Shootist* promoted the film as the successor to classics like *Stagecoach, Red River, Shane, High Noon*, and *The Magnificent Seven.* In this way, the foregrounding of Wayne's long association with the Western can be viewed at least in part as an attempt to add a certain prestige to *The Shootist* by drawing a lineage between it and some of the genre's most revered classics. In this particular case, however, the notion that Wayne's previous roles were, in a sense, interchangeable cannot help but promote the stubborn idea that, in the end, he was always playing the same character: John Wayne. This conflation between star and character actually stands to work in the film's dramatic favor, because it is then not just Books who is dying, but all the Western heroes Wayne has portrayed over the course of his long career. *It has all come down to this.*

Or has it?

As we know, Wayne already died once in the 1970s, in *The Cowboys.* Was that on-screen passing somehow less meaningful because the film's opening credits failed to appropriate scenes from, say, *Red River* to represent Wil Andersen's past?

A number of points can be made here. While many of the Western heroes played by Wayne over the course of his career have clear similarities, to say they are "the same" lacks specificity. If we are to assert that, even with some exceptions, and while acknowledging that there are important though minor differences between Wayne's characters, the parallels are still pronounced, the question we need to ask is *why?* Why are the roles similar? What function does this serve? The usual answer is that Wayne was playing himself; that his individual roles were not really different characters but expressions of his own personality. But why this proposition necessarily follows the observation of similitude across his body of work is unclear. Taken on its own, the premise that Wayne's characters are similar because Wayne was playing all of the characters is a circular argument that offers nothing in the way of explanation. The idea that Wayne was playing himself cannot be justified by any evidence found within the films themselves, but instead requires appealing to aspects of Wayne's star persona.

An alternative approach to accounting for the continuity of characters we find across Wayne's films—more specifically, the recurrence of certain character types and traits—might be to consider his Western heroes as conventions of the Western genre. In this way, what we observe in the films is actually the same play of repetition and difference expected of other genre conventions. In Hawks's Westerns, for example, it is through minor variations in character that new narrative scenarios are created. Much of the appeal of the character of Rooster Cogburn is how he alternately violates and upholds the conventions of Wayne's heroes.

In the opening credits of *The Shootist,* the series of excerpts are presented to us outside of their original narrative context. Yet the continuity between them is not simply that they each feature Wayne (and thus Books) in a different stage of his career. The continuity is, instead, an understanding about the types of characters Wayne has played that results from our recognizing certain coded elements and actions. Each excerpt features Wayne dressed in familiar cowboy attire—buckskin for the first two instances, which take place in wilderness settings, and denim with familiar vest for the last two, which occur in towns—and each presents the same scenario: the hero faced with an armed adversary. In each case, the other man draws first. And in each case, Wayne draws faster. These devices are central components of the conventional Western representation of frontier heroism. In this way, the clips from previous movies do not merely show John Wayne, but actually stress the conventions of the Western that Wayne has happened to incarnate over the course of his long career. This not only shapes expectations about the character he will play in the present picture, but also gives us reason to expect that Wayne will play this kind of character again in the future. Importantly, these expectations are shaped less by Wayne's personal biography than by the films themselves.

Questions of which is a better movie aside, Andersen's death in *The Cowboys* is not afforded the significance of Books's in *The Shootist*, less because of the latter's credit sequence—which is really just a more explicit way of invoking the history of the Western genre—than because of the significance the later film has taken on in light of Wayne's death. With the knowledge that this would be the last of Wayne's frontier protagonists, *The Shootist* is often read as *the* end, rather than a possible end. The unfortunate effect of this kind of interpretation is that it tends to overshadow the film itself, which does an effective job on its own terms of conveying the finality of Books's situation—thanks in large measure to a superb performance by Wayne.

In a variation on a theme observed in each of Wayne's later pictures, Books is presented not simply as part of an older order, but as the last of that order. He has even outlived the historical personality on whom his character is based. After Carson City's undertaker offers Books his finest funeral services only "for the privilege," Books replies: "You're gonna do to me what they did to John Wesley Hardin. You're gonna lay me out, let the public come by and gawp at me for fifty cents a head, ten cents for the children. When the curiosity peters out you're gonna stuff me in a gunny sack and stick me in a hole while you hurry to the bank with your loot." Books has no surviving friends from the Civil War, no companions to speak admiringly of his courage. His past is spoken about mostly by those who were not there to experience it, so do not understand it.

Following Hostetler's counsel, Books resolves to die a death befitting a man of his courage. Death is a far more abstract villain than a land baron or cattle rustler, however, and so Books engineers a final confrontation between himself and three of Carson City's most notorious personalities: Jay Cobb (Bill McKinney), Gillom Rogers's boss at the town's dairy; Mike Sweeney (Richard Boone), a longtime resident of Carson City; and Jack Pulford (Hugh O'Brien), the faro dealer at the Metropole Saloon. His reasons for their selection vary. Books had a short verbal altercation with Cobb, who is routinely jailed for his brutality, upon his arrival in Carson City. The derisive Sweeney is an old acquaintance of sorts; as Books tells Bond, "I had some dealings with his brother Albert once." Finally, Pulford recently shot and a killed a man—at a distance of over eighty feet—who first took exception to Pulford's assertion that he "could have taken" Books and then proceeded to shoot first.

While the film provides patent motivation for Books's decision to die the way he lived, it is difficult not to conceive of the arranged final confrontation in mythic terms. At the start of the film, Books literally rides out of both the past and the wilderness and into the bustling streets of Carson City, where he determines to rid that nascent civilization of three of its more scandalous characters. In spite of this, Books is viewed by most of the town's residents as part of the problem rather than the solution. He is referred to as "bloodthirsty" and "savage," having no place in changing times. As Thibido, the town's marshal, tells him: "Once we're rid of people like you, we'll have a goddamn Garden of Eden here!"

The character of Pulford presents a challenge to conceiving of Books's final act as a symbolic purging of society's evils. Although his impressive feat of marksmanship is later recounted to Books by other characters, Pulford only appears once prior to the film's climactic shoot-out. While portrayed as confident in his abilities, he is nonetheless honorable in his actions: he fires second. Books's selection of Pulford can be seen as drawing on a tradition of gentlemanly rivalry in the Western genre where two skilled gunmen will inevitably cross paths—less to settle the question of right and wrong than the question of who is faster. When that final confrontation occurs, however, Pulford breaks the cardinal rule of Western good guys: he shoots first. After Books has dispensed with Cobb and

Sweeney, Pulford, rather than standing and challenging Books to a test of skill like we might expect, instead quickly fires and then ducks for cover. Not unlike the irony that belies the opening credits of *Big Jake,* Pulford's cowardice provides yet another example of how, in the later Wayne Westerns, the supposedly fixed conceptual boundary between savagery and civilization are undermined. It is Books, savage man of the past, who proves to be the civilized one. He is the one with the code to live by.

After Books kills Pulford, Gillom Rogers enters the saloon just before Books is shot in the back by the bartender—"revenge for all those shattered mirrors and wrecked saloons," as Philip French has said.[26] Gillom grabs one of Books's .45s and guns down the bartender. Books, bleeding to death on the floor, looks up at Gillom expectantly. Gillom looks to Books, and then to the gun in his hand. The music in the scene swells then goes silent. Gillom throws the pistol away. Books nods, then dies.

Books's approval of Gillom's final act indicates that, as in most of the other Wayne Westerns of the 1970s, knowledge has been passed successfully down from one generation to the next. Yet this legacy, involving a rejection of the way of the gun, is quite unlike those earlier instances. That a Western film would end with an explicit renunciation of violence is not uncommon, even if such assertions tend to be undermined by the fact that a large measure of nearly any Western's appeal is that very

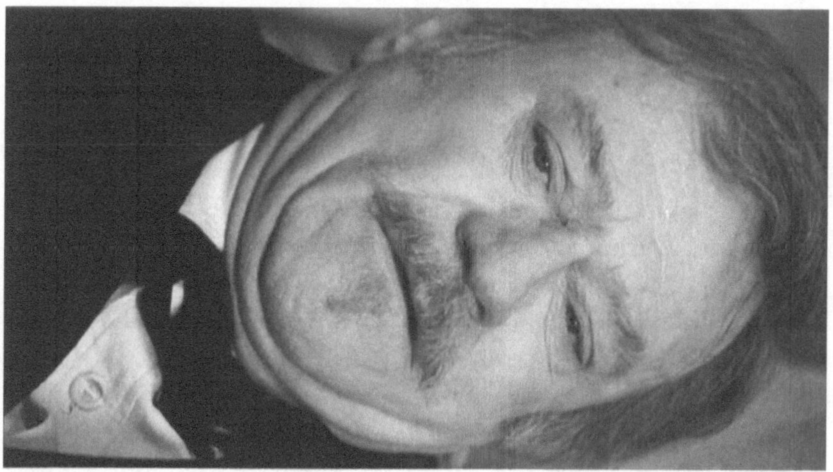

The death of J. B. Books in *The Shootist* (1976)

violence being renounced. There exists a long tradition of Western heroes who know their lifestyle should not be emulated. As Shane tells Joey after he rids the valley of hired guns: "There's no livin' with a killing." This does not necessarily mean, however, that Westerns that conclude in this way are intending to make larger points about the genre as a whole.

Books is unquestionably a heroic character, but unlike Chisum or Lane, he now finds himself alone in the world. Like McCandles, Andersen, and Cahill, he is offered a chance at redemption, to recapture what he has lost, but unlike those men his chance comes too late. His path has led to lying dead on a barroom floor, unceremoniously shot in the back by the bartender. This is not a legacy to be passed on to subsequent generations. As Books tells Gillom earlier in the film, "There's more to being a man than handling a gun." Removed from the knowledge of Wayne's terminal cancer, there is little reason to see this end as *the* end—for either the Western hero or the genre. It is simply one of any number of possible ends, the result of a selected deployment of the genre's conventions in a slightly new way.

The Western Hero Fights On

Wayne's were not the only Westerns of the time to emphasize the handing down of knowledge from one generation to the next. Director Henry Hathaway and producer Hal B. Wallis attempted, without much success, to recapture the magic of *True Grit* in *Shoot Out* (Henry Hathaway, 1971), which stars Gregory Peck as an outlaw just released from prison whose plans for revenge against his double-crossing former partners are complicated by the arrival of an 8-year-old girl who may be his daughter. Peck also played surrogate father to Desi Arnaz in *Billy Two Hats.* William Holden's characters find themselves paired with younger men in *The Revengers* and *Wild Rovers* (Blake Edwards, 1971), as do Glenn Ford in *Santee,* Charlton Heston in *The Last Hard Men,* and Richard Widmark in *Death of a Gunfighter.*

This theme is also present in the more favored Westerns of the time. The most engaging aspect of *Little Big Man* is Crabb's relationship with his adoptive grandfather, Old Lodge Skins, and we have also seen how *Ulzana's Raid* recasts the central pairing of greenhorn and veteran from

The Searchers, only tilting the balance in favor of the Burt Lancaster's wily scout. Another of Lancaster's pictures, *Lawman,* includes a subplot that has one of the villain's young hands, Crowe (Richard Jordan), come to grudgingly admire the outnumbered Marshal Maddox. This is the same relationship, very loosely based on Wyatt Earp and Billy Clanton, which is the focus of *Young Billy Young.*

In contrast, many of the most bleak, critical Westerns of the period are those in which there are few or no prospects for the perpetuation of the values of the Western hero. Many of these Westerns draw on conventional scenarios and iconography and then subvert them. In *Doc,* Holliday develops a friendship with Billy Clanton; he even gives Billy a shooting lesson. At the final confrontation at the O.K. Corral, Billy is left standing at the end. Holliday eyes him for a moment, then shoots him dead. When Earp asks why he killed the kid, Holliday replies, "I guess he reminded me of too many things." *McCabe & Mrs. Miller* introduces a minor character named Cowboy (Keith Carradine), an innocent range hand in chaps and a ten-gallon hat drawn to Presbyterian Church by the reputation of McCabe's whorehouse. During his enthusiastic visit there, he is mocked behind his back my Mrs. Miller's prostitutes because of the size of his penis. On his way out of town, Cowboy is murdered in cold blood by one of the gunmen hired by the mining company to kill McCabe. As Self notes, the "sudden and inexplicable killing violates the mythic code of the gunfight" and foreshadows the impending confrontation between McCabe and the three gunmen.[27] Not unlike McCabe, Cowboy is a character to be pitied, caught up in events beyond his control, saddled with a reputation as empty as his oversized hat.

Such pessimism is not limited to "revisionist" Westerns, however. Later in 1971, Carradine appeared as another nameless character—"Young Gunfighter," per the closing credits—in *A Gunfight* (Lamont Johnson, 1971). The movie is about a pair of aging gunmen, Will Tenneray and Abe Cross (Kirk Douglas and Johnny Cash), who agree to stage a duel before a large crowd in a bullfight arena across the border in Mexico, with proceeds from the ticket sales going to the winner. The young gunslinger arrives in town hoping to eliminate one of the two participants and take his place in the final duel. When Cross asks the stranger why he wants to fight, he replies, "Money. Same reason you want at each other." He succeeds in provoking Tenneray into a contest, but loses.

A trio of young would-be bank robbers suffers a similar fate in *The Spikes Gang* (Richard Fleischer, 1974). Gary Grimes plays Will, another pent-up youngster who with two friends (Ron Howard and Charles Martin Smith) embarks on a life of crime, falling in with charismatic outlaw Harry Spikes (Lee Marvin). Spikes eventually turns on the boys when offered a reward for their arrest, and in a final shootout Will kills Spikes. Gut-shot, Will stumbles outside and dies on a train platform. His final thoughts flash back to his friends and their naïve plans to conquer the West.

These films assert that the gunfighter's legacy is inseparable from his violent ways. "Young Gunfighter" in *A Gunfight* cannot apprehend that the way of the gun has led both Cross and Tenneray to a dead end, from which a final act of violence provides the only escape: the money to live out his remaining days in peace, or death. Harry Spikes proves there is no such thing as a noble outlaw. *McCabe & Mrs. Miller* demonstrates how even the accouterments of the gunfighter are enough to mark a man for death. Even with this pessimism and disillusionment, the message is still about the tragedy and ugliness of violence, and it is a message conveyed by playing off of familiar Western scenarios. A close consideration of how a given Western engages with conventions from the genre's history often reveals even greater complexities.

Perhaps the most famous off-screen story from the production of *The Shootist* involves the composition of the climactic shoot-out in the Metropole saloon. Although the exact details vary depending on who is recounting the incident, it generally goes something like this: because Wayne's illness forced him to be away from the set for extended periods of time, Siegel and the remainder of his cast had to shoot around Wayne as much as possible, including lensing portions of the final sequence that did not involve Books. Wayne was eventually able to return to work and film his parts of the movie's finale. When viewing the finished product, however, the Duke took exception to the portrayal of Cobb's death, which included a shot filmed in Wayne's absence: Cobb being shot by Books in the back. The degree to which Wayne objected, again, varies by source. Whether he simply stated that he did not do that in his pictures, or whether he cited the fact that he had starred in over one hundred films and never once shot a man in the back is ultimately uncertain. But what is certain is that the final product was changed in accordance with his wishes: Cobb dies after being shot in the chest.

This is certainly an evocative story. It suggests that not only was there a patently moral, core motivation behind Wayne's acting choices, but that that moral center could be interpreted as the difference between Wayne's Westerns and other films of the time. Wayne would not shoot a man in the back, whereas other anti-heroes of the 1970s would.

Biographies of John Wayne are filled with anecdotes like this, providing a tempting source of rhetorical ammunition that could be used to counter the kind of criticism—grounded in a more disparaging view of Wayne—encountered over the course of this chapter. Needless to say, selectively drawing on evidence because it presents Wayne in a favorable light would be more than a little hypocritical. Moreover, the productivity of using a more flattering abstraction of Wayne as a critical lens would prove just as questionable in the face of close analysis of the films.

The problem with the anecdote from *The Shootist* is that Wayne's characters have, in fact, shot men in the back. The first example to spring to mind would likely be *The Man Who Shot Liberty Valance*—although Wayne apologists would likely contend, with merit, that Doniphon shot Valance not in the back but in the side. A better example comes from *The Searchers.* Midway through the film, Edwards shoots and kills three men attempting to ambush him and Martin. Any doubt as to where he hit them is erased later in the film, when Captain Clayton (Ward Bond) tells Edwards: "The fact that all three of them was shot in the back was the only thing that raised some question." That a Western hero played by John Wayne would shoot a man in the back is certainly unexpected, but this transgression has an important function. In *The Searchers,* much of the complexity of Edwards's character comes from how he varyingly upholds and violates our expectations about the how the conventional Western hero will behave. *The Shootist,* by contrast, places great emphasis on the gentlemanly code of the Western hero, and it is for this reason—less than because of Wayne's acting history—that we expect Books to face his adversaries head on.

The more general point to be made here is a caution against the use of generalized models as starting points for examining films, as opposed to beginning with the films themselves. When Wayne's political personality is not used to explain the Wayne Western's divergence from other Westerns of their time, the recourse is frequently to an accustomed interpretive schemata that posits the Western as articulating the conflict between binary oppositions: savagery and civilization, wilderness and society, west and east, past and present, and so on. The justification for such a methodology is made on cultural grounds, where the recurrence of certain themes and meanings is taken as a form of collective response, reflecting the American zeitgeist. At this point, though, we may question whether the recurrent detection of the same meanings is not due to the recurrent use of the same critical models.

While many of the later Wayne Westerns do include elements suggestive of the oppositions listed above, a close analysis of the films reveals them to be functioning quite unlike we would expect based on those interpretive schemata. Contrary to critical models that conceive of the Western hero's tragic role as vanquishing a savagery that threatens the establishment of society—a society in which the hero cannot himself be a part of—the later Wayne Westerns, like most Westerns of the time, are about continuity across perceived boundaries. As the credit ballad from *Chisum* tells us, for the heroes of the later Western, "the fight keeps goin' on." There is a place for the Western hero in changing times, because the values he embodies will always be needed, even *after* he is dead and gone. As such, the legacy must be passed down to successive generations.

6

To the '80s, and Beyond!

> There was a director who was lauded with an Academy Award and called an artist, and then turns around and makes a movie that *The New York Times* said was about as exciting as touring your own living room. . . . [T]hat casts a giant pall on the idea of the director as the creative captain of the ship.
>
> —John Carpenter, on Michael Cimino

> Cimino accomplishes nothing in *Heaven's Gate* that was not accomplished already, with more facility, in Walter Hill's *The Long Riders*.
>
> —Jay Scott, *The Globe and Mail,* April 25, 1981

> The society which enjoyed the Western believed in itself. The society which devours *Star Wars* is frightened and desperate.
>
> —Will Wright, 1982

Most notions about the Western's evolution toward a period of self-conscious formalism and critical revisionism in the 1970s do not hold when considering the films in their generic and historical contexts. Furthermore, the limitations of the concept of the revisionist Western are evident when we consider the number of Westerns from the 1970s that have been excluded from film history because they don't fit the revisionist paradigm. Hypothetically, though, it is possible to construct an alternative account of the Western during this same period. This alternate version takes the following into account:

- the genre's greatest star, John Wayne, wins an Academy Award in 1969 and continues to star in Westerns for the next eight years, most of which are more popular with audiences than contemporaneous "revisionist" offerings;
- Burt Kennedy and Andrew V. McLaglen are the most prolific Western filmmakers;
- other classic Western actors like Burt Lancaster, Gregory Peck, Henry Fonda, and Kirk Douglas continue to star in Westerns;
- and an arguably "traditional" Western about Jesse James is number one at the box office its opening weekend in 1980.

The Long Riders

The Long Riders, directed by Walter Hill, opened on May 16, 1980, earning $2.3 million in rentals over its first three days in release.[1] In a clever feat of casting, real-life siblings play the various brothers that comprised the James–Younger Gang. James and Stacy Keach, who also co-wrote the screenplay, star as Jesse and Frank James; David, Keith, and Robert Carradine play Cole, Jim, and Bob Younger; Dennis and Randy Quaid play Ed and Clell Miller; and Christopher and Nicholas Guest play Charlie and Bob Ford. The episodic narrative follows the members of the gang as they balance various robberies with family and personal life, disband, and then reform for the doomed job in Northfield, Minnesota. They are pursued without success by agents of the Pinkerton Detective Agency, whose actions, including the accidental murder of Jesse and Frank's younger brother, only increase sympathy for the outlaws.

In contrast to the earlier portrayals of Jesse James, here the legendary bandit is presented as a quiet, noble protagonist—yet one whose motivations are never made entirely clear to us, thus leaving the matter of his heroism open to question. This is, perhaps, to be expected from a movie described in its theatrical trailer with the ambiguous line, "This is the story of the James–Younger gang, and it's as close to truth as legends can ever be."

At the beginning of the film, after Ed Miller nearly botches a bank robbery by getting Jesse shot, he is kicked out of the gang. When Ed asks why, Jesse angrily snaps back, "Panickin' and shootin' innocent folks! And for goddamn getting' me near killed!" A concern for innocent life is the hallmark of an honorable bandit, but it is not clear in this scene whether Jesse is more upset about the threat to innocent bystanders or to himself. Later, Jesse speaks of his outlaw activities in the context of needing to support his family, but mentions little else—not the Civil War or the plight of the South. In an early scene, Clell Miller gives a matter-of-fact account of the gang's inception to an admiring prostitute: "We was all in the war. Robbed our first Yankee bank 'cause we didn't know no better. Seemed like a good idea at the time. After that we was . . . just in the habit. So I guess we'll just keep on 'a going till they lock us up 'n hang us." *The Long Riders* makes a point of emphasizing that it is the youngest member of the group, Bob Younger, who has the most veneration for the Southern cause despite never having formally fought for it. Bob is not held up to any ridicule for his enthusiasm, however, either by other characters in the movie or by the narration. He is shown to be just as capable as the other members of the gang, and just as cognizant of the realities of violence and gunplay. This is typical of the movie, which balances attention to detail—from period atmosphere to the minutiae of interpersonal relationships—with a kind of moral detachment. By virtue of it being about Jesse James, *The Long Riders* sides with the outlaws, but the gang's pursuers are not depicted as corrupt or vindictive. Just as other characters in the film never question the outlaw activities of the Jameses and Youngers, the narration too refrains from passing judgment.

The Long Riders also displays arguably the largest degree of genre consciousness of any cinematic James story before or since. The climactic, failed robbery of the First National Bank of Northfield is a telling example. The sequence features an overtly stylized depiction of violence highly reminiscent of the Westerns of Sam Peckinpah. Quickly cut footage of the outlaws desperately trying to escape the town is interspersed with slow-motion shots of the gang members being bloodily slashed by bullets.

Yet present in equal measure, and not incongruously, are devices we can recognize from much earlier Westerns, including Henry King's *Jesse James* from 1939. During the aftermath of the failed bank robbery, *The Long Riders* reproduces the slow-motion spectacle of riders on horseback

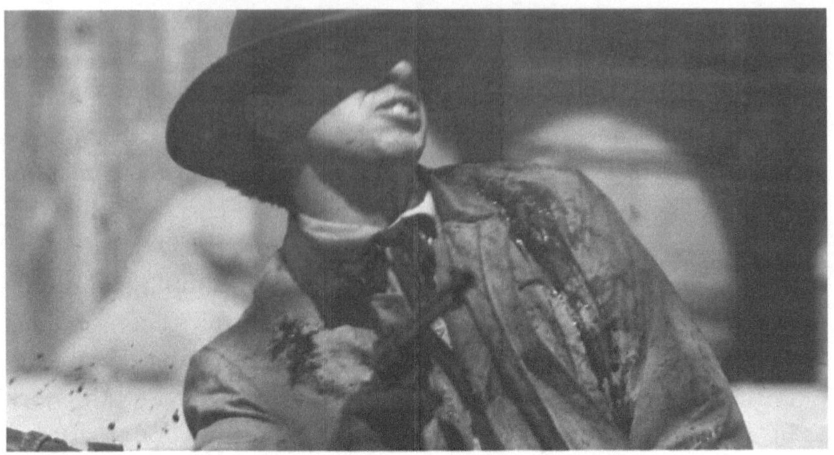

The bank robbery goes wrong in *The Long Riders* (1980)

crashing through a shop window. Jesse meets his demise in the picture in familiar fashion—shot in the back by the coward Robert Ford—but the representation of the act, with Ford appearing to shoot directly at the camera, draws not only on myth, but a far earlier act of screen violence: the assassination of the audience at the end of Porter's *The Great Train Robbery.*

Considered in concert with the picture's relative dispassion towards the events and characters it portrays, this attention to crafting visually fluid sequences that maximize the mise-en-scène and exploit genre conventions could suggest that *The Long Riders* is ultimately a shallow film. A lack of character development certainly affects the movie in negative ways. The famous antagonism between Jesse and Cole, for example, does not so much build as simply appear when the gang reunites to plan the Northfield raid. The charge of superficiality is also likely to bring to mind other Westerns we have examined, like *The Culpepper Cattle Co.* and *Doc,* which similarly devoted considerable attention to Western convention and period detail. Those films, however, intend to criticize the Western (and make larger political points). This is not the case in *The Long Riders*

The movie's narrative does have a "greatest hits" quality. We see the gang raiding a bank, robbing a stagecoach, holding up a train; the failed Northfield raid and its aftermath, as Frank and Jesse escape while the Younger brothers are apprehended; and, finally, Jesse's death at the hands

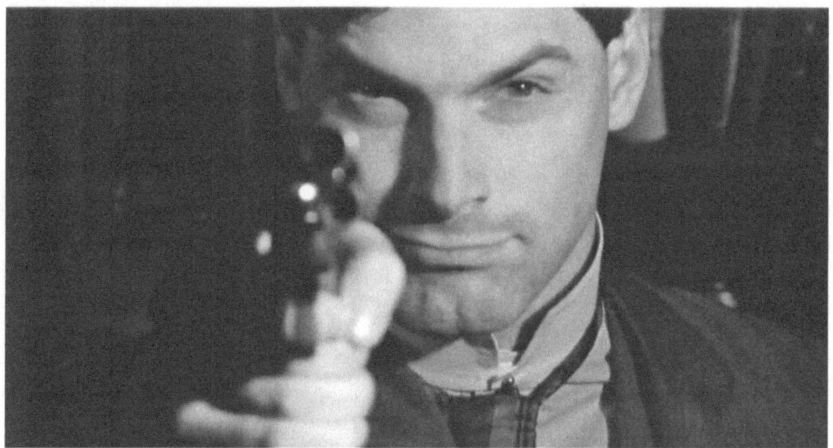

Bob Ford shoots Jesse James, and us, in *The Long Riders* (1980)

of the Fords. In contrast to earlier Jesse James movies that cover the same terrain, *The Long Riders* is decidedly lacking in exposition. Just as judgment is withheld, so is the kind of contextualizing information—dates, places—common to Westerns, especially those that make claims to be more historically accurate than those that came before. The opening credits appear over a series of slow-motion shots of the outlaw gang riding through green hills. At the conclusion of the sequence, the following title appears: "Missouri after the Civil War . . ." The imprecision of this title not only sets the standard for the remainder of the film, but also stands in stark contrast to information conveyed by the opening credits of many other Westerns. In a way, *The Long Riders* preempts attempts to equate updates with "corrections," as if earlier cinematic representations of James and other frontier heroes were somehow "wrong." At the same time, it also resists making direct connections to elements of the James mythology—that is, Jesse James as the last rebel of the Civil War, or the Robin Hood of the Ozarks. This makes *The Long Riders* the rare Western that not only acknowledges the distinction between myth and history, but also the distinction between history and truth.

As for the movie's invocation of genre conventions, we would be ill advised to immediately interpret this kind of referencing as a symptom of self-consciousness rather than an instance of the cyclical play of repetition and variation that we have observed in every other Western examined to this point. Indeed, it would make little sense to read a dramatic, updated restaging of certain iconic scenes as desperation and not say the same, or worse, about a 1957 film that incorporates entire sequences from a movie released in 1939.

Some critics who gave *The Long Riders* positive notices nevertheless questioned whether the modern moviegoer's unfamiliarity with the Western would work to the movie's detriment. The review in *The Washington Post* connected this concern to larger questions about the vitality of the genre:

> The catch is that I suspect that only moviegoers with a deep regard for western lore and classic western moviemaking will be drawn to the film's graceful, revealing authenticity and then strongly impressed by it. Hill has certainly brought pictorial class to this project without obscuring or romanticizing the characters. For all one knows, *The Long Riders* is destined to take its place among the most respected examples of the genre. What it doesn't seem to do is transcend the genre. Will it appeal to people who usually ignore westerns? Highly unlikely. And if it doesn't, westerns will continue in their current state of eclipse.[2]

How valid are these concerns? An awareness of the conventional nature of the film is not necessary to comprehend or enjoy it, and as much as the references to earlier movies are intentional, it would make little sense for a movie released in 1980 to suppose its audience all shared the same knowledge of the Western—especially a knowledge of movies going back forty years. The sight of riders crashing through a shop window makes for a spectacular scene, and the image of an outlaw pointing his gun at us still retains a certain power, despite our sophisticated awareness of motion picture conventions. The matter of the movie's "appeal" is harder to address with any certainty. That a genre's success depends on the ability of a given film to "transcend" that genre may seem like a paradox, but, as we shall see, it reflects recent developments in the American film industry.

Although a marginal film today, *The Long Riders* was supposed to mark the beginning of a Western revival—a revival that, sadly, did not come to pass.

"The Hollywood Western Rides into Favor Again"

That was the headline gracing the front page of the Arts section of the *New York Times* on Sunday, June 8, 1980. "[A]fter a recent dry spell when it seemed headed for the last roundup," writes Miles Beller in the accompanying article, "the western is staging a remarkable comeback." The year 1980 had already seen the release of two Westerns, *The Long Riders* and *Tom Horn,* and two more, *Heaven's Gate* and *The Legend of the Lone Ranger,* were due out before the end of the year. According to Beller, even more Westerns were on the horizon: a return of the Cisco Kid, possibly to star television's Erik Estrada; *The Desperadoes,* about outlaw Emmet Dalton; a new Sam Peckinpah effort called *The Texans; Cattle Annie and Little Britches,* about "two teen-agers who sign on with the Dalton Gang"; and an untitled project at Warner Bros. for which Beller, likely quoting the studio's publicity, offers a vague description: "a fast-paced period piece, complete with two heroes and a villain."

That the release of four or five films in a given year could constitute a "remarkable comeback" for the genre implies that even fewer, or perhaps no, Westerns were released in the preceding years. The most recent, pre-"comeback" Western cited by the *Times* article is the parody *Blazing Saddles,* released in 1974. At that point the genre had become, according to Beller, a "cheap joke," its "cowboys and gunslingers too ridiculous to be taken seriously." While, on reexamination, Mel Brooks's Western farce is mediocre and ham-fisted, it was very popular at the time, and remained the highest-earning Western ever released until the arrival of *Dances with Wolves* in 1990. That the most successful Western ever could come at a time when production of Westerns was in serious decline supports the notion that the genre was no longer taken seriously by audiences, so the one way to make a successful Western would be to play to those sentiments. The success of *Blazing Saddles* also supports theories of genre evolution, where parody is the final stage of a genre's development before its death.

This account both overstates the impact of *Blazing Saddles* and misrepresents Western production during the 1970s. While it is well known that production of Westerns dropped from the early 1960s onward, Hollywood never stopped making theatrical Westerns outright. The trend throughout the 1970s was decreasing production, but *Blazing Saddles* did not signal any kind of turning point. Some Westerns released after *Blazing Saddles* were comedies, but they failed to replicate that movie's appeal, and those that were marginally popular, like *The Duchess and the Dirtwater Fox* (Melvin Frank, 1976) and *The Villain* (Hal Needham, 1979), are dreadful. More importantly, by any measure detailed in chapter 2, Western productions actually *increased* in 1975 and 1976 before declining again in the final years of the decade. In particular, 1976—the year of America's Bicentennial—saw the release of a number of notable Westerns, including *The Shootist* and *The Outlaw Josey Wales.* Without discounting either the ridiculousness or cheapness of *Blazing Saddles,* it is likely that *New York Times* readers even casually familiar with the genre would have been able to name at least a couple of Westerns released in the intervening years.

In general, the number of Westerns produced over the latter half of the 1970s makes 1980's total of four Westerns appear, at least numerically, to be less a revival than consistent with current production levels. Why, then, did these new Westerns seem like a return to form?

The question at the heart of the *Times* article is, "Why, in the 1980s, is the classic Hollywood western staging a comeback?" The answers, from respondents including a literary scholar, an actor, a psychologist, and a Western novelist, are cultural. Americans were tired of the "malaise" that resulted from the introspection and self-criticism of the past two decades, which had produced a certain type of Western. "During the activist, protest-filled late 1960's and early 1970's, producers and directors tried breathing new life into westerns by making them 'socially relevant commentaries.' Films like *Little Big Man* reworked the established conventions, railing against oppression of minorities (Indians) by the brutish military-industrial complex of cavalry, bankers, railroad tycoons and Federal bureaucrats." Now, Americans were looking to the past for inspiration and to reclaim "basic values." This change in cultural mood is reflected not only in the resurgence of the Western, but in the type of Western being made. It is not simply the Western that was returning, but the "classic, old-style, action-packed" Western.

The only dissenting voice to the cultural explanation is Walter Hill, director of *The Long Riders.* For him, the return of the Western owes less to cultural relevance or Hollywood's interest in the genre than a concern for *who* is making Westerns.

> What studio executives do find alluring about the current crop of westerns, he says, is the talent behind them. "They know *The Warriors* and *Alien* were successful films," says Mr. Hill (a coauthor and director of *The Warriors* and a producer of *Alien.*) "So when the studio (United Artists) saw I was involved with *The Long Riders,* a western, they nonetheless were receptive." The fact that Michael Cimino's *The Deer Hunter* did well at the box office, adds Mr. Hill, was doubtless a key factor in the decision by United Artists to back Mr. Cimino's big budget western, *Heaven's Gate.*

Whatever the reason for its return, in 1980 the future of the Western was bright. As Beller concludes, "The noble cowboy—the durable embodiment of an art form that seems destined to survive as long as America—is coming back, his moral convictions still unshaken."

Looked at today, the article is a fascinating historical document. For one, it is indicative of the fluid boundaries between scholarly and popular writing about movie genres, the Western in particular. Although argued less forcefully than in scholarly criticism, Beller's article nevertheless articulates a number of the fundamental ideas about the Western that persist to this day: the genre is quintessentially American, responds to and reflects changes in American culture, and is the product of important filmmakers.

The article is also part of a trend in commentaries on the Western, which we could call the "Western is back!" article. While its less optimistic counterpart, the "Western is dead" exposé, is more common, comparable examples of articles touting the Western's return can be found throughout the subsequent decades: in the mid-1980s, after the release of *Silverado* (Lawrence Kasdan, 1985) and *Pale Rider* (Clint Eastwood, 1985); in the mid-1990s, after the Academy Award-winning successes of *Dances with Wolves* and *Unforgiven;* and in the mid-2000s, with the debut of the acclaimed television series *Deadwood* (2004–2006) as well as theatrical Westerns *Open Range* (Kevin Costner, 2004), *The Assassination of Jesse James by the Coward Robert Ford* (Andrew Dominik, 2007), and the remake of *3:10 to Yuma* (James Mangold, 2007). Of these three comebacks, the 1990s revival proved most legitimate, but production of Westerns again waned at the end of the decade. As was the case in 1980, each of these "comebacks" proved short-lived at best and illusory at worst.

Four Westerns were ultimately released in 1980. *The Legend of the Lone Ranger* (William A. Fraker) was plagued by production problems and delayed until 1981, but another picture not mentioned in the *Times* article, *The Mountain Men* (Richard Lang) with Charlton Heston, was released in June of 1980. Of the five future features mentioned by the article, only one, *Cattle Annie and Little Britches* (Lamont Johnson) was made. It was released, briefly, in 1981, bringing that year's Western total to two.

That the 1980 comeback failed to resuscitate the Western comes as no surprise to us today, of course, given the disastrous and well-documented fate of 1980's fourth and final Western, *Heaven's Gate.* Given complete artistic control by United Artists over what was initially envisioned as a modest Western about the Johnson County War, Michael Cimino, the movie's meticulous and temperamental director, went ridiculously over time and budget, shooting a million and a half feet of film, firing crewmembers at will, and tearing down million-dollar sets for no discernable reason. Cimino first delivered to the studio a five-hour version of the movie, which he was convinced to reduce to three-and-a-half hours. Intended for a prestige roadshow release, *Heaven's Gate* was so poorly received that the studio promptly withdrew it. A 149-minute cut of the movie released in 1981 fared no better. The movie's failure led to the sale of United Artists by Transamerica Corporation to MGM in 1981, effectively bringing to an end the independent studio formed by Mary Pickford, Charles Chaplin, Douglas Fairbanks, and D. W. Griffith in 1919.[3]

The failure of *Heaven's Gate* is held to mark the end of a period of profound creativity in the American film industry, when a generation of young filmmakers took advantage of new artistic freedoms to produce innovative, boundary-breaking movies influenced by European art cinema, many of which took up the cause of reexamining the genres, stories, and themes of classical Hollywood. The most famous example of this reexamination is the revisionist Western, which, it is argued, became the dominant form of the genre during the period. As such, when *Heaven's Gate* brought the Hollywood Renaissance to an end, the Western went with it.

This account is not entirely inaccurate, but what truth is there requires a great deal of context. As a force in Hollywood, the art cinema movement reached its apogee in the mid-1970s, after which it declined as an even younger group of filmmakers ushered in a new era of high-concept, front-loaded blockbusters: the "New Hollywood." Thomas Schatz describes this transition by remarking that, while Francis Ford Coppola was in the Philippines filming *Apocalypse Now*, a "brilliant though self-indulgent, self-destructive venture of Wellsian proportions," his protégés George Lucas and Steven Spielberg were refining a new aesthetic of visceral thrills and technical polish, "replacing the director-as-author with a director-as-superstar ethos."[4] John Belton observes that as Hollywood's filmmakers became younger, their audience grew younger still. The result, he argues, was a cinema that was stylistically youthful but politically conservative:

> Exploitation-type genre films continued to dominate the marketplace, but in the 1970s they cost much more to make and much more was at risk if they failed. As a result, their potential for subversive statements had been severely restricted. If, in the late 1960s and early 1970s, the counterculture had struck back, then by the mid-1970s it found itself seriously compromised by changes in the marketplace, which heralded yet another turn in the revolutionary progress of the cinema.[5]

Looked at this way, *Heaven's Gate* was out of step with contemporary cinema not only artistically but also politically. This may have contributed to adverse response to the film. Christian Keathly comments: "It seems likely that much of the negative press that greeted *Heaven's Gate* on its release was due, in part, to the fact that the film revisited themes that many viewers and critics simply no longer wanted to face. The blockbuster cycle was well underway, and there was every initial indication that Cimino's film would participate in the cultural rebuilding of American ideological confidence."[6] To anyone who has seen it, the idea that *Heaven's Gate* could have in any way have been an exercise in rebuilding ideological confidence will seem absurd.

Shot by cinematographer Vilmos Zsigmond, the movie is visually stunning, making extensive use of magic hour photography and taking full advantage of the natural beauty of its Montana shooting locations. Paradoxically, the film's portrait of nineteenth century life is exceedingly bleak. The story pits Marshal Jim Averill (Kris Kristofferson) against a consortium of businessmen led by cattle baron Frank Canton (Sam

Waterston), who, with the support of the Wyoming government, have drafted a "death list" of suspected cattle rustlers and hired bounty hunters to execute them. The "rustlers" are really starving, oppressed immigrants from eastern Europe, but because the government has sided with big business, neither they nor Averill stand a chance. As Keathly goes on to note, it is hard to imagine a less reassuring Hollywood film than *Heaven's Gate.*

With that said, the Beller *New York Times* piece confirms that at least some people expected the movie to be a "classic" Western, upholding basic American values and affirming the moral code of the cowboy. This was, after all, a film whose promotional poster featured Kristofferson and co-star Isabelle Huppert enrobed in an American flag below the tagline, "The only thing greater than their passion for America . . . was their passion for each other." Moreover, such expectations conform to the account of the emerging New Hollywood given by Belton, where controversial or subversive subject matter became a box office liability—explaining the felt imperative to misrepresent the film's subject matter in its advertising. The foundering of *Heaven's Gate* thus takes on a political dimension, wherein the movie contravened not only industrial and aesthetic trends, but ideological ones as well. It is this final incongruity that later critics find most appealing about the film—a "$36 million critique of frontier capitalism," as Cook calls it, at a time when capitalism was on the comeback.[7]

Interest in *Heaven's Gate* increased throughout the 1980s after the wide dissemination of Cimino's 219-minute cut of the film, famously first shown on Z Channel, a Los Angeles-area pay cable station, in 1983, and then released commercially on VHS by MGM. One of the first, and still the most famous, scholarly endeavors to recover and vindicate the film was Robin Wood's 1986 essay, "Heaven's Gate Reopened."[8] Hailing the film as a masterpiece, Wood found the movie's culture prescience noteworthy: "The tragic statement the film offers, while concerned with choices and failures in the distant (and largely mythical) American past, takes on particular resonance in the context of the Reagan administration, with its shameless bolstering of the rich camouflaged and given spurious validity by its 'moral' crusade: the present political context makes Cimino's conception of the film, some years ago, curiously prophetic."[9]

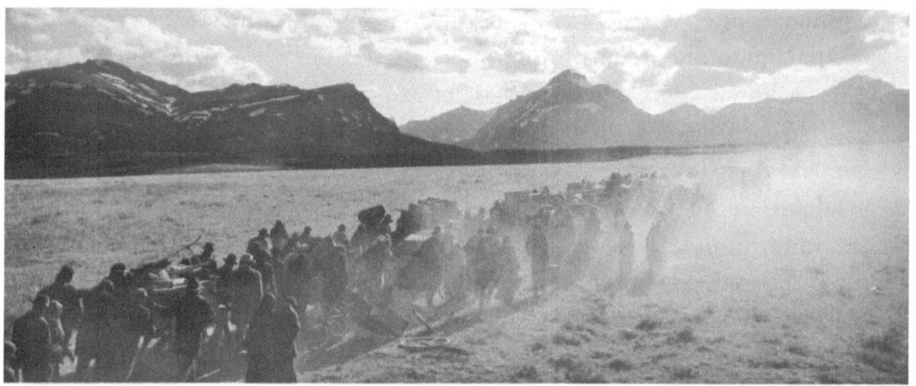

Impoverished European immigrants make their way across the American west in *Heaven's Gate* (1980)

Although Wood addresses the ways in which *Heaven's Gate* responds to Western conventions, in particular the representation of community, appreciations of the film within the specific context of the Western would not come until the 1990s—after the genre had "come back," thereby exonerating *Heaven's Gate* of the crime of "killing" the Western. Kitses writes that *Heaven's Gate* was "a disaster not because it silenced the form during the years of crimes and misdemeanors presided over by Ronald Reagan, the most prominent Western actor-auteur of them all, but because it failed to realize its epic, post-modern, revisionist vision."[10] As a Western, then, the failure of *Heaven's Gate* is neither commercial nor critical, but aspirational—which is understandable, perhaps, given that by this point the revisionist Western was supposedly crashing against the bulwark of 1980s conservatism.[11]

The roping of the Western's fortunes to larger cultural forces is no less problematic when explaining the genre's failures than when accounting for its successes. In this case, the distinction between the Hollywood Renaissance and the New Hollywood—and any broader cultural forces we could associate with each—is less clear than the terminology suggests. We have already seen that the two periods in fact overlap, but *Heaven's Gate* is not simply a vestige of the older order. It is also a product of the newer one. As much as the financial logic and aesthetic of the blockbuster marked certain changes in Hollywood production, the authorial cachet afforded to key figures like Spielberg and Lucas was an outgrowth of the Hollywood Renaissance. As Geoff King observes, in ceding control to

Cimino, United Artists was "using the status of the [director] as part of its strategy to design and promote prestigious blockbuster productions. This backfired, especially in the case of *Heaven's Gate.*"[12]

If *Heaven's Gate* made little sense as a viable blockbuster production, it made even less sense as a Western. A look at the types of Westerns produced in the twenty years preceding *Heaven's Gate* reveals a poor track record for films with "epic" aspirations, which also suggests that the picture, true to the essence of the blockbuster, was intended to transcend the boundaries of any one genre. With the notable exception of 1962's *How the West Was Won,* in the 1960s no Western released with a running time that approached or exceeded 2½ hours had been a critical or commercial hit. The list of notable failures includes *Cimmaron* (Anthony Mann, 1960), *Cheyenne Autumn, Hallelujah Trail* (John Sturges, 1965), and *Custer of the West* (Robert Siodmak, 1967). The lengthy Westerns *Paint Your Wagon* and *Little Big Man* were among the highest-earning movies in their respective release years, but each was an expensive production. *Little Big Man* just broke even, while *Paint Your Wagon* lost money. With regards to both cost and running time, many of the Westerns that followed were considerably leaner.[13]

The failure of *Heaven's Gate* certainly contributed in some way to the Western's subsequent hibernation. The Westerns released to cinemas in 1981 were produced in 1979 with the intention of an earlier release date. Two minor Westerns of note, *Barbarosa* (Fred Schepisi), starring country singer Willie Nelson, and *The Grey Fox* (Phillip Borsos), were released in 1982, but no Westerns appeared in either 1983 or 1984. We have already seen, however, that Western production had already been reduced to only a handful of pictures annually in the final years of the 1970s, so it is not as though the failure of *Heaven's Gate* extinguished a vibrant segment of Hollywood's output.

The same grand theories that account for the advent of the revisionist Western also explain the genre's wane: as the failure of the frontier myth to resolve contemporary societal conflicts in the face of cultural change; the end-point of an intrinsic evolutionary process; or the rise of new moviemakers only interested in using the genre as a vehicle for social commentary. Although the Western's quiescence is taken as proof that revisionism—in the sense of critiquing the genre's mythology or allegorically condemning present-day injustices—is the harbinger of death for movie genres, by this point we know better. The methodological parameters of each theory are actually blinders, first restricting our purview to a small selection of movies and then directing our focus to particular aspects of each. Nevertheless, the appeal of the revisionist account, with its privileging of social relevance and celebrated filmmakers, is such that rebuttals to the equation of genre revision with a genre's death never involve widening the scope of inquiry to include Westerns that fall outside the revisionist canon (and, we may suspect, the sympathies of the critic). Instead, the favored tactic that we have encountered is to argue that, when the Western does eventually return, especially in the 1990s, it is *still* the revisionist Western. There is, however, an alternative approach that involves going outside the genre—and all the way to a galaxy far, far away.

Blame the Russians

In *Toy Story 2* (John Lasseter, 1999), cowboy doll Woody learns that he—or, more precisely, the character whom he represents in toy form—was once the star of "Woody's Roundup," a popular children's television series of the 1950s. The fictional show's status as a cultural phenomenon, established by a range of tie-in merchandise and magazine covers, is clearly based on *The Howdy Doody Show* (1947–1960), but the program itself, a self-contained play of marionettes without any visible human actors, is more like *Four Feather Falls* (1960), a short-lived series produced by Gerry Anderson, who would go on to create *Thunderbirds* (1965–1966) and other popular "Supermarionation" television programs.

Surrounded by relics of his former glory, Woody watches the series with delight, right up to a dramatic cliffhanger ending that promises to be concluded in the next episode, titled "Woody's Finest Hour." When Woody asks where the next tape is, he is told there is none—the series was cancelled. The reason? As worded by his co-star Stinky Pete, "Two words: Sput nik. Once the astronauts went up, children only wanted to play with *space toys.*"

This example from *Toy Story 2* is a rather obvious segue to a consideration of the relationship between the Western and science fiction. That the latter "replaced" the former in the 1970s as the genre exemplifying

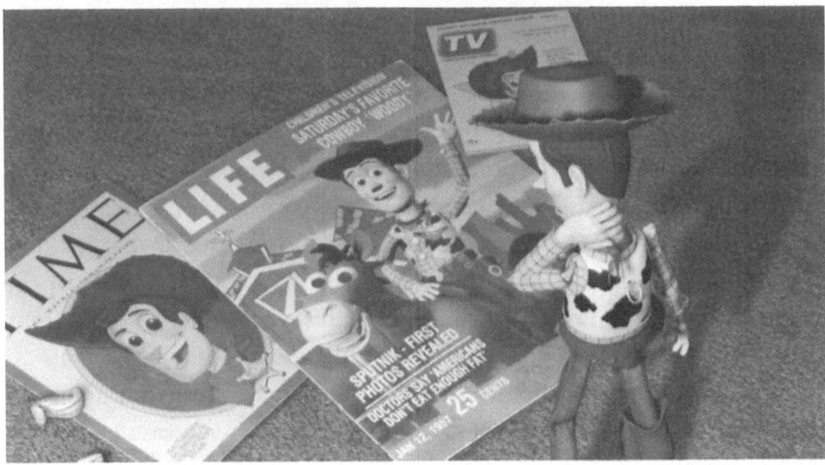

Cowboy toy Woody confronts his past in *Toy Story 2* (1999)

the American character is a well-worn argument, often reasoned using the same kinds of cultural and ideological thinking commonly applied to the Western. The following excerpt from a study of science fiction is a good example:

> During the 1970s, when the Western was in a rapid demise, films like *Star Wars* (1977) offered the USA a new way forward, a new sense of destiny. It was a way of rearranging, if not rewriting, its national mythology in the same forward-looking way as the Western, but in a new arena, one not tied to historical detail. The cultural earthquakes of the 1960s reverberated through [science fiction] as much as any other genre, but not to the same destructive degree as in the Western. So, while the Western collapsed in the 1970s, science fiction inspired the big screen.[14]

Following this line of thought, we could trace the end of the Western back to the dawn of the Space Age. The young adults who abandoned the movie Western in the late 1960s and 1970s were presumably the children who traded in their six-shooters and Howdy Doody dolls for ray guns and space helmets in the late 1950s and early 1960s.

That they so willingly did so has led a number of critics to refine claims about the Western being superseded by science fiction into the Western strongly influencing, or even *becoming,* science fiction, wherein the mythical frontier of American history is transposed, along with its ideological significance, into outer space—the final frontier. It is common to argue that, along with the urban police action movie, the science fiction film succeeded the Western in the great chain of genre, being—as pioneers and gun-slinging heroes set their sights on the "final frontier"—a reflection of changing preoccupations in American society that began in the 1950s with the escalation of the Cold War and the ensuing "space race" between the United States and the Soviet Union. As Barry Keith Grant writes in *Film Genre: From Iconography to Ideology* (2007), "The western myth survives within a different genre, one with a technological iconography rather than a pastoral one, perhaps because it is more relevant to our daily experience."[15] No less than the two most popular science fiction franchises in modern times are often cited as proof of this lineage: *Star Trek,* described by creator Gene Roddenberry as "*Wagon Train* in space," and *Star Wars,* with its galactic gunfighters and rescue narrative inspired by *The Searchers.*[16]

The Western-to-science-fiction argument also provides an answer to why the traditional or classic Western failed to return in the 1980s, despite its apparent sympathies with the prevailing cultural climate. The Western was too far removed from "daily experience"; its situation in the historical past, ambivalence about technology, and emphasis on community were at odds with the dynamism, technophilia, and individualism of the day. Not all critics were positive about this state of affairs. Will Wright agrees with the general premise that the Western lives on in the "space opera" of *Star Wars* and *The Empire Strikes Back* (Irvin Kershner, 1982), but observes crucial differences that he finds troubling because of what they say about contemporary American society. In these films, oppressive technology and bureaucracy are represented as pervasive and all-powerful, and the only possible form of resistance is a greater mystical force—both a problem and solution that are alien to the concerns of the Western.

> It seems that the only upbeat, heroic imagery available to us today must involve fantasy and religion, paranoia, and escape. . . . It is the imagery of dreams, of transcendence, and it suggests that collectively we are increasingly ready to have a great power look after us,

> for we no longer feel capable of doing it ourselves. Nineteen eighty-four is almost upon us, and perhaps the brave new world will not require either systematic tyranny or daily drugs for its order. Perhaps the fantasies inspired by our social fears will finally succeed in separating understanding and allegiance from reality.[17]

From either a hopeful or despondent perspective on science fiction's succession of the Western, it is still (as in theories that restrict themselves to the Western) cultural change that effects alterations and revisions in movie genres. Consider, though, how all of these positions rely on the same simplified social history of the United States in the 1980s, emphasizing features like technological innovation, consumerism, conservatism, and nostalgia for the 1950s.

This is to be expected, given that most symptomatic readings of the revisionist Western also rely on streamlined conceptions of the preceding decades. Here the argument is no more persuasive, although it is likely to displease liberals just as much as conservatives. Taking the line of reasoning to its logical end, we can conclude that it was the Soviets who were ultimately responsible for both inaugurating and finalizing the Western's decline: the launch of Sputnik in 1957, and the election in 1980 of Ronald Reagan, who had his sights set on the "bear in the woods."

Grant finds support for the Western-to-sci-fi lineage in a genre theory that does not depend on symptomatic cultural interpretation: the semantic/syntactic approach to genre developed by Rick Altman. Altman distinguishes between semantic approaches that emphasize a genre's iconographic and conventional "building blocks" and syntactic approaches that privilege the narrative and thematic "structures" into which those blocks are arranged. To insist on one approach to the exclusion of the other is, according to Altman, to ignore the dual nature of any generic corpus.

> For every film that participates actively in the elaboration of a genre's syntax there are numerous others content to deploy in no particular relationship the elements traditionally associated with the genre. We need to recognize that not all genre films relate to their genre in the same way or to the same extent. By simultaneously accepting semantic and syntactic notions of genre we avail

> ourselves of a possible way to deal critically with differing levels of 'genericity.' In addition, a dual approach permits a far more accurate description of the numerous intergeneric connections typically suppressed by single-minded approaches.[18]

Citing Altman's claim that the Western's durability as a popular genre owes to its establishment of a notably coherent syntax, Grant concludes that the "successful transformation of the western into the imagery of science fiction would seem to be a case in point."[19]

Altman, however, frames the relationship between the Western and science fiction within the development of the latter: a movie genre initially defined by a stable semantics that first borrowed the syntax of the horror film, and then of the Western. He writes, "By maintaining simultaneous descriptions according to both [semantic and syntactic] parameters, we are not likely to fall into the trap of equating *Star Wars* with the Western (as numerous recent critics have done), even though it shares certain syntactic patterns with that genre."[20] That is to say, science fiction persisted by drawing upon elements from the Western, and not the other way around. Because science fiction cinema—or, more specifically, one period of science fiction cinema—only borrowed from a narrative structure established by the Western, while largely retaining its own semantics, the identities of both genres remained intact. As Altman elaborates in his 1999 book *Film/Genre:* "When *Star Wars* took American theatres by storm, many viewers recognized in its structures the familiar epic configuration of the Western. In fact, some critics described *Star Wars* as a Western. Their desire to integrate this film into the corpus of the Western did not hold sway, however, for the general tendency of genre theorists and the popular audience alike is to recognize genre only when both subject and structure coincide."[21] Using Altman's terminology, *Star Wars* could be said to employ a structure, or syntax, common to the Western but to populate it with a different subject, or semantics. We should also add that if a science fiction film contains elements from the Western, there is at least some conscious will behind it. And those transpositions have consequences. Consider how the attitudes toward technology on display in the Western and science fiction genres are very different. In sci-fi, technology is usually embraced, if only by virtue of its ubiquity. It is the rare science fiction film that questions humankind's increasing reliance on technology, and this questioning is often halfhearted (as technology is usually part of the solution to whatever problem technology has caused). By contrast, the Western consistently displays a conflicted attitude toward technological advancement. If something is gained by the march of time, something is also lost.

Even when acknowledging that aspects of the Western have diffused into other movie genres, we must be careful not to lapse too far into generalities lest we lose sight of the genre's intricacies and complexities. For one, it is important to emphasize that syntax is not synonymous with plot. To say a genre has a recognizable syntax does not mean the genre tells the same story over and over again. While more recent criticism speaks of science fiction, in general, Wright distinguishes a particular type of contemporary science fiction film, the "space opera" of *Star Wars,* as being influenced by the Western. We recognize, however, that it is one particular Western, *The Searchers,* that especially influences *Star Wars. The Searchers* is a Western, indeed an important Western, but is it representative of *all* Westerns? No.

Conclusion

Old Westerns, New Frontiers

HOTEL CLERK: I thought you were dead.
JACOB: Dead? The next person who says that I'm gonna shoot, so help me.

—From *Big Jake* (1971)

In 1977—three years after the release of "Whatever Happened to Randolph Scott?"—the Statler Brothers overcame their dislike of contemporary cinema with a song called "The Movies." Opening with a catchy clarinet solo, the song is a laundry list of film titles cleverly strung together in rhyming sentences, with verses separated by the memorable (if historically inaccurate) chorus: "The movies are great medicine / Thankyou Thomas Edison / For giving us the best years of our lives." While most of the movies mentioned in the song are Hollywood classics, recent pictures about contemporary "doubts and fears," including *The Way We Were* and *One Flew Over the Cuckoo's Nest* (Milos Foreman, 1975), are mentioned. When it comes to Westerns, however, the Statlers sing about classics like *Rio Grande* and *Shane* but do not mention any films from the 1970s. Is there some underlying significance to this reluctance to move beyond the canon of classic Westerns?

Probably not.

Given the how commonplace invocations of the genre's classic films are, it is admittedly easy to overlook just how remarkable the Western is. Consider, for example, how no other major American film genre, past or present, has ever operated within comparably narrow temporal and geographical parameters, which in turn limit the range of subject matter than can be addressed. Science fiction can claim every movie that takes place in "the future," or features technology that has yet to be invented. A study of the horror genre is deemed controversial and too narrow because of the mundane claim that horror proper requires a patently supernatural element.[1] Film noir, more a theory than an actual genre (in the historical sense), grows more expansive with every article and monograph published on the subject.

Interest in the Western genre has yielded some of the most significant studies of American cinema and American cultural history ever produced, the shoulders upon which this study stands. Too often, however, efforts to reconcile the Western's longevity and popularity with its comparatively limited scope have resulted in essentialism. Appeals to notions about how the Western functions as a foundational myth for American society feed into the natural historiographical tendency to want to establish orderly narratives. A repeated emphasis on classic films can lead us to overlook, or even forget, the tremendous diversity of Westerns produced at any given time, even when the genre was in decline.

What this book has endeavored to recover is some of the multiplicity and complexity of the Western genre during a defined period of time, 1969 to 1980, drawing out connections between canonical and lesser-known works as well as continuities between these and older Westerns. By doing so, we see how existing accounts of the revisionist Western, shaped by general narratives about American film and culture in the 1960s and 70s, are often limited and one-dimensional. The point has not been to uncover any single intrinsic quality of the genre, but to explore an ongoing, cyclical process of regeneration in which conventional iconography, themes, and narratives are updated, rearranged and combined by filmmakers in order to meet the varied desires of moviegoers. It is ultimately regeneration, rather than revision, that emerges as the key theme of the period, transcending but also elucidating divisions within the Western of the time.

The theme of regeneration that characterized the narratives of Western films produced in the 1970s receded as the movie Western continued to appear in fits and spurts from the 1980s onward, replaced in large part by an increased emphasis on the camaraderie of the professional group—from the motley crew of gunmen in *Silverado* to the companies of heroes in 1990s Westerns like *Unforgiven, Tombstone, Posse* (Mario Van Peebles, 1993), *Bad Girls* (Jonathan Kaplan, 1994), and *Wyatt Earp,* up to more recent entries like *Open Range* and *True Grit* (Joel and Ethan Coen, 2010). And yet, in many of these films, and even some others like *3:10 to Yuma* and *The Lone Ranger* (Gore Verbinski, 2013), we find a continued emphasis on a central pair of protagonists who serve as foils for each other, a storytelling device we can trace back through celebrated Westerns of the late 1960s and 1970s like *True Grit* and *The Wild Bunch* to films of earlier decades. Moreover, it is the broader regenerative impulse characteristic of Western filmmaking from 1969 to 1980—and not "revisionism"—that persists in subsequent Western filmmaking.

Few, if any, Westerns made in the 1980s onward set out to "kill" the genre by openly attacking its conventions and mythology. Contemporary reviews touted *Silverado* and *Pale Rider,* both released in 1985, as renewals of the classic or traditional Western. *New York Times* critic Janet Maslin observed that *Silverado*'s director, producer and co-writer Lawrence Kasdan "doesn't seem to be commenting ironically on the western form. Nor is he determined to update it. He simply approaches it from a present-day standpoint, and the result is an energetic revival with some significant differences in scale."[2] Eastwood's *Pale Rider* inserts the director's "Man with No Name" character into the story of *Shane,* where he serves as supernatural protector of a group of small miners against a powerful hydraulic-mining outfit—in effect bringing together two parts of the Western's past and injecting a measure of 1980s ecological

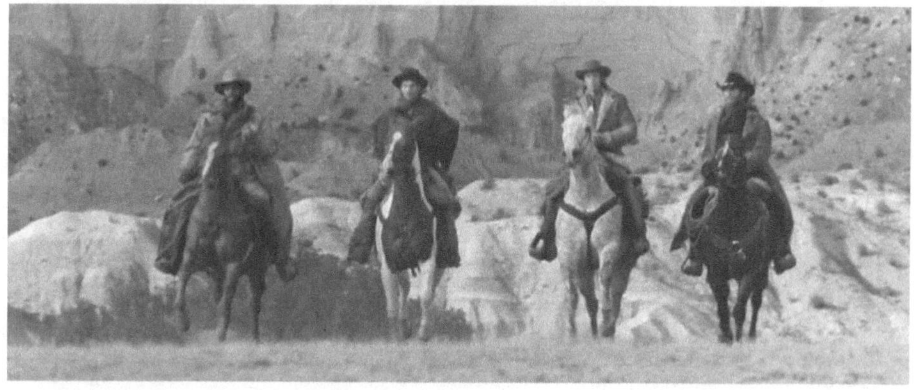

The company of heroes in *Silverado* (1985)

topicality. *Silverado,* the more ambitious of the two films, attempts to weave together nearly every conventional Western plot and populate it with every stock character. The results are entertaining, and *Silverado,* like *Pale Rider,* was judged a success upon its release. Even among the positive notices, though, were charges of superficiality, the films' uncritical invocation of the Western's rituals seen as postmodernism of the bad kind. *Silverado* and *Pale Rider* may thus strike us as symptomatic of the blockbuster era in which they appeared, when the films of George Lucas and Steven Spielberg offered eager viewers healthy doses of nostalgia and pastiche. One review of *Silverado* was even titled "The Sins Spielberg Must Answer For."[3]

Silverado and *Pale Rider* certainly bear the marks of the culture and filmmaking tendencies of the 1980s, but, as we've seen countless times over the course of this study, there are almost always precedents for features that are initially accounted for as responses to or reflections of contemporary social circumstance. With regard to the former, we could observe how earlier Westerns like *How the West Was Won* (1962) and *Red River* (1948) feature comparable assemblages of familiar genre plots. More significantly for the purposes of this study, however, is the degree to which *Silverado* and *Pale Rider* are more like the "traditional" Westerns that made up the majority of Western films produced between 1969 and 1980. As Loy observes, both pictures reach back into the genre's history and end with the triumph of the mythological West.[4] Those on-screen triumphs did not correspond with a revival of the Western as a popular genre, though.

The same can be said for the cycle of Westerns that appeared in the 1990s. Although these films are often seen as either a continuation or revival of the revisionist Western, they do not substantially critique the genre. Films unsparing in their presentation of the Western hero, like *Unforgiven* and *Wyatt Earp,* still end with that hero's legend intact, while movies that seek to redress the genre's treatment of women and minorities, like *Bad Girls* and *Posse,* appeal to conventions of frontier heroism to mythologize their consciously gendered and raced protagonists. Regeneration remained the order of the day, but it did not restore the Western to a regular role in Hollywood moviemaking. Instead, spurred by the successes of *Dances with Wolves* and *Unforgiven,* each of which won the Academy Award for Best Picture, Western production both big and small from the 1990s onward has been characterized by serious films made by auteur directors that are intended to garner awards and critical acclaim. Scholarship on the Western of the 1990s onward needs to acknowledge this change in the genre's status from a popular to a specialty form and consider the consequences for the Western's purported social function.[5] If a reflectionist approach to genre is problematic under ideal conditions, where dozens of films are consumed by thousands of moviegoers, then what happens when only one or perhaps two films are released to cinemas annually? Can anyone credibly argue that the Western still enjoys a privileged relationship with the American consciousness?

With respect to the genre's past, 1969 to 1980 is by no means the only period in which Westerns that fall outside or on the margins of the critically privileged canon have been given the short shrift. There are hundreds of Westerns from the 1940s, 1950s, and 1960s waiting to be rediscovered. Many such films, like *The Westerner, Yellow Sky, Devil's Canyon, Man with the Gun, Warlock, Last Train from Gun Hill*, and *Hour of the Gun,* have served as evidence over the course of this book, helping to situate developments in the later Western within the broader trends and transformations that have occurred during the genre's history. Certain canonical Westerns like *High Noon* and *The Searchers* have figured prominently in this study, but on account of their places in the genre's history—modifying themes and plots of films that came before and influencing subsequent developments—and not because of their political resonance or artistic greatness. It is also not a coincidence that the influence of each film on later cinema intensifies around the same time that film criticism is erecting its canons of great films and filmmakers.

As much as no movie can ever be fully explained or exhausted of meaning, even when subjected to the most comprehensive of analyses, we should not be content to simply return time and again to the same Westerns. As undeniably brilliant as many of these films are, the prominence given to the canon of great Western films and filmmakers too often obscures the genre's rich and vibrant history—a history we should not be deterred from exploring more fully.

APPENDIX

Filmography

I. American Westerns, 1969–1980

Alien Thunder. Claude Fournier. 1974.
Bad Company. Robert Benton. 1972.
The Ballad of Cable Hogue. Sam Peckinpah. 1970.
The Beguiled. Don Siegel. 1971.
Big Jake. George Sherman. 1971.
Billy Two Hats. Ted Kotcheff. 1974.
Bite the Bullet. Richard Brooks. 1975.
Blazing Saddles. Mel Brooks. 1974.
Boss Nigger. Jack Arnold. 1975.
Breakheart Pass. Tom Gries. 1975.
Buck and the Preacher. Sidney Poitier. 1972.
Buffalo Bill and the Indians, or Sitting Bull's History Lesson. Robert Altman. 1976.
Butch and Sundance: The Early Days. Richard Lester. 1979.
Butch Cassidy and the Sundance Kid. George Roy Hill. 1969.
Cahill: United States Marshal. Andrew V. McLaglen. 1973.
Charro. Charles Marquis Warren. 1969.
Chato's Land. Michael Winner. 1972.
The Cheyenne Social Club. Gene Kelly. 1970.
China 9, Liberty 37. Monte Hellman. 1978.
Chisum. Andrew V. McLaglen. 1970.
The Cowboys. Mark Rydell. 1972.
Cry Blood Apache. Jack Starrett. 1970.

The Culpepper Cattle Co. Dick Richards. 1972.
The Deadly Trackers. Barry Shear. 1973.
Death of a Gunfighter. Alan Smithee. 1969.
The Deserter. Burt Kennedy. 1971.
The Desperados. Henry Levin. 1969.
Dirty Dingus Magee. Burt Kennedy. 1970.
Dirty Little Billy. Stan Dragoti. 1972.
Doc. Frank Perry. 1971.
The Duchess and the Dirtwater Fox. Melvin Frank. 1976.
El Condor. John Guillermin. 1970.
The Frisco Kid. Robert Aldrich. 1979.
From Noon Till Three. Frank D. Gilroy. 1976.
The Gatling Gun. Robert Gordon. 1973.
Goin' South. Jack Nicholson. 1978.
The Good Guys and the Bad Guys. Burt Kennedy. 1969.
The Great Northfield Minnesota Raid. Philip Kaufman. 1972.
The Great Scout and Cathouse Thursday. Don Taylor. 1976.
Greyeagle. Charles B. Pierce. 1977.
A Gunfight. Lamont Johnson. 1971.
Guns of the Magnificent Seven. Paul Wendkos. 1969.
Hannie Caulder. Burt Kennedy. 1971.
Heaven with a Gun. Lee H. Katzin. 1969.
Heaven's Gate. Michael Cimino. 1980.
High Plains Drifter. Clint Eastwood. 1973.
The Hired Hand. Peter Fonda. 1971.
The Hunting Party. Don Medford. 1971.
Jeremiah Johnson. Sydney Pollack. 1972.
Jory. Jorge Fons. 1973.
Kid Blue. James Frawley. 1974.
Kid Vengeance. Joseph Manduke. 1977.
The Last Hard Men. Andrew V. McLaglen. 1976.
The Last Rebel. Denys McCoy. 1971.
Lawman. Michael Winner. 1971.
The Life and Times of Judge Roy Bean. John Huston. 1972.
Little Big Man. Arthur Penn. 1970.
The Long Riders. Walter Hill. 1980.
MacKenna's Gold. J. Lee Thompson. 1969.

The Magnificent Seven Ride. George McCowan. 1972.
A Man Called Horse. Elliot Silverstein. 1970.
A Man Called Sledge. Vic Morrow. 1970.
Man in the Wilderness. Richard C. Sarafian. 1971.
The Man Who Loved Cat Dancing. Richard C. Sarafian. 1973.
McCabe & Mrs. Miller. Robert Altman. 1971.
The Missouri Breaks. Arthur Penn. 1976.
Monte Walsh. William A. Fraker. 1970.
The Mountain Men. Richard Lang. 1980.
100 Rifles. Tom Gries. 1969.
One More Train to Rob. Andrew V. McLaglen. 1971.
The Outlaw Josey Wales. Clint Eastwood. 1976.
Paint Your Wagon. Joshua Logan. 1969.
Pat Garrett and Billy the Kid. Sam Peckinpah. 1973.
Posse. Kirk Douglas. 1975.
The Return of a Man Called Horse. Irvin Kershner. 1976.
The Revengers. Daniel Mann. 1972.
Rio Lobo. Howard Hawks. 1970.
Rooster Cogburn. Stuart Millar. 1975.
Sam Whiskey. Arnold Laven. 1969.
Santee. Gary Nelson. 1973.
Shoot Out. Henry Hathaway. 1971.
The Shootist. Don Siegel. 1976.
Showdown. George Seaton. 1973.
Soldier Blue. Ralph Nelson. 1970.
Something Big. Andrew V. McLaglen. 1971.
The Spikes Gang. Richard Fleischer. 1974.
Support Your Local Gunfighter. Burt Kennedy. 1971.
Support Your Local Sheriff! Burt Kennedy. 1969.
Tell Them Willie Boy Is Here. Abraham Polonsky. 1969.
There Was a Crooked Man. Joseph L. Mankiewicz. 1970.
A Time for Dying. Budd Boetticher. 1969.
Tom Horn. William Wiard. 1980.
The Train Robbers. Burt Kennedy. 1973.
True Grit. Henry Hathaway. 1969.
Two Mules for Sister Sara. Don Siegel. 1970.
Ulzana's Raid. Robert Aldrich. 1972.

The Undefeated. Andrew V. McLaglen. 1969.
Valdez is Coming. Edwin Sherin. 1971.
The Villain. Hal Needham. 1979.
The White Buffalo. J. Lee Thompson. 1977.
The Wild Bunch. Sam Peckinpah. 1969.
Wild Rovers. Blake Edwards. 1971.
Young Billy Young. Burt Kennedy. 1969.

II. Other Westerns Cited

3:10 to Yuma. Delmar Daves. 1957.
3:10 to Yuma. James Mangold. 2007.
Annie Oakley. George Sherman. 1935.
Arrowhead. Charles Marquis Warren. 1953.
Bandolero! Andrew V. McLaglen. 1968.
The Big Country. William Wyler. 1958.
Blood on the Moon. Robert Wise. 1948.
Broken Arrow. Delmar Daves. 1950.
Buchanan Rides Alone. Budd Boetticher. 1958.
Cat Ballou. Elliot Silverstein. 1965.
Cattle Annie and Little Britches. Lamont Johnson. 1981.
Cheyenne Autumn. John Ford. 1964.
Dances with Wolves. Kevin Costner. 1990.
Devil's Canyon. Alfred L. Werker. 1953.
Dodge City. Michael Curtiz. 1939.
Drum Beat. Delmar Daves. 1954.
Duel at Diablo. Ralph Nelson. 1966.
El Dorado. Howard Hawks. 1967.
Fire Creek. Vincent McEveety. 1968.
Fort Apache. John Ford. 1948.
Forty Guns. Samuel Fuller. 1957.
Frontier Marshall. Alan Dwan. 1939.
The Gunfight at O.K. Corral. John Sturges. 1956.
The Gunfighter. Henry King. 1950.
Hang 'Em High. Ted Post. 1968.
High Noon. Fred Zinnemann. 1952.

Hondo. John Farrow. 1953.
Hour of the Gun. John Sturges. 1967.
How the West Was Won. John Ford, Henry Hathaway, George Marshall. 1962.
Jesse James. Henry King. 1939.
Johnny Guitar. Nicholas Ray. 1954.
Kansas Raiders. Ray Enright. 1950.
The Last Sunset. Robert Aldrich. 1961.
Last Train from Gun Hill. John Sturges. 1959.
Law and Order. Nathan Juran. 1953.
The Left Handed Gun. Arthur Penn. 1958.
Legend of the Lone Ranger. William A. Fraker. 1981.
The Magnificent Seven. John Sturges. 1960.
The Man Who Shot Liberty Valance. John Ford. 1962.
Man with the Gun. Richard Wilson. 1955.
The Maverick Queen. Joe Kane. 1956.
McLintock! Andrew V. McLaglen. 1963.
My Darling Clementine. John Ford. 1946.
My Name is Nobody. Tonino Valerii. 1973.
Once Upon a Time in the West. Sergio Leone. 1968.
The Ox-Bow Incident. William Wellman. 1943.
Pale Rider. Clint Eastwood. 1985.
The Professionals. Richard Brooks. 1966.
Pursued. Raoul Walsh. 1947.
Quantrill's Raiders. Edward Bernds. 1958.
Rancho Notorious. Fritz Lang. 1952.
Red River. Howard Hawks. 1948.
Return of the Bad Men. Ray Enright. 1948.
Return of the Gunfighter. James Neilson. 1967.
Ride the High Country. Sam Peckinpah. 1962.
Rio Bravo. Howard Hawks. 1959.
Run of the Arrow. Samuel Fuller. 1957.
The Scalphunters. Sydney Pollock. 1968.
The Searchers. John Ford. 1956.
Shane. George Stevens. 1953.
Silverado. Lawrence Kasdan. 1985.
Silver Lode. Allan Dwan. 1954.

Stagecoach. John Ford. 1939.
Tennessee's Partner. Allan Dwan. 1955.
Terror in a Texas Town. Joseph H. Lewis. 1958.
The Texas Rangers. Phil Karlson. 1951.
The Tin Star. Anthony Mann. 1957.
Trooper Hook. Charles Marquis Warren. 1957.
The True Story of Jesse James. Nicholas Ray. 1957.
Unforgiven. Clint Eastwood. 1992.
Vera Cruz. Robert Aldrich. 1954.
Warlock. Edward Dmytryk. 1959.
The War Wagon. Burt Kennedy. 1967.
The Westerner. William Wyler. 1940.
White Feather. Robert D. Webb. 1955.
Wichita. Jacques Tourneur. 1955.
Yellow Sky. William A. Wellman. 1948.

Notes

Introduction

1. See, for example, Richard Abel, "The Imagined Community of the Western," in *American Cinema's Transitional Era: Audiences, Institutions, Practices,* ed. Charlie Keil and Shelley Stamp (Berkeley: University of California Press, 2004), 131; Andrew Brodie Smith, *Shooting Cowboys and Indians: Silent Western Films, American Culture and the Birth of Hollywood* (Boulder: University of Colorado Press, 2003); Peter Stanfield, *Hollywood, Westerns and the 1930s: The Lost Trail* (Exeter, UK: University of Exeter Press, 2001); and Stanfield, *Horse Opera: The Strange History of the 1930s Singing Cowboy* (Urbana/Chicago: University of Illinois Press, 2002).

Chapter 1

Epigraph 1. Tom Shales, "Myths of the Old West, Again," *Washington Post,* January 28, 1980, B3.

Epigraph 2. Paul Andrew Hutton, "Showdown at the Hollywood Corral: Wyatt Earp at the Movies," *Montana: The Magazine of Western History* 45, no. 3 (Summer 1995): 25.

Epigraph 3. Quoted in Jason Wilson, "The State of Westerns," *GamePro,* June 22, 2010, http://www.gamepro.com/article/features/215612/the-state-of-westerns/.

1. Richard A. Maynard, "The Rise of the Cowboy Anti-Hero—Trends in Westerns since 1960," in *The American West on Film: Myth and Reality,* ed. Richard A. Maynard (Rochelle Park, N.J.: Hayden Book Company, 1974), 93.

2. Jack Nachbar, "Riding Shotgun: The Scattered Formula in Contemporary Western Movies," *The Film Journal* 2, no.3 (September 1973), reprinted in *Focus on the Western,* ed. Jack Nachbar (Inglewood Cliffs, N.J.: Prentice-Hall, 1974), 102–108.

3. Nachbar, "Riding Shotgun," 109.

4. John G. Cawelti, "The Western: A Look at the Evolution of a Formula," in *Adventure, Romance and Mystery* (Chicago: University of Chicago Press, 1976), 252–59.

5. Cawelti, "The Western," 259.

6. Noël Carroll, "The Future of Allusion: Hollywood in the Seventies (and Beyond)," *October* 20 (Spring 1982): 60.

7. Ibid.

8. Michael T. Marsden and Jack Nachbar, "The Modern Popular Western: Radio, Television, Film and Print," in *A Literary History of the American West* (Fort Worth, Tex.: Texas Christian University Press, 1987), 1273.

9. Marsden and Nachbar, "Modern Popular Western," 1271.

10. Ibid.

11. John H. Lenihan, *Showdown: Confronting Modern America in the Western Film* (Urbana: University of Illinois Press, 1985), 166; Michael Coyne, *The Crowded Prairie: American National Identity in the Hollywood Western* (London: I. B. Tauris, 1998), 73. Patrick McGee, *From Shane to Kill Bill: Rethinking the Western* (Malden, Mass.: Blackwell Publishing, 2007), 133, 151; Deborah Knight and George McKnight, "The Northwestern: McCabe and Mrs. Miller," in *The Philosophy of the Western,* ed. Jennifer L. McMahon and B. Steve Csaki (Lexington, Ky.: University Press of Kentucky, 2010), 241. Scott Simmon also uses "classic Western" extensively in *The Invention of the Western Film: A Cultural History of the Genre's First Half-Century* (Cambridge, Mass.: Cambridge University Press, 2003) to distinguish Westerns of the 1930s and early 1940s from later Westerns influenced by film noir.

12. Jim Kitses, "Post-modernism and the Western," *The Western Reader,* ed. Jim Kitses and Gregg Rickman (New York: Limelight Editions, 1996), 17.

13. Ibid.

14. Kristin Thompson, *Breaking the Glass Armor: Neoformalist Film Analysis* (Princeton, N.J.: Princeton University Press, 1988), 12 (original emphasis).

15. Steve Neale, "Questions of Genre," *Film and Theory: An Anthology,* ed. Robert Stam and Toby Miller (Malden, Mass.: Blackwell Publishing, 2000), 172–73.

16. David Bordwell, *Poetics of Cinema* (New York: Routledge, 2008), 31.

17. Frederick Jackson Turner, *The Frontier in American History* [1920] (New York: Henry Holt, 1937), 2.

18. Cawelti, "The Western," 252.

19. Richard Maltby, *Hollywood Cinema,* 2nd ed. (Malden, Mass.: Blackwell Publishing, 2003), 100.

20. Thomas Schatz, *Hollywood Genres: Formulas, Filmmaking and the Studio System* (New York: Random House, 1981), 41.

21. Although frequently cited as "the first Western," the 1903 Edison film *The Great Train Robbery,* directed by Edwin S. Porter, is more accurately described as an example of early cinema's infatuation with trains and crime. Successive film adaptations of *The Virginian,* released in 1914, 1923, and 1929, reflect less the popularity of movie cowboys than of Owen Wister's 1902 novel. The 1930 prestige releases *The Big Trail* (Raoul Walsh) and *Billy the Kid* (King Vidor), each in a nascent 70 mm widescreen format, did not find favor with audiences. Even as popular a cowboy star as Gene Autry was confined to making B-movies at Mascot and then Republic Studios.

22. Kitses, "Post-modernism and the Western," 18–19.

23. While the seminal example of this approach remains *Horizons West,* with its influential fusion of structuralism and auteurism, even studies that purposely avoid auteurist methodologies have difficulty evading the director-defined canon of important Westerns. Michael Coyne's *The Crowded Prairie* (1998), which traces the genre's changing relationship to American politics, is commendable for devoting attention to a number of successful but disregarded Westerns, including *The Last Sunset*

(Robert Aldrich, 1961) and *Bandolero!* (Andrew V. McLaglen, 1968). Nevertheless, of the twenty-five films that comprise the book's "principle focus of analysis," seven are directed by John Ford—eight if we include the episodic *How the West Was Won* (1962). One of the only major studies of the Western to avoid focusing on the genre's signature filmmakers is *Sixguns and Society* by Will Wright (1975), which does so by dint of addressing only films that earned $4 million or more in domestic rentals—a criterion that excludes, for example, *My Darling Clementine* (1946) and *The Man Who Shot Liberty Valance* (1962), two of Ford's most celebrated Westerns, as well as *McCabe & Mrs. Miller.*

24. Geoff King, *New Hollywood Cinema* (London: I. B. Tauris, 2002), 13.

25. Peter Biskind, *Easy Riders, Raging Bulls* (London: Bloomsbury, 1999), 17; David A. Cook, *Lost Illusions: American Cinema in the Shadow of Watergate and Vietnam 1970–1979* (Berkeley: University of California Press, 2000), 182.

26. Raphaëlle Moine, *Cinema Genre,* trans. Alistair Fox and Hilary Radner (Oxford: Blackwell Publishing, 2008), 135.

27. Jim Kitses, *Horizons West* (London: Thames and Hudson, 1969), 26.

28. Kitses, *Horizons West,* 26–27.

29. Kristin Thompson, *Storytelling in the New Hollywood* (Cambridge, Mass.: Harvard University Press, 1999), 5.

30. Steve Neale, "'The Last Good Time We Ever Had?' Revising the Hollywood Renaissance," in *Contemporary American Cinema,* ed. Linda Ruth Williams and Michael Hammond (London: Open University Press, 2006), 106.

31. Kitses, "Post-modernism and the Western," 19.

32. Ibid.

33. Kitses, "Post-modernism and the Western," 18.

34. Nachbar, "Riding Shotgun," 111.

35. "AFI's 10 Top 10: Top 10 Westerns," http://www.afi.com/10top10/category.aspx?cat=3.

36. The complete list of eligible movies is available at http://www.afi.com/100Years/downloads.aspx.

37. See "Appendix Table 1: Production of Westerns 1921–77," *The BFI Companion to the Western,* new ed., ed. Edward Buscombe (Andre Deutsch/BFI Publishing: London, 1993), 426.

38. For more on *Unforgiven*'s status as "revisionist" Western, see Andrew Patrick Nelson, "Revisionism 2.0? *Unforgiven* and the Hollywood Western of the 1990s," *Contemporary Westerns: Film and Television since 1990,* ed. A. P. Nelson (Lanham, Md.: Scarecrow Press, 2013), 15–30.

39. Will Wright, *Sixguns and Society: A Structural Study of the Western* (Berkeley: University of California Press, 1975), 34; Andre Bazin, "The Evolution of the Western," in *What Is Cinema?,* vol. 2, trans. Hugh Gray (Berkeley: University of California Press, 2005), 149–57.

40. Kitses, "Post-modernism and the Western," 21.

41. For a good indication of the prevalence of these trends in recent scholarship on the genre, one can turn to the tables of contents in two collections of essays released around the turn of the century: *Back in the Saddle Again,* ed. Edward Buscombe and Roberta E. Pearson (London: BFI Publishing, 1998), and *Westerns: Films Through History,* ed. Janet Walker (New York: Routledge, 2001).

42. Take, for example, two significant studies of the Western genre published in the 1990s: *West of Everything: The Inner Life of Westerns* (1993) by Jane Tompkins, and *Westerns: Making the Man in Fiction and Film* (1998) by Lee Clark Mitchell. Both books examine masculinity in the Western. Tompkins argues that the genre gained prominence as a patriarchal reaction against women's encroachment into the public spear in the 19th and 20th centuries, whereas Mitchell sees the Western as an ongoing, obsessive negotiation of "what it means to be a man" in the face of generational change. Each author traces the genre from literature to film, but in doing so neither strays from the established canon. As it happens, the two movies examined at greatest length by both Tompkins and Mitchell are *Shane* and *High Noon.*

43. See also, for example, McGee's *From Shane to Kill Bill* and Barry Langford, "Revisiting the 'Revisionist' Western," *Film and History* 33, no. 2 (September 2003): 26–35.

44. David Bordwell, "Contemporary Film Theory and the Vicissitudes of Grand Theory," in *Post-Theory: Reconstructing Film Studies,* ed. David Bordwell and Noël Carroll (Madison: University of Wisconsin Press, 1996), 3.

45. Ibid., 9.

46. Ibid., 10.

47. Ibid., 9.

48. Bordwell, *Poetics of Cinema,* 30.

49. Bordwell, "Contemporary Film Theory," 26–30.

50. Ibid., 27.

51. The proliferation of available titles that followed the advent of DVD is not responsible for this, either. With the exception, again, of *Dirty Little Billy,* all were released on VHS, meaning they have been available for some time. *Monte Walsh,* available on VHS, wasn't released on DVD until 2011. *Dirty Little Billy,* which was independently produced by Jack L. Warner and distributed by Columbia Pictures, has only recently been made commercially available as part of Warner's DVD-to-order Warner Archive service.

Chapter 2

Epigraph. "Press violent about film's violence, prod Sam Peckinpah following 'Bunch,'" *Daily Variety*, July 2, 1969, reprinted in *Sam Peckinpah's The Wild Bunch,* ed. Stephen Prince (Cambridge: Cambridge University Press, 1999), 211.

1. Richard Slotkin, *Gunfighter Nation: The Myth of the Frontier in Twentieth-Century America* [1992] (Norman: University of Oklahoma Press, 1998), 594.

2. Ibid., 595–6.

3. Coyne, *The Crowded Prairie*, 152 (see chap 1, n. 11).

4. Stephen Prince, *Savage Cinema: Sam Peckinpah and the Rise of Violent Movies* (London: The Athlone Press, 1998), 27.

5. Prince, *Savage Cinema*, 25.

6. Ibid.

7. "Press violent about film's violence," 210.

8. Ibid., 209–10.

9. Garner Simmons, *Peckinpah: A Portrait in Montage* (Austin: University of Texas Press, 1982), 106.

10. Sheldon Hall and Steve Neale, *Epics, Spectacles and Blockbusters: A Hollywood History* (Detroit, Mich.: Wayne State University Press, 2010), 195.

11. Maynard, "The Rise of the Cowboy Anti-Hero," 108 (see chap. 1, n. 1).

12. Graham Fuller, "Sending Out a Search Party for the Western," *New York Times,* March 5, 2000, http://www.nytimes.com/2000/03/05/movies/film-sending-out-a-search-party-for-the-western.html.

13. "Press violent about film's violence," 212.

14. Even Robert Aldrich, who made six Westerns over the course of a three-decade-long career in Hollywood, is not identified principally with the genre. He is also not considered to be an auteur filmmaker.

15. Kitses, *Horizons West,* new ed. (London: BFI Publishing, 2004), 201.

16. Ibid., 246.

17. Richard Warren Lewis, "John Wayne: The Playboy Interview," *Playboy* 18, no. 5 (May 1971), http://www.playboy.com/articles/john-wayne-interview/.

18. "National Review's Best Conservative Movies," *National Review,* October 24, 1994, 53.

19. "High Noon: Trivia and Other Fun Stuff," *Turner Classic Movies,* http://www.tcm.com/tcmdb/title/24083/High-Noon/articles.html.

20. Quoted in Joseph McBride, *Hawks on Hawks* (Berkely: University of California Press, 1982), 161. In interviews Hawks mistakenly refers to Van Heflin's character in *3:10 to Yuma* as a sheriff. The character of Dan Evans is, in fact, not a lawman but a small-time rancher who has volunteered to help bring in outlaw Ben Wade (Glenn Ford)—which helps motivate his nervous, timid behavior in the face of danger.

21. Wright, *Sixguns and Society,* see especially pages 85–123 (see chap. 1, n. 39).

22. Ibid., 86.

23. Richard Coombs, review of *Doc* (Perry, 1971), *Monthly Film Bulletin* 39, no. 456 (January 1972), 4.

24. Ibid.

25. Leighton Grist, "Unforgiven," in *The Book of Westerns,* ed. Ian Cameron and Douglas Pye (New York: Continuum, 1996), 294.

26. "Appendix Table 1," *BFI Companion to the Western,* 426.

27. The two other cited sources of the BFI table's data are Les Adams and Buck Rainey, *Shoot Em Ups: The American Film Issue Catalog of Motion Pictures Produced in the United States: Feature Films, 1921–1930* and *Film Daily Yearbook,* which ceased publication in 1970.

28. Hardy's criterion for including a film is, "has it developed from or does it contribute to the Western tradition in the broadest sense?" For the late 1960s and 1970s, this leads him to take account of a number of Italian Westerns; movies with contemporary Westerns settings and themes like *Junior Bonnor* (Sam Peckinpah, 1972) and *The Electric Horseman* (Sydney Pollock, 1979), but also a movie like *Coogan's Bluff* (Don Siegel, 1968); and genre crossovers like *Westworld* (Michael Crichton, 1973).

29. Unless otherwise indicated, all box office information comes from *Daily Variety.* $4.0 million is the measure by which a movie is included in *Variety*'s list of "All Time Rental Champs."

30. For perspective, the highest earning feature films (U.S. rentals) for each year from 1969 to 1980 are as follows: 1969, *Butch Cassidy and the Sundance Kid,* $45.9 million; 1970, *Love Story,* $80 million; 1971, *Fiddler on the Roof,* $49.4 million; 1972, *The*

Godfather, $127.6 million; 1973, *The Sting,* $115 million; 1974, *The Towering Inferno,* $88.6 million; 1975, *Jaws,* $193.7 million; 1976, *Rocky,* $77.1 million; 1977, *Star Wars,* $270.9 million; 1978, *Grease,* $96.3 million; 1979, *Rocky II,* $42.2 million; 1980, *The Empire Strikes Back,* $173.8.

31. Goldman tells this story in numerous interviews, including in *Screenwriters: Word into Image: William Goldman* (Terry Sanders and Freida Lee Mock, 1981), and in both the commentary track and the making of documentary on the 2006 DVD release of *Butch Cassidy and the Sundance Kid.*

32. For one thing, it fails to take into account alternatives. That a majority of moviegoers choose to see a particular movie on a given weekend does not mean they all did so for the same reason, and it says nothing of the people who chose not to attend the cinema.

33. Roger Ebert, review of *Bad Company, Chicago Sun-Times,* October 25, 1972, http://rogerebert.suntimes.com/apps/pbcs.dll/article?AID=/19721025/REVIEWS/210250301/1023.

34. Steve Neale, "Westerns and Gangster Films Since the 1970s," *Genre and Contemporary Hollywood,* ed. Steve Neale (London: BFI, 2002), 28.

35. Cook, *Lost Illusions,* 180 (see chap. 1, n. 25).

36. Countless other familiar faces from Westerns of the 1940s, 1950s, and 1960s also continued to find work, including Arthur Hunnicutt, Andy Devine, Slim Pickens, Ben Johnson, Jack Elam, Woody Strode, Iron Eyes Cody, Forrest Tucker, Dub Taylor, Strother Martin, Richard Jaeckel, and Harry Carrey, Jr.

37. Cook, *Lost Illusions,* 339. In spite of his popularity, moviegoers were less interested in seeing Wayne outside the Western; the actor's later attempts to branch out beyond the genre—*The Hellfighers* (Andrew V. McLaglen, 1968), based on the life of oil well firefighter Red Adair, and two police movies, *McQ* (John Sturges, 1974) and *Brannigan* (Douglas Hickox, 1975)—were not successful.

38. Cook, *Lost Illusions,* 180.

39. Gary Wills, *John Wayne's America: The Politics of Celebrity* (New York: Touchstone, 1998), 285.

40. Ibid.

41. Christopher Frayling, *Once Upon A Time in Italy* (New York: Harry N. Abrams, 2005), 59–63.

42. Coyne, *The Crowded Prairie,* 137.

43. Kim Newman, *Wild West Movies: How the West Was Found, Won, Lost, Lied about, Filmed and Forgotten* (London: Bloomsbury, 1990), 195.

Chapter 3

Epigraph. From the catalogue of the "International Cinema Meetings," Sorrento, Italy, September 1970. Quoted in George N. Fenin and William K. Everson, *The Western: From Silents to the Seventies* (New York: Penguin Books, 1973), 368.

1. Brian Henderson, "'The Searchers': An American Dilemma," *Film Quarterly,* 34 (1981): 12.

2. For opposing views that assert the "pro-Indian" Western of the 1950s did, in fact, address both the historical and contemporary situation of American Indians, see

Steve Neale, "Vanishing Americans: Racial and Ethnic Issues in the Interpretation and Context of Post-war 'Pro-Indian' Westerns," in *Back in the Saddle Again: New Essays on the Western* (London: BFI Publishing, 1998), 8–28; and Edward Buscombe, *"Injuns!": Native Americans in the Movies* (London: Reaktion, 2006), 101–50.

3. John O'Connor, "The White Man's Indian: An Institutional Approach," in *Hollywood's Indian: The Portrayal of the Native American in Film,* ed. Peter C. Rollins and John E. O'Connor (Lexington: University Press of Kentucky, 1998), 37.

4. Fenin and Everson, *The Western*, 368.

5. "Soldier Blue," in *The BFI Companion to the Western,* new ed., ed. Edward Buscombe (Andre Deutsch/BFI Publishing: London, 1993), 300.

6. Philip French, *Westerns* [1973] (Manchester: Carcenet Press, Ltd., 2005), 56.

7. See French, *Westerns*, 47–61; Robert Baird, "Going Indian: Discovery, Adoption and Renaming Toward a 'True American,' from '*Deerslayer*' to '*Dances with Wolves*'" [1996], in *The Western Reader*, 277–292 (see chap. 1, n. 12); Arthur M. Eckstein, "Introduction: Main Critical Issues in 'The Searchers,'" in *The Searchers: Essays and Reflections on John Ford's Classic Western,* ed. Arthur M. Eckstein and Peter Lehmen (Detroit: Wayne State University Press, 2004), 11; Mark Mordue, "Dead Men Walking," *Frieze Magazine,* 114 (April 2008), http://www.frieze.com/issue/article/dead_men_walking/.

8. Buscombe, *"Injuns!",* 135.

9. Douglas Pye, "Ulzana's Raid," in *The Book of Westerns,* ed. Ian Cameron and Douglas Pye (New York: Continuum, 1996), 263.

10. Buscombe, *"Injuns!",* 135.

11. Ibid., 136–37.

12. Paul Simpson, *The Rough Guide to Westerns* (London: Rough Guides Ltd., 2006), 210

13. Kenneth Turan, "A Fistful of Memories: Interview with Clint Eastwood" [1992], in *The Western Reader,* 249.

14. White actors also continued to play characters of other races, with the exception of blacks. Burt Lancaster, for example, "darkens up" his complexion to play the Hispanic lead in *Valdez Is Coming* (Edwin Sherin, 1970).

15. Patricia Nelson Limerick, *The Legacy of Conquest: The Unbroken Past of the American West* (New York: W. W. Norton & Company, 1987), 19.

16. Two of the better, albeit partisan, accounts of the American Indian Movement are Paul Chaat Smith and Robert Allen Warrior, *Like a Hurricane: The Indian Movement from Alcatraz to Wounded Knee* (New York: The New Press, 1996), and Dennis Banks with Richard Erdoes, *Ojibwa Warrior: Dennis Banks and the Rise of the American Indian Movement* (Norman: University of Oklahoma Press, 2004); for an oppositional view of the AIM, see Joseph H. Trimbach and John M. Trimbauch, *American Indian Mafia: An FBI Agent's True Story About Wounded Knee, Leonard Peltier, and the American Indian Movement* (Parker, Colo.: Outskirts Press, 2007).

17. Slotkin, *Gunfighter Nation*, 367 (see chap. 2, n. 1). Making Westerns, according to Slotkin, also allowed liberal filmmakers to make implicitly political movies while avoiding raising the suspicions of the House Un-American Activities Committee and offending "southern sensibilities."

18. Joseph McBride, *Searching for John Ford: A Life* (London: Faber and Faber, 2003), 652.

19. Ibid.

20. Tak Fujiwara, "Who Will Tell The People? 'Cheyenne Autumn,'" *Undercurrent*, 5 (March 2009), http://www.fipresci.org/undercurrent/issue_0509/cheyenne.htm.

21. Leigh Brackett, *Follow the Free Wind* [1963] (New York: Ballantine Books, 1980), 138–39.

22. Angela Aleiss, *Making the White Man's Indian* (Westport, Conn.: Praeger Publishers, 2005), 130.

23. Aleiss, *Making the White Man's Indian*, 131–33; Ralph E. Friar and Natasha A. Friar, *The Only Good Indian . . . The Hollywood Gospel* (New York: Drama Book Specialists, 1972), 116; Bob Herzberg, *Savages and Saints: The Changing Image of American Indians in Westerns* (Jefferson, N.C.: McFarland & Co., 2008), 233–37.

24. Aleiss, *Making the White Man's Indian*, 130–31.

25. Quoted in Friar and Friar, *The Only Good Indian*, 124.

26. In the 1976 sequel, *The Return of a Man Called Horse* (Irvin Kirshner), Morgan rejoins the Sioux to lead them against a more conventional threat: trappers operating with the support of the government. He again undergoes a slightly altered (and, on balance, more graphic) version of the Vow to the Sun rite.

27. Fenin and Everson, *The Western*, 370.

28. Kimberly Lindbergs, "Little Big Man's Big Impact," *TCM Movie Morlocks* (May 6, 2010), http://moviemorlocks.com/2010/05/06/little-big-mans-big-impact/.

29. Cook, *Lost Illusions*, 75 (see chap. 1, n. 25).

30. The number of reported causalities varied greatly at the time, and there is still much debate about many aspects of the battle, including whether or not it was a "massacre." See Stan Hoig, *The Battle of the Washita: The Sheridan-Custer Indian Campaign of 1867–69* [1976] (Lincoln: University of Nebraska Press, 1980); Jerome A. Green, *Washita, The Southern Cheyenne and the U.S. Army* (Norman: University of Oklahoma Press, 2004); Richard G. Hardorff, ed., *Washita Memories: Eyewitness Views of Custer's Attack on Black Kettle's Village* (Norman: University of Oklahoma Press, 2006).

31. Jan Aghed and Bernard Cohn, "Interview with Arthur Penn," *Positif*, April 1971, reprinted in Michael Chaiken and Paul Cronin, eds., *Arthur Penn: Interviews* (Jackson: University Press of Mississippi, 2008), 66.

32. Lindbergs, "Little Big Man's Big Impact," http://moviemorlocks.com/2010/05/06/little-big-mans-big-impact/.

33. Ward Churchill, "Smoke Signals in Context: A Historical Overview," *Z Magazine* (November 1998), http://www.zcommunications.org/smoke-signals-in-context-by-ward-churchill.

34. Austin Fisher, "A Marxist's Gotta Do What a Marxist's Gotta Do: Political Violence on the Italian Frontier," *Scope: An Online Journal of Film and Television Studies*, 15 (November 2009), http://www.scope.nottingham.ac.uk/cultborr/chapter.php?id=14.

35. Damien Love, "The Miracle Worker: An Interview with Arthur Penn" [2004], *Bright Lights Film Journal* 65 (August 2009), http://www.brightlightsfilm.com/65/65arthurpenniv.php.

36. Mel Brooks's portrayal of a Jewish Indian chief in *Blazing Saddles* may owe something to *Little Big Man*. In his review of *Little Big Man*, critic Vincent Canby detects "borrowed Yiddish humor" in Old Lodge Skins; on the charge that the Cheyenne in *Little Big Man* are less Indians than New York Jews, Philip French counsels,

"We should of course remember that it was the belief of Joseph Smith and the Mormons that Indians were in fact Jewish, the descendents of lost Hebrew tribes." Vincent Canby, "Movie Review: 'Little Big Man,'" *New York Times*, December 15, 1970, http://movies.nytimes.com/movie/review?res=EE05E7DF1739E56FBC4D52DFB467838B669EDE; French, *Westerns*, 58.

37. Buscombe, "*Injuns!*", 132.

38. Cawelti, "The Western," 258 (see chap. 1, n. 4).

39. Slotkin, *Gunfighter Nation*, 590–91 (see chap. 2, n.1).

40. "Pollution: Keep American Beautiful—Iron Eyes Cody (1961–1983)," Historic Campaigns, *Ad Council*, http://www.adcouncil.org/Our-Campaigns/The-Classics/Pollution-Keep-America-Beautiful-Iron-Eyes-Cody.

41. "Ad Age Advertising Century: Top 100 Advertising Campaigns," *AdAge.com*, http://adage.com/century/campaigns.html.

42. Barbara Mikkelson, "Iron Eyes Cody," *snopes.com* (August 9, 2007), http://www.snopes.com/movies/actors/ironeyes.asp. Angela Aleiss was the first to discover Cody's Italian identity, which she reported in an article entitled "Native Son" in the *New Orleans Times-Picayune* (May 26, 1996), D1.

43. Buscombe, "*Injuns!*", 161. For a discussion of the implications of Cody's passing for Indian, see 158–64.

Chapter 4

Epigraph. Bruce Williamson, interview with Robert Altman, *Playboy* 23, no. 8 (August 1976), reprinted in *Robert Altman: Interviews*, ed. David Sterritt (Jackson: University Press of Mississippi, 2000), 39.

1. "The Culpepper Cattle Co.," in *The BFI Companion to the Western*, new ed., ed. Edward Buscombe (Andre Deutsch/BFI Publishing: London, 1993) 257.

2. Roger Greenspun, "'Culpepper Cattle': Hero Quits Trail Drive to Help Pacifists," review of *The Culpepper Cattle Co., New York Times*, April 17, 1972, http://movies.nytimes.com/movie/review?res=9403E5D8143AE73ABC4F52DFB2668389669EDE.

3. Randy Roberts and James S. Olson, *John Wayne, American* (New York: The Free Press, 1995), 584.

4. Hutton, "Showdown at the Hollywood Corral," 25 (see chap. 1, epigraph 2).

5. Christopher D. Geist and Jack Nachbar, "Popular Heroes: Introduction," *The Popular Culture Reader*, 3rd ed., ed. Christopher D. Geist and Jack Nachbar (Bowling Green, Ohio: Bowling Green University Popular Press, 1983), 208.

6. Marsden and Nachbar, "The Modern Popular Western," 1271 (see chap. 1, n. 8).

7. Frank Waters, *The Earp Brothers of Tombstone: The Story of Mrs. Virgil Earp* [1960] (Lincoln, Nebr.: Bison Books, 1976), 7.

8. Quoted in Wayne Michael Sarf, *God Bless You, Buffalo Bill: A Layman's Guide to History and the Western Film* (East Brunswick, N.J.: Associated University Presses, 1983), 58.

9. See Sarf, *God Bless You, Buffalo Bill*, 60, and Hutton, "Showdown at the Hollywood Corral," 24.

10. Review of *Doc* (Perry, 1971), *Variety*, August 11, 1971, 16.

11. Quoted in Hutton, "Showdown at the Hollywood Corral," 24.

12. Jon Tuska, *The American West in Film: Critical Approaches to the Western* (London: Greenwood Press, 1985), 195.

13. Howard Thompson, "An Enigmatic 'Doc,'" *New York Times*, August 19, 1972, http://movies.nytimes.com/movie/89636/Doc/overview.

14. Both pictures offer a more balanced portrayal of the lawman, but he emerges from each with his mythic heroism intact.

15. Peter Buckley, review of *Doc* (Perry, 1971), *Films and Filming,* January 1972, 52.

16. Tag Gallagher, "Shoot-Out at the Genre Corral: Problems in the 'Evolution' of the Western," in *Film Genre Reader* (Austin: University of Texas Press, 1986), 204.

17. Quoted in Peter Stanfield, *Hollywood, Westerns and the 1930s* (Exeter, UK: University of Exeter Press, 2001), 182–83.

18. Ibid., 183.

19. Ibid., 182.

20. Ibid., 182.

21. The Jesse James myth also produced one of the worst Westerns of the decade, *The Last Rebel* (Denys McCoy, 1971), in which American football star Joe Namath gives an exceedingly awkward, sheepish performance as a Confederate soldier who refuses to surrender at the conclusion of the Civil War.

22. Geoffrey C. Ward, *The Civil War: An Illustrated History* (New York: Knopf, 1990), 264

23. Williamson, Interview with Robert Altman, 39 (see chap. 4, epigraph).

24. Gerard Plecki, *Robert Altman* (Boston: Twayne, 1985), 45.

25. Aljean Harmetz, "The 15th Man Who Was Asked to Direct *M*A*S*H* (and Did) Makes a Peculiar Western," *The New York Times Magazine*, June 20, 1971, reprinted in *Robert Altman: Interviews*, ed. David Sterritt (Jackson: University Press of Mississippi, 2000), 7.

26. Quoted in Robert T. Self, *Robert Altman's McCabe & Mrs Miller: Reframing the American West* (Lawrence: University Press of Kansas, 2007), 135.

27. Quoted in Harmetz, "The 15th Man," 7.

28. Ibid., 7.

29. Self, *Robert Altman's McCabe & Mrs. Miller*, 137.

30. Ibid., 136.

Chapter 5

Epigraph. Richard Warren Lewis, "John Wayne: The Playboy Interview," *Playboy* 18, no. 5 (May 1971), http://www.playboy.com/articles/john-wayne-interview/.

1. Quoted in Simpson, *The Rough Guide to Westerns*, 16 (see chap. 3, n. 12).

2. According to Jim Kitses in his commentary track for the film's DVD release, Budd Boetticher reportedly detested (with good reason) the awkward, studio-mandated song added to the opening credits of *Seven Men From Now* (1956). In other cases, the opening credit ballad is used to great effect. There is no question that Stan Jones's theme to *The Searchers*—with forlorn voices asking, "*What makes a man to wander? What makes a man to roam? What makes a man leave bed and board and turn*

his back on home? Ride away . . . ride away . . . "—aids considerably in establishing the appropriate tone of longing. This practice takes a more pop-oriented turn in the late 1970s following the improbable success of Burt Baccarat's "Raindrops Keep Falling on My Head" from *Butch Cassidy and the Sundance Kid.* The opening song to *True Grit,* sung by the "Rhinestone Cowboy" Glenn Campbell (who also co-starred in the film), is typical of the more pop-oriented approach to the credit ballad. *Chisum* features a comparable number midway through the picture in the sappy "Turn Me Around."

3. R. Philip Loy, *Westerns in a Changing America: 1955–2000* (Jefferson, N.C.: McFarland and Co., 2004), 159.

4. Deborah Thomas, "John Wayne's Body," in *The Book of Westerns,* ed. Ian Cameron and Douglas Pye (New York: Continuum Publishing Co., 1996), 75–87.

5. French, *Westerns,* 20–21 (see chap. 3, n. 6); Stephen Tatum, *Inventing Billy the Kid* (Tucson: University of Arizona Press, 1997), 154–56 n. 221.

6. John Woolley and Gerhard Peters, *The American Presidency Project* (Santa Barbara: University of California), http://www.presidency.ucsb.edu/ws/?pid=2608.

7. Tatum, *Inventing Billy the Kid,* 156.

8. For a detailed analysis of Nixon's movie watching and a listing of the films he screened during his presidency (including date and screening site), see Mark Feeney, *Nixon at the Movies: A Book about Belief* (Chicago: University of Chicago Press, 2004). Note that Nixon did not watch *Chisum* the evening prior to his Denver appearance, as French and Tatum claim. The movie he actually screened the night before was *The Swiss Family Robinson* (Ken Annakin, 1962).

9. Nachbar, "Riding Shotgun," 111 (see chap. 1, n. 2).

10. Quoted in David Lusted, *The Western* (Essex, UK: Pearson Longman, 2003), 208.

11. Todd McCarthy, *Howard Hawks: The Grey Fox of Hollywood* (New York: Grove Press, 1997), 640.

12. Cawelti, "The Western," 255 (see chap. 1, n. 4).

13. Roberts and Olson, *John Wayne, American,* 583 (see chap. 4, n. 3).

14. Wills, *John Wayne's America:,* 289 (see chap. 2, n. 39); Simpson, *The Rough Guide to Westerns,* 190. Wills attributes the neglect of *Big Jake* in part to critics being "snobbish about its over-the-hill director [Sherman], who was second-rate even in his prime." Wills writes that Wayne, displeased with early rushes from the film, took over much of the directing from Sherman. Wills credits this information as having come from an interview with Harry Carey, Jr., who starred in the film and choreographed the final shootout.

15. Curiously, the shot from *The Great Train Robbery* is presented inversed, with the passenger fleeing from left to right rather than right to left.

16. Wills, *John Wayne's America,* 289–91. Wills never elaborates on how *Big Jake* echoes *Fort Apache,* the first of John Ford's cavalry pictures. As noted above, in its presentation of the strained relations between the Wayne and O'Hara characters, *Big Jake* would seem to more strongly recall *Rio Grande.*

17. Cawelti, "The Western," 255.

18. Nachbar, "Riding Shotgun," 109.

19. Loy, *Westerns in a Changing America,* 153–54.

20. Roberts and Olsen, *John Wayne, American*, 596–97.

21. Cawelti, "The Western," 256.

22. Ibid. The concept of the "Western Godfather" also ties into the history of scholarship on the genre in an interesting way. Cawelti is arguing, in a sense, that in the "traditional" Western of the 1970s, the difference between the Western hero and the gangster, first articulated by Robert Warshow in his seminal 1954 article "Movie Chronicle: The Westerner," has collapsed.

23. David Lusted, *The Western* (Essex, UK: Pearson Longman, 2003), 215.

24. Coyne, *The Crowded Prairie*, 180 (see chap. 1, n. 11).

25. Lusted, *The Western*, 212.

26. Quoted in Newman, *Wild West Movies*, 195 (see chap. 2, n. 43).

27. Self, *Robert Altman's McCabe & Mrs. Miller*, 177 (see chap. 4, n. 26).

Chapter 6

Epigraph 1. Quoted in Robert C. Cumbow, *Order in the Universe: The Films of John Carpenter* (Lanham, Md.: Scarecrow Press, 2000), 183.

Epigraph 2. Jay Scott, "Heaven's Gate Makes a Near Miraculous Recovery," review of *Heaven's Gate* (1980), *The Globe and Mail*, April 25, 1981, C10.

Epigraph 3. Will Wright, "The Empire Bites the Dust," *Social Text* 6 (Autumn 1982), 124–25.

1. Unfortunately—at least for Western fans—*The Empire Strikes Back* (Irvin Kirshner) opened the following weekend.

2. Gary Arnold, "'Easy Riders'; 'The Long Riders'; An Elegant Entry In the Western Genre," *The Washington Post*, May 16, 1980, D1.

3. The most comprehensive account of the production of *Heaven's Gate* is Steven Bach, *Final Cut: Dreams and Disaster in the Making of Heaven's Gate* (New York: William Morrow, 1985). Bach was senior vice-president and head of worldwide productions for United Artists during the production of the film. Also see Biskind, *Easy Riders, Raging Bulls*, 376–407 (see chap. 1, n. 25).

4. Thomas Schatz, "The New Hollywood," in *Film Theory Goes to the Movies*, ed. Jim Collins, Hilary Radner, and Ava Preacher Collins (London: Routledge, 1993), 20.

5. John Belton, *American Cinema/American Culture* (New York: McGraw-Hill, 1994), 296.

6. Christian Keathly, "Trapped in the Affection Image: Hollywood's Post-traumatic Cycle (1970–1976)," in *The Last Great American Picture Show: New Hollywood Cinema in the 1970s*, ed. Thomas Elsaesser, Alexander Horwath, and Noel King (Amsterdam: Amsterdam University Press, 2004), 305.

7. Cook, *Lost Illusions*, 63 (see chap. 1, n. 25).

8. Robin Wood, "Heaven's Gate Reopened," *Movie* 31–32 (1986), 72. The essay is reprinted as part of a chapter on Cimino in Robin Wood, *Hollywood from Vietnam to Reagan* (New York: Columbia University Press, 1986), 270.

9. Wood, *Hollywood from Vietnam to Reagan*, 317.

10. Kitses, "Post-modernism and the Western," 19 (see chap. 1, n. 12).

11. See, for example, analyses of *Heaven's Gate*'s depiction of class struggle in the context of the Western in McGee, *From Shane to Kill Bill,* 216–34 (see chap. 1, n. 11), and Brian Woolland, "Class Frontiers: The View through Heaven's Gate," in *The Book of Westerns,* ed. Ian Cameron and Douglas Pye (New York: Continuum Publishing Co., 1996), 277–83.

12. King, *New Hollywood Cinema,* 91 (see chap. 1, n. 24).

13. This may partly account for the difficulties Sam Peckinpah experienced with *Pat Garrett & Billy the Kid,* the initial cut of which exceeded 2½ hours.

14. Jan Johnson-Smith, *American Science Fiction TV:* Star Trek, Stargate *and Beyond* (New York: I. B. Tauris, 2005), 57.

15. Barry Keith Grant, *Film Genre: From Iconography to Ideology* (London: Wallflower, 2007), 39.

16. Other science fiction movies of the 1980s like *Battle Beyond the Stars* (Jimmy T. Murmaki, 1980) and *Outland* (Peter Hyams, 1981) were clear remakes of Westerns (*The Magnificent Seven* and *High Noon,* respectively).

17. Wright, "The Empire Bites the Dust," 25.

18. Rick Altman, "A Semantic/Syntactic Approach to Film Genre," *Cinema Journal* 23, no. 3 (Spring 1984), reprinted in *Film/Genre* (London: BFI Publishing, 1999), 221.

19. Grant, *Film Genre,* 39.

20. Altman, "A Semantic/Syntactic Approach to Film Genre," 222.

21. Rick Altman, "What Is Generally Understood by the Notion of Film Genre?," in *Film/Genre* (London: BFI Publishing, 1999), 24.

Conclusion

1. Noël Carroll, *The Philosophy of Horror, or Paradoxes of the Heart* (New York: Routledge, 1990).

2. Janet Maslin, "'Silverado': A Western," *New York Times,* July 10, 1985, C21.

3. David Robinson, "Cinema: The Sins Spielberg Must Answer For/Review of Recent Films," *The Times* (London), December 20, 1985.

4. Loy, *Westerns in a Changing America,* 140–141 (see chap. 5, n. 3).

5. See Nelson, "Introduction: The American Western, 1990–2010," *Contemporary Westerns,* xiii–xxi (see chap. 1, n. 38).

Bibliography

Abel, Richard. "The Imagined Community of the Western." In *American Cinema's Transitional Era: Audiences, Institutions, Practices,* 131. Berkeley: University of California Press, 2004.

Aghed, Jan, and Bernard Cohn. "Interview with Arthur Penn." *Positif,* April 1971. Reprinted in *Arthur Penn: Interviews,* edited by Michael Chaiken and Paul Cronin, 3. Jackson: University Press of Mississippi, 2008.

Aleiss, Angela. *Making the White Man's Indian.* Westport, Conn.: Praeger Publishers, 2005.

Altman, Rick. *Film/Genre.* London: BFI Publishing, 1999.

Ansen, David. "Saddled Up and Rarin' to Go." *Newsweek,* July 15, 1985, 54.

Arnold, Gary. "'Easy Riders'; 'The Long Riders'; An Elegant Entry In the Western Genre." *Washington Post,* May 16, 1980, D1.

Bach, Steven. *Final Cut: Dreams and Disaster in the Making of Heaven's Gate.* New York: William Morrow and Company, Inc., 1985.

Baird, Robert. "Going Indian: Discovery, Adoption and Renaming Toward a 'True American,' from *Deerslayer* to *Dances with Wolves*" [1996]. In *The Western Reader,* edited by Jim Kitses and Gregg Rickman, 277. New York: Limelight Editions, 1996.

Banks, Dennis with Richard Erdoes. *Ojibwa Warrior: Dennis Banks and the Rise of the American Indian Movement.* Norman: University of Oklahoma Press, 2004.

Bazin, André. "The Evolution of the Western." In *What is Cinema?* Vol. 2, 149. Translated by Hugh Gray. Berkeley: University of California Press, 2005.

Belton, John. *American Cinema/American Culture.* New York: McGraw-Hill, 1994.

Biskind, Peter. *Easy Riders, Raging Bulls.* London: Bloomsbury, 1999.

Bordwell, David. "Contemporary Film Studies and the Vicissitudes of Grant Theory." In *Post-Theory: Reconstructing Film Studies,* edited by David Bordwell and Noël Carroll, 3–36. Madison: University of Wisconsin Press, 1996.

Bordwell, David. *Poetics of Cinema.* New York: Routledge, 2008.

Brackett, Leigh. *Follow the Free Wind* [1963]. New York: Ballantine Books, 1980.

Buckley, Peter. Review of *Doc* (Perry, 1971). *Films and Filming,* January 1972, 51.

Buscombe, Edward, ed. *The BFI Companion to the Western: New Edition.* London: Andre Deutsch/BFI Publishing, 1988.

Buscombe, Edward. *"Injuns!": Native Americans in the Movies*. London: Reaktion, 2006.

Canby, Vincent. Review of *Little Big Man* (1970). *New York Times,* December 15, 1970. http://movies.nytimes.com/movie/review?res=EE05E7DF1739E56FBC4D52DFB467838B669EDE.

Carroll, Noël. "The Future of Allusion: Hollywood in the Seventies (and Beyond)." *October* 20 (Spring 1982): 60.

Carroll, Noël. *The Philosophy of Horror, or Paradoxes of the Heart*. New York: Routledge, 1990.

Cawelti, John G. *The Six-Gun Mystique*. Bowling Green, Ohio: Bowling Green University Popular Press, 1971.

Cawelti, John G. "The Western: A Look at the Evolution of a Formula." In *Adventure, Romance and Mystery*, 192. Chicago: University of Chicago Press, 1976.

Churchill, Ward. "Smoke Signals in Context: A Historical Overview." *Z Magazine,* November 1998. http://www.zcommunications.org/smoke-signals-in-context-by-ward-churchill.

Cook, David. A. *Lost Illusions: American Cinema in the Shadow of Watergate and Vietnam 1970–1979*. Berkeley: University of California Press, 2000.

Coombs, Richard. Review of *Doc* (1971). *Monthly Film Bulletin* 39, no. 456 (January 1972): 4.

Coyne, Michael. *The Crowded Prairie: American National Identity in the Western.* New York: I. B. Tauris, 1998.

Cumbow, Robert C. *Order in the Universe: The Films of John Carpenter*. Lanham, Md.: Scarecrow Press, 2000.

Eckstein, Arthur M. "Introduction: Main Critical Issues in *The Searchers*." In *The Searchers: Essays and Reflections on John Ford's Classic Western,* edited by Arthur M. Eckstein and Peter Lehmen, 1. Detroit: Wayne State University Press, 2004.

Feeney, Mark. *Nixon at the Movies: A Book about Belief*. Chicago: University of Chicago Press, 2004.

Fenin, George N., and William K. Everson. *The Western: From Silents to the Seventies.* New York: Penguin Books, 1973.

Fieldler, Leslie. *The Return of the Vanishing American*. New York: Stein & Day, 1968.

Fisher, Austin. "A Marxist's Gotta Do What a Marxist's Gotta Do: Political Violence on the Italian Frontier." *Scope: An Online Journal of Film and Television Studies* 15 (November 2009). http://www.scope.nottingham.ac.uk/cultborr/chapter.php?id=14.

Frayling, Christopher. *Once Upon A Time in Italy*. New York: Harry N. Abrams, 2005.

French, Philip. *Westerns* [1973]. Manchester: Carcenet Press, Ltd., 2005.

Friar, Ralph E., and Natasha A. Friar. *The Only Good Indian . . . The Hollywood Gospel.* New York: Drama Book Specialists, 1972.

Fujiwara, Chris. "Who Will Tell The People? *Cheyenne Autumn*." *Undercurrent* 5 (March 2009). http://www.fipresci.org/undercurrent/issue_0509/cheyenne.htm.

Gallagher, Tag. "Shoot-Out at the Genre Corral: Problems in the 'Evolution' of the Western." In *Film Genre Reader,* edited by Barry Keith Grant, 202. Austin: University of Texas Press, 1986.

Geist, Christopher D., and Jack Nachbar. "Popular Heroes: Introduction." In *The Popular Culture Reader,* 3rd ed., edited by Christopher D. Geist and Jack

Nachbar, 206–211. Bowling Green, Ohio: Bowling Green University Popular Press, 1983.

Grant, Barry Keith. *Film Genre: From Iconography to Ideology*. London: Wallflower, 2007.

Green, Jerome A. *Washita, The Southern Cheyenne and the U.S. Army*. Norman: University of Oklahoma Press, 2004.

Greenspun, Roger. "'Culpepper Cattle': Hero Quits Trail Drive to Help Pacifists." Review of *The Culpepper Cattle Co. New York Times,* April 17, 1972. http://movies.nytimes.com/movie/review?res=9403E5D8143AE73ABC4F52DFB2668389669EDE.

Grist, Leighton. "Unforgiven." In *The Book of Westerns*, edited by Ian Cameron and Douglas Pye, 294. New York: Continuum, 1996.

Hall, Sheldon, and Steve Neale. *Epics, Spectacles and Blockbusters: A Hollywood History*. Detroit, Mich.: Wayne State University Press, 2010.

Hardorff, Richard, ed. *Washita Memories: Eyewitness Views of Custer's Attack on Black Kettle's Village*. Norman: University of Oklahoma Press, 2006.

Hardy, Phil. *The Encyclopedia of Western Movies*. London: Octopus Books, 1985.

Harmetz, Aljean. "The 15th Man Who Was Asked to Direct *M*A*S*H* (and Did) Makes a Peculiar Western." *New York Times Magazine,* June 20, 1971. Reprinted in *Robert Altman: Interviews,* edited by David Sterritt, 3. Jackson: University Press of Mississippi, 2000.

Henderson, Brian. "*The Searchers:* An American Dilemma." *Film Quarterly* 34 (1981): 9–23.

Herzberg, Bob. *Savages and Saints: The Changing Image of American Indians in Westerns*. Jefferson, N.C.: McFarland, 2008.

Hoig, Stan. *The Battle of the Washita: The Sheridan-Custer Indian Campaign of 1867–69* [1976]. Lincoln: University of Nebraska Press, 1980.

Hutton, Paul Andrew. "Showdown at the Hollywood Corral: Wyatt Earp at the Movies." *Montana: The Magazine of Western History* 45, no. 3 (Summer 1995): 5.

Johnson-Smith, Jan. *American Science Fiction TV:* Star Trek, Stargate *and Beyond,* New York: I. B. Tauris, 2005.

Keathly, Christian. "Trapped in the Affection Image: Hollywood's Post-traumatic Cycle (1970–1976)." In *The Last Great American Picture Show: New Hollywood Cinema in the 1970s,* edited by Thomas Elsaesser, Alexander Horwath, and Noel King, 293. Amsterdam: Amsterdam University Press, 2004.

King, Geoff. *New Hollywood Cinema.* London: I. B. Tauris, 2002.

Kitses, Jim. *Horizons West.* London: Thames and Hudson, 1969.

Kitses, Jim. *Horizons West: Directing the Western from John Ford to Clint Eastwood.* New ed. London: BFI Publishing, 2004.

Kitses, Jim. "Post-modernism and the Western." In *The Western Reader*, edited by Jim Kitses and Gregg Rickman, 15. New York: Limelight Editions, 1996.

Lake, Stuart N. *Wyatt Earp: Frontier Marshall* [1931]. New York: Pocket Books, 1994.

Langford, Barry. "Revisiting the 'Revisionist' Western." *Film and History* 33, no. 2 (September 2003): 26.

Lewis, Richard Warren. "John Wayne: The Playboy Interview." *Playboy* 18, no. 5 (May 1971). http://www.playboy.com/articles/john-wayne-interview/.

Limerick, Patricia Nelson. *The Legacy of Conquest: The Unbroken Past of the American West.* New York: W. W. Norton, 1987.

Lindbergs, Kimberly. "Little Big Man's Big Impact." *TCM Movie Morlocks*, May 6, 2010. http://moviemorlocks.com/2010/05/06/little-big-mans-big-impact/.

Love, Damien. "The Miracle Worker: An Interview with Arthur Penn" [2004]. *Bright Lights Film Journal* 65 (August 2009). http://www.brightlightsfilm.com/65/65arthurpenniv.php.

Loy, R. Philip. *Westerns in a Changing America: 1955–2000*. Jefferson, N.C.: McFarland, 2004.

Lusted, David. *The Western*. Essex, UK: Pearson Longman, 2003.

Marsden, Michael T., and Jack Nachbar. "The Modern Popular Western: Radio, Television, Film and Print." *A Literary History of the American West*, 1273. Fort Worth: Texas Christian University Press, 1987.

Maslin, Janet. "'Silverado': A Western." *New York Times*, July 10, 1985, C: 21.

Maynard, Richard A. "The Rise of the Cowboy Anti-Hero—Trends in Westerns since 1960." In *The American West on Film: Myth and Reality*, edited by Richard A. Maynard, 93. Rochelle Park, N.J.: Hayden, 1974.

McBride, Joseph. *Hawks on Hawks*. Berkely: University of California Press, 1982.

McBride, Joseph. *Searching for John Ford: A Life*. London: Faber and Faber, 2003.

McCarthy, Todd. *Howard Hawks: The Grey Fox of Hollywood*. New York: Grove Press, 1997.

McGee, Patrick. *From Shane to Kill Bill: Rethinking the Western*. Oxford: Blackwell Publishing, 2007.

Mikkelson, Barbara. "Iron Eyes Cody." *Snopes.com*, August 9, 2007. http://www.snopes.com/movies/actors/ironeyes.asp.

Mitchell, Lee Clark. *Westerns: Making the Man in Fiction and Film*. Chicago: University of Chicago Press, 1998.

Moine, Raphaëlle. *Cinema Genre*. Translated by Alistair Fox and Hilary Radner. Oxford: Blackwell, 2008.

Mordue, Mark. "Dead Men Walking." *Frieze Magazine* 114 (April 2008). http://www.frieze.com/issue/article/dead_men_walking/.

Nachbar, Jack. "Riding Shotgun: The Scattered Formula in Contemporary Western Movies." *Film Journal* 2, no. 3 (September 1973). Reprinted in *Focus on the Western*, edited by Jack Nachbar, 102–108. Inglewood Cliffs, N.J.: Prentice-Hall, 1974.

Neale, Steve. "'The Last Good Time We Ever Had?' Revising the Hollywood Renaissance." In *Contemporary American Cinema*, edited by Linda Ruth Williams and Michael Hammond, 90. London: Open University Press, 2006.

Neale, Steve. "Questions of Genre." In *Film and Theory: An Anthology*, edited by Robert Stam and Toby Miller, 157. Malden, Mass.: Blackwell Publishing, 2000.

Neale, Steve. "Vanishing Americans: Racial and Ethnic Issues in the Interpretation and Context of Post-war 'Pro-Indian' Westerns." In *Back in the Saddle Again: New Essays on the Western*, edited by Edward Buscombe and Roberta E. Pearson. London: BFI, 1998.

Neale, Steve. "Westerns and Gangster Films Since the 1970s." In *Genre and Contemporary Hollywood*, 27. London: BFI Publishing, 2002.

Newman, Kim. *Wild West Movies: How the West Was Found, Won, Lost, Lied About, Filmed and Forgotten*. London: Bloomsbury, 1990.

O'Connor, John "The White Man's Indian: An Institutional Approach." In *Hollywood's Indian: The Portrayal of the Native American in Film*, edited by Peter C.

Rollins and John E. O'Connor, 27. Lexington: University Press of Kentucky, 1998.

Plecki, Gerard. *Robert Altman*. Boston: Twayne, 1985.

Prince, Stephen. *Savage Cinema: Sam Peckinpah and the Rise of Violent Movies*. London: The Athlone Press, 1998.

Prince, Stephen, ed. *Sam Peckinpah's The Wild Bunch*. Cambridge: Cambridge University Press, 1999.

Pye, Douglas. "Ulzana's Raid" [1981]. *The Book of Westerns*, edited by Ian Cameron and Douglas Pye, 262. New York: Continuum, 1996.

Roberts, Randy, and James S. Olson. *John Wayne, American*. New York: The Free Press, 1995.

Robinson, David. "Cinema: The Sins Spielberg Must Answer For/Review of Recent Films." *The Times* (London), December 20, 1985.

Sarf, Wayne Michael. *God Bless You, Buffalo Bill: A Layman's Guide to History and the Western Film*. East Brunswick, N.J.: Associated University Presses, 1983.

Schatz, Thomas. *Hollywood Genres: Formulas, Filmmaking and the Studio System*. New York: Random House, 1981.

Schatz, Thomas. "The New Hollywood." In *Film Theory Goes to the Movies*, edited by Jim Collins, Hilary Radner, and Ava Preacher Collins. London: Routledge, 1993.

Scott, Jay. "*Heaven's Gate* Makes a Near Miraculous Recovery." Review of *Heaven's Gate* (1980). *The Globe and Mail*, April 25, 1981, C10.

Self, Robert T. *Robert Altman's McCabe & Mrs. Miller: Reframing the American West*. Lawrence, Kans.: University Press of Kansas, 2007.

Shales, Tom. "Myths of the Old West, Again." *The Washington Post*, January 28, 1980, B3.

Simmons, Garner. *Peckinpah: A Portrait in Montage*. Austin: University of Texas Press, 1982.

Simpson, Paul. *The Rough Guide to Westerns*. London: Rough Guides, 2006.

Smith, Andrew Brodie. *Shooting Cowboys and Indians: Silent Western Films, American Culture and the Birth of Hollywood*. Boulder: University of Colorado Press, 2003.

Smith, Paul. *Clint Eastwood: A Cultural Production*. Minneapolis: University of Minnesota Press, 1993.

Smith, Paul Chaat, and Robert Allen Warrior. *Like a Hurricane: The Indian Movement from Alcatraz to Wounded Knee*. New York: The New Press, 1996.

Stanfield, Peter. *Hollywood, Westerns and the 1930s: The Lost Trail*. Exeter, UK: University of Exeter Press, 2001.

Stanfield, Peter. *Horse Opera: The Strange History of the 1930s Singing Cowboy*. Urbana: University of Illinois Press, 2002.

Tatum, Stephen. *Inventing Billy the Kid*. Tucson: University of Arizona Press, 1997.

Thomas, Deborah. "John Wayne's Body." *The Book of Westerns*, edited by Ian Cameron and Douglas Pye. New York: Continuum, 1996.

Thompson, Kristin. *Breaking the Glass Armor: Neoformalist Film Analysis*. Princeton, N.J.: Princeton University Press, 1988.

Thompson, Kristin. *Storytelling in the New Hollywood*. Cambridge, Mass.: Harvard University Press, 1999.

Thompson, Howard. "An Enigmatic 'Doc.'" *New York Times*, August 19, 1972. http://movies.nytimes.com/movie/89636/Doc/overview.

Tompkins, Jane. *West of Everything: The Inner Life of Westerns.* Oxford: Oxford University Press, 1993.

Trimbach, Joseph H., and John M. Trimbach. *American Indian Mafia: An FBI Agent's True Story About Wounded Knee, Leonard Peltier, and the American Indian Movement.* Parker, Colo.: Outskirts Press, 2007.

Turan, Kenneth. "A Fistful of Memories: Interview with Clint Eastwood" [1992]. *The Western Reader,* edited by Jim Kitses and Gregg Rickman, 245. New York: Limelight Editions, 1996.

Turner, Frederick Jackson. *The Frontier in American History* [1920]. New York: Henry Holt, 1937.

Tuska, Jon. *The American West in Film: Critical Approaches to the Western.* London: Greenwood Press, 1985.

Ward, Geoffrey C. *The Civil War: An Illustrated History.* New York: Knopf, 1990.

Waters, Frank. *The Earp Brothers of Tombstone: the Story of Mrs. Virgil Earp* [1960]. Lincoln, Nebr.: Bison Books, 1976.

Williamson, Bruce. Interview with Robert Altman. *Playboy* 23, no. 8 (August 1976). Reprinted in *Robert Altman: Interviews,* edited by David Sterritt, 34–62. Jackson: University Press of Mississippi, 2000.

Wills, Gary. *John Wayne's America: The Politics of Celebrity.* New York: Touchstone, 1998.

Wilson, Jason. "The State of Westerns." *GamePro,* June 22, 2010.

Wright, Will. "The Empire Bites the Dust." *Social Text* 6 (Autumn 1982): 120.

Wright, Will. *Sixguns and Society: A Structural Study of the Western.* Berkeley: University of California Press, 1975.

Wollen, Peter. *Signs and Meaning in the Cinema.* London: BFI, 1969.

Wood, Robin. *Hollywood from Vietnam to Reagan.* New York: Columbia University Press, 1986.

Woolland, Brian. "Class Frontiers: The View through Heaven's Gate." In *The Book of Westerns,* edited by Ian Cameron and Douglas Pye, 277. New York: Continuum, 1996.

Woolley, John, and Gerhard Peters. *The American Presidency Project.* Santa Barbara: University of California [hosted]. http://www.presidency.ucsb.edu/ws/?pid=2608.

Index

Page numbers in *italics* indicate photographs.

Index

Index

www.ingramcontent.com/pod-product-compliance
Lightning Source LLC
LaVergne TN
LVHW091040080826
845145LV00002B/566
* 9 7 8 0 8 0 6 1 4 8 2 1 2 *